"In taking us straight to the hec
served us magnificently. We so nee
let the Scriptures get into us. The f
and with such submission to Biblic
genuinely helped to be shape

– Terry Virgo

"Fresh. Solid. Simple. Really good stuff."

– R. T. Kendall

"Phil makes the deep truths of Scripture alive and accessible. If you want to grow in your understanding of each book of the Bible, then buy these books and let them change your life!"

***– P J Smyth** – GodFirst Church, Johannesburg, South Africa*

"Most commentaries are dull. These are alive.
*Most commentaries are for scholars. These are for **you**!"*

– Canon Michael Green

*"These notes are amazingly good. Lots of content and depth of research, yet packed in a **Big Breakfast** that leaves the reader well fed and full. Bible notes often say too little, yet larger commentaries can be dull – missing the wood for the trees. Phil's insights are striking, original, and fresh, going straight to the heart of the text and the reader! Substantial yet succinct, they bristle with amazing insights and life applications, compelling us to read more. Bible reading will become enriched and informed with such a scintillating guide. Teachers and preachers will find nuggets of pure gold here!"*

***– Greg Haslam** – Westminster Chapel, London, UK*

"The Bible is living and dangerous. The ones who teach it best are those who bear that in mind – and let the author do the talking. Phil has written these studies with a sharp mind and a combination of creative application and reverence."

***– Joel Virgo** – Leader of Newday Youth Festival*

"Phil Moore's new commentaries are outstanding: biblical and passionate, clear and well-illustrated, simple and profound. God's Word comes to life as you read them, and the wonder of God shines through every page."

– *Andrew Wilson* – *Author of* Incomparable *and* If God, Then What?

"Want to understand the Bible better? Don't have the time or energy to read complicated commentaries? The book you have in your hand could be the answer. Allow Phil Moore to explain and then apply God's message to your life. Think of this book as the Bible's message distilled for everyone."

– *Adrian Warnock* – *Christian blogger*

"Phil Moore presents Scripture in a dynamic, accessible and relevant way. The bite-sized chunks – set in context and grounded in contemporary life – really make the Word become flesh and dwell among us."

– *Dr David Landrum* – *The Bible Society*

"Through a relevant, very readable, up to date storying approach, Phil Moore sets the big picture, relates God's Word to today and gives us fresh insights to increase our vision, deepen our worship, know our identity and fire our imagination. Highly recommended!"

– *Geoff Knott* – *former CEO of Wycliffe Bible Translators UK*

"What an exciting project Phil has embarked upon! These accessible and insightful books will ignite the hearts of believers, inspire the minds of preachers and help shape a new generation of men and women who are seeking to learn from God's Word."

– *David Stroud* – *Newfrontiers and ChristChurch London*

For more information about the Straight to the Heart series, please go to **www.philmoorebooks.com**.
You can also receive daily messages from Phil Moore on Twitter by following **@PhilMooreLondon**.

STRAIGHT TO THE HEART OF

Solomon

60 BITE-SIZED INSIGHTS FROM PROVERBS, ECCLESIASTES AND SONG OF SONGS

Phil Moore

MONARCH BOOKS

Oxford, UK & Grand Rapids, Michigan, USA

Published by Monarch Books
an imprint of
Lion Hudson plc
Wilkinson House, Jordan Hill Road,
Oxford OX2 8DR, England
Email: monarch@lionhudson.com
www.lionhudson.com/monarch

ISBN 978 0 85721 426 3
e-ISBN 978 0 85721 427 0

First edition 2013

A catalogue record for this book is available from the British Library.

Printed and bound in the UK, May 2013, LH26

This book is for my wife Ruth,

the greatest co-pilot of them all.

CONTENTS

LESSON FOUR: KEEP TO GOD'S WAY (ECCLESIASTES)

About the *Straight to the Heart* Series

On his eightieth birthday, Sir Winston Churchill dismissed the compliment that he was the "lion" who had defeated Nazi Germany in World War Two. He told the Houses of Parliament that *"It was a nation and race dwelling all around the globe that had the lion's heart. I had the luck to be called upon to give the roar."*

I hope that God speaks to you very powerfully through the "roar" of the books in the *Straight to the Heart* series. I hope they help you to understand the books of the Bible and the message which the Holy Spirit inspired their authors to write. I hope that they help you to hear God's voice challenging you, and that they provide you with a springboard for further journeys into each book of Scripture for yourself.

But when you hear my "roar", I want you to know that it comes from the heart of a much bigger "lion" than me. I have been shaped by a whole host of great Christian thinkers and preachers from around the world, and I want to give due credit to at least some of them here:

Terry Virgo, David Stroud, Dave Holden, John Hosier, Adrian Holloway, Greg Haslam, Lex Loizides and all those who lead the Newfrontiers family of churches. Friends and encouragers, such as Stef Liston, Joel Virgo, Stuart Gibbs, Scott Taylor, Nick Sharp, Nick Derbridge, Phil Whittall, and Kevin and Sarah Aires. Tony Collins, Jenny Ward and Simon Cox at Monarch Books. Malcolm Kayes and all the elders of The Coign Church, Woking.

My fellow elders and church members here at Everyday Church in Southwest London. My great friend Andrew Wilson – without your friendship, encouragement and example, this series would never have happened.

I would like to thank my parents, my brother Jonathan, and my in-laws, Clive and Sue Jackson. Dad – your example birthed in my heart the passion which brought this series into being. I didn't listen to all you said when I was a child, but I couldn't ignore the way you got up at five o' clock every morning to pray, read the Bible and worship, because of your radical love for God and for his Word. I'd like to thank my children – Isaac, Noah, Esther and Ethan – for keeping me sane when publishing deadlines were looming. But most of all, I'm grateful to my incredible wife, Ruth – my friend, encourager, corrector and helper.

You all have the lion's heart, and you have all developed the lion's heart in me. I count it an enormous privilege to be the one who was chosen to sound the lion's roar.

So welcome to the *Straight to the Heart* series. My prayer is that you will let this roar grip your own heart too – for the glory of the great Lion of the Tribe of Judah, the Lord Jesus Christ!

Introduction: Life Works God's Way

Does not wisdom call out? Does not understanding raise her voice?... "Those who find me find life and receive favour from the Lord."

(Proverbs 8:1, 35)

Very few people ever get to pilot an F-35 fighter jet. With a top speed of 1,200 miles per hour and enough onboard weaponry to destroy a small city, it's probably just as well. Would-be pilots have to pass a gruelling set of physical, intellectual and psychological tests even to make it into flight school, and only the very best graduates are ever trusted to handle a jet as

powerful as the F-35. Air force commanders know that only a fool would try to pilot an F-35 without the proper training.

Solomon grasped this principle when he visited the Tabernacle at Mount Gibeon in 970 BC. He sacrificed 1,000 burnt offerings because he knew that he was in desperate need of God's attention. The Lord responded by appearing to him that night in a dream with an incredible offer: *"Ask for whatever you want me to give you."*[1]

Solomon didn't hesitate. If piloting an F-35 is difficult, piloting life is even harder. It didn't matter that his father David had assured him when he named him king of Israel that *"You are a man of wisdom"*; Solomon knew that he couldn't pilot his life on his own. *"I am only a little child and do not know how to carry out my duties,"* he pleaded. *"So give your servant a discerning*

---

[1] 1 Kings 3:5. See also 1 Chronicles 21:29; 2 Chronicles 1:3–6.

heart."[2] Solomon had seen the smoking wreckage caused by his father's adulterous affair with his mother, and he had seen three of his older brothers wreck their own lives too by ignoring God's shouts from the control tower. Amnon had copied his father's sexual sin, Absalom had chased fame and Adonijah had lusted after power. All three of them were dead, and the new King Solomon was determined that he would not fly solo any more. *"Give your servant a hearing heart,"* he asked God literally in Hebrew. He asked to enrol in the Lord's flight school because he had seen firsthand that life only works God's way.

The Lord was delighted with Solomon's reply. Offered carte blanche, he hadn't asked for women or worship or wealth, but for wisdom to handle the flight path of his life better than his father and his brothers. *"I will do what you have asked,"* the Lord promised. *"I will give you a wise and discerning heart, so that there will never have been anyone like you, nor will there ever be."*[3] 1 Kings 4:29–34 tells us that God gave him such great wisdom that he outclassed the finest teachers of the world and received visitors from every nation who shared his passion to find out how to live life God's way. It also tells us that he wrote 3,000 proverbs and over 1,000 songs to preserve his wisdom for anyone humble enough to ask God if they can enrol in his flight school too.

Although some modern scholars have questioned whether Solomon actually wrote the three Old Testament books which we know as Proverbs, Ecclesiastes and Song of Songs, the text of the three books seems to support the almost 3,000 years of consensus among Jews and Christians that he did so. Proverbs 1:1 describes the book as *"The proverbs of Solomon son of David,*

---

[2] 1 Kings 2:9; 3:7–9. Solomon must have only been about 18 years of age when he became king.

[3] 1 Kings 3:12. You can read about the smoking wreckage of David and his eldest sons' lives in 2 Samuel 11–20 and 1 Kings 1–2. You can read about the wisdom and later folly of Solomon's life in 1 Kings 1–11.

king of Israel".[4] Song of Songs 1:1 explains that it is *"Solomon's Song of Songs"*, which is a Hebrew way of saying *"Solomon's Best Song"*.[5] Ecclesiastes 1:1 and 12 describe the author as *"The Teacher, son of David, king in Jerusalem... king over Israel in Jerusalem"*, which is something only Solomon could ever say since all subsequent kings of Jerusalem ruled over Judah but not Israel. We should therefore view these books as a description of the lessons which Solomon learned through the ups and downs of his life's flight path. We should treat them as a warning that we need help to live life God's way.

Solomon reigned for forty years from 970 to 930 BC, and during the first half of his reign he succeeded in living life God's way. 1 Kings 10:23 celebrates the fact that *"King Solomon was greater in riches and wisdom than all the other kings of the earth. The whole world sought audience with Solomon to hear the wisdom God had put in his heart."* Not content with sharing his wisdom with visitors in his own generation, he devised a way that he could put succeeding generations of believers through God's flight school too.[6] He began to compile the book which we know as Proverbs, starting with lesson one in **Proverbs 1–9**, which is a call to **Learn God's Way**. He created lesson two by picking 375 of his 3,000 proverbs to form the bulk of **Proverbs 10–31** and spell out in detail what it means to **Live God's Way**.[7] If this longest lesson appears to jump from one theme to another, with

---

[4] His authorship is reiterated in Proverbs 10:1 and 25:1.

[5] This was simply the normal Hebrew way of expressing an absolute superlative. We can also see this in the way they referred to *"The Most Holy Place"* in the Tabernacle as *"The Holy of Holies"*.

[6] Solomon may have written specifically for his eldest son and heir Rehoboam, since he repeatedly addresses Proverbs 1–9 to *"my son"*. However, Proverbs 4:1 also makes it clear he had a wider readership in mind.

[7] Solomon's Top 375 forms the bulk of lesson two (10:1–22:16), but by no means all of it. It also includes some of Solomon's favourite wise sayings from around the world (22:17–24:34), as well as 125 more of Solomon's proverbs which were selected by King Hezekiah's wise men over two centuries later (25:1–29:27), and some of their own favourite wise sayings from around the world (30:1–31:31).

little sense of thematic grouping, it is deliberate. Life is more complicated than flying an F-35, and it defies our attempts to compartmentalize its challenges. Since love is perhaps the most complicated aspect of them all, Solomon gave us **Song of Songs** as lesson three in order to teach us how to **Love God's Way**.

Sadly, in the second half of his reign, Solomon failed to practise what he preached. The star student of God's flight school, who had proved in his twenties and thirties that life works God's way, attempted to fly solo and wrecked his life even more seriously than his father David had before him. He nosedived in his forties and fifties into the misery and despair which he describes in the book of **Ecclesiastes** and which serves as lesson four and as a warning that we need to **Keep to God's Way**. Ecclesiastes charts his discovery that life makes no sense without God at the centre, and it describes his homeward path to a recommitment of his life to the Lord and to the fact that life only works God's way.

So let's enrol together in God's flight school and go straight to the heart of the three Old Testament books which were written by Solomon. Let's allow the wisest Old Testament writer to tell us how we can learn God's way, live God's way and love God's way, just as he did. Let's heed his warnings not to deviate from God's flight path, as he did, but to keep to God's way until we reach the landing lights at the end of our life's journey.

Let's ask the God who appeared to Solomon at the Tabernacle to give us wisdom too. Let's ask him to teach us how to live life to the full in the world which he has made. Let's surrender to Solomon's ancient conclusion that life only works God's way.

Lesson One:

Learn God's Way

(Proverbs 1–9)

Two Won't Do (1:1–7)

The fear of the Lord is the beginning of knowledge,
but fools despise wisdom and instruction.

(Proverbs 1:7)

There is an old Chinese proverb about what it takes to become a good painter: *"You need the hand, the eye and the heart. Two won't do."* As Solomon sits us down and begins to deliver our first lesson in God's flight school, he tells us in these opening verses that the same is true of wisdom.

Many people think that wisdom is all about the eye and the heart, and not about the hand. They equate wisdom with the endless debating of Greek philosophers, so Solomon uses a dozen different Hebrew words in these seven verses to make it clear that two out of three won't do. He starts with the Hebrew word *hokmāh* in verse 2, which means *wisdom* in the sense of know-how as opposed to mere head knowledge. It is the same word which was used in Exodus 31:3 to describe a master craftsman's skill at making artwork out of the simple material in his hand. Lucille Ball captured the practical nature of *hokmāh* when she pointed out that *"A man who correctly guesses a woman's age may be smart, but he's not very bright."*[1] Like Jesus ten centuries later, Solomon insists that *"Now that you know these things, you will be blessed if you* ***do*** *them."*[2]

To reinforce this point, he also uses the Hebrew word *mūsār* in verses 2 and 3. This word means *discipline, chastisement*

[1] She said this in her classic 1950s comedy series *I Love Lucy*. Note that verses 20–21 tell us Wisdom calls out in the streets and public square, and not just in the library and university.

[2] John 13:17. Jesus also said the same thing in a parable in Matthew 7:24–27.

or *correction*, and it reminds us that wisdom is often learned through personal failure and negative feedback on our actions from others. One of my first employers used to tell me before a reprimand that *"Feedback is the breakfast of future champions."* Solomon wants us to know that it is served as an all-day breakfast in the canteen at God's school of wisdom.

Other people think that wisdom is all about the heart and the hand, and not about the eye. They ask God for wisdom and expect to get it as an effortless download from heaven, but Solomon warns that two out of three won't do. He crams these seven verses with Hebrew words which reinforce the need to use our eyes to learn wisdom through keen observation and analysis of the world we live in. In verse 2 it is *bīnāh*, the same word for *understanding* which is used in Ezra 8:15 when the writer tells us that *"When I checked among the people and the priests, I found no Levites there."* Wisdom comes through checking and making a thoughtful examination of the facts. Solomon tells us to *sākal* or *be circumspect* in order to gain *'ormāh* or *prudence* and *da'ath* or *knowledge*. He tells us to tax our brains and feast our eyes on the facts in order to form a *mizmāh* or *discerning plan* in order to understand the *hīdāh* or *dark riddles*, which are fathomed by the wise. His word for *proverb* is *māshāl*, which means literally a *lesson by comparison*, and his word for *parable* in verse 6 is *melītsāh*, which was the normal word used for an *interpretation* offered after careful study of a foreign language.

Sherlock Holmes tells Dr Watson the difference between mere sight and observation in one of Conan Doyle's short stories:

> *You see, but you do not observe. The distinction is clear. For example, you have frequently seen the steps which lead up from the hall to this room... Then how many are there?... Quite so! You have not observed. And yet you have seen. This is just my point. Now, I know that*

there are seventeen steps, because I have both seen and observed.[3]

Like any flight school instructor, Solomon tells us that piloting begins with seeing and perceiving. He promises in verse 5 that if we use the senses God has given us, we will find they give us *tahbulōth* or *guidance*, the Hebrew word which was used for the ropes held by a steersman in order to guide the rudder of a cargo boat or warship.

Other people think that wisdom is all about the hand and the eye, and not about the heart. That's what sets Solomon's wisdom literature apart from that of his pagan contemporaries, because he tells us that two out of three won't do. Whereas pagan philosophers treat wisdom as a commodity to be acquired in its own right, Solomon fills these verses with reminders that true wisdom only comes through relationship with God. The man who asked God for a *"hearing heart"* at the Tabernacle in 970 BC uses the same word *shāma* again in verse 5 to emphasize that wise people are those who have learned to still their hearts before God and listen. His word *māshāl* or *proverb* is used in Numbers 23:7 and 18 to describe an *oracle* from God, and his word *leqah* or *learning* is used in Deuteronomy 32:2 to record Moses teaching God-given *doctrine*. If Adam and Eve's sin was to eat from the tree of knowledge in order to gain wisdom without reference to God, Solomon points us back to the tree of life and to dependency on God instead.[4] Paul unpacks what Solomon means in New Testament language in 1 Corinthians 1:24 and 30, when he tells us that Jesus is *"the wisdom of God"* and *"has become for us wisdom from God"*. Solomon warns us

---

[3] He says this in Sir Arthur Conan Doyle's short story "A Scandal in Bohemia" (1891).

[4] We will examine this contrast further in the chapter entitled "The Tree of Life", but for now simply note that Solomon hints at this in Proverbs 3:18, 11:30, 13:12 and 15:4.

not to grasp for wisdom as a thing, but to receive him as a person into our hearts.[5]

Enough of Hebrew words.[6] Solomon has made his point, so he moves to a conclusion in verse 7. Unlike most of the Old Testament writers, he starts Proverbs with a clear statement of the book's purpose.[7] He tells us that our quest for wisdom will require us to use our eye and hand and heart. When we feast our eyes on who God is, on what he calls us to do, and on his offer to let us feast on his Messiah in our hearts, it silences our boasting in human wisdom and it causes us to bow before the only wise God. *"The fear of the Lord is the beginning of wisdom,"* Solomon explains. Of course it is if Wisdom is not a substance, but a person.[8]

Solomon looks up at us from these opening verses of our first lesson in God's flight school. He offers us the perfect co-pilot to help us – the one he is about to describe as Wisdom personified, and whom the New Testament tells us is none other than Jesus Christ himself. Solomon tells us to offer this co-pilot our hand and eye and heart. If we want to find out that life works God's way, he warns us that two out of three won't do.

---

[5] Paul tells us in 1 Corinthians 2:7–16 and Ephesians 1:17 that we receive Jesus as God's Wisdom in our hearts through receiving the Holy Spirit as the Spirit of Jesus and the Spirit of Wisdom. We will look at how much Solomon understood he was prophesying about the coming of the Messiah in the chapter "Choose".

[6] If you are enjoying this Hebrew and want a little more, here you go: In the whole of Proverbs and Ecclesiastes, Solomon uses the word *hokmāh* and its sister words 129 times, *mūsar* 30 times, *bīnāh* 13 times, *da'ath* 46 times, *mizmāh* 10 times, *sākal* 14 times, and *'ormāh* and its sister words 11 times.

[7] He restates this purpose again in 9:10 and 15:33. He defines *"the fear of the Lord"* in 8:13 as hating sin and loving obedience, which is why he tells us here in 1:3 that it means *"doing what is right and just and fair"*.

[8] Solomon repeats this summary of the message of Proverbs in 9:10 and 15:33. Job and David had already said something similar in Job 28:28 and Psalm 111:10.

The Five Faces of a Fool (1:8–33)

How long will you who are simple love your simple ways? How long will mockers delight in mockery and fools hate knowledge?

(Proverbs 1:22)

Solomon must have had high hopes for his eldest son Rehoboam. He gave him a name which meant *The People Have Grown Bigger,* because he knew that following in his footsteps would not be easy. Success without a successor spells failure, so Solomon started to train his crown prince early.

Some readers of Proverbs struggle to understand why the book seems to be mainly addressed to men and not women, to rulers and not subjects, to the rich and not the poor, and to the young and not the old, but this is why. Solomon makes it clear in 4:1, 5:7 and 7:24 that he has a wider readership in mind than simply Rehoboam, but he also makes it clear that his number one reader is the son who will reign after him.[1] Proverbs 1–9 takes the form of twelve fatherly talks, the first eleven of which begin with a passionate appeal to *"my son"*.[2] Other people can

[1] In the broadest sense Solomon is *"giving prudence to those who are simple, knowledge and discretion to the young"* (1:4), but these verses also make it clear he has a particular simple youth in mind.

[2] These twelve fatherly talks are 1:8–19; 2:1–22; 3:1–20, 21–35; 4:1–9, 10–19, 20–27; 5:1–23; 6:1–19, 20–35; 7:1–27 and 8:1–9:18. In the twelfth talk, it is Wisdom rather than Solomon who speaks as parent. Rehoboam is not named so that *"my son"* can refer to anyone, but for Solomon one son mattered more than all the others.

enrol in God's flight school, but the head boy of the school is the crown prince Rehoboam.

If you have read 1 Kings 12, you will know that Solomon's high hopes for his eldest son were not to be. When he came to the throne in 930 BC, Rehoboam wore the five faces of a fool which his father warned against in these verses. Let's look together at five Hebrew words which Solomon uses to describe the different aspects of human folly. As we do so, let's commit ourselves to heed his fivefold warning more than Rehoboam did.

The first word is *'ewīl* in verse 7, and this word for fool occurs nineteen times in Proverbs. It doesn't mean someone who lacks mental ability, but rather someone who lacks moral humility. An *'ewīl* is not a good-hearted person who fails to grasp God's will with his head, but a rebellious person who refuses to submit to it with his heart.[3] Rehoboam was an *'ewīl* in 1 Kings 12 because he took his dilemma to his friends instead of to the Lord. While his father began his reign by visiting the Tabernacle and listening to the Lord, Rehoboam began his reign by closing his ears to God and setting out to make his own moral choices. He ignored his father's call in Proverbs 1:8–19 to listen to the Lord and not to sinful human counsellors,[4] and he discovered to his cost that Solomon was right to insist in verse 19 that life only works God's way.[5] 2 Chronicles 12:14 tells us that Rehoboam's evil deeds were not due to his ignorance, but his wilfulness: *"He did evil because he had not set his heart on seeking the Lord."*

The second word is *pethī* in verse 22, and this word for

---

[3] Compare 1:13 with 8:18–21 to grasp the stupidity of the wicked fool. He disobeys God in the hope of getting what would have been his anyway if he had simply obeyed him.

[4] Rehoboam's mother appeals to him too in 1:8. She was an Ammonite foreigner named Naamah (1 Kings 14:21), but she had learned from her husband that life only works God's way.

[5] This theme of wicked life decisions destroying the lives of the wicked occurs repeatedly in wisdom literature. See Proverbs 26:27; 28:10: Ecclesiastes 10:8–9; Psalms 5:10; 7:15–16; 9:15–16; 57:6.

fool occurs sixteen times in Proverbs. It means a *simple* or *gullible* or *naïve* person – anyone weak-minded enough to fall for flattery and temptation. Rehoboam was a *pethī* when he ignored the voice of Wisdom calling out in the public square in Proverbs 1:20–33, and listened to the voice of his flattering friends instead. Wisdom shouted that *"the waywardness of* pethī *people will kill them, and the complacency of fools will destroy them; but whoever listens to me will live in safety and be at ease, without fear of harm."* Rehoboam refused to listen to her or to the ten northern tribes of Israel when they pointed out quite reasonably that his father's fiscal and labour policies had been unfair towards them.[6] He listened to his friends and was flattered into acting like a macho despot. As a result, his waywardness and complacency destroyed his kingdom. The ten northern tribes broke away from his rule, and he was left with a fraction of the power which his father had bequeathed to him.

The third word is *lēts* in verse 22, and this word for fool occurs fifteen times in Proverbs. It means a *mocker* or *scoffer* and describes the person who refuses to take the truth or the advice of wise counsellors seriously.[7] When Solomon's experienced counsellors pointed out to Rehoboam that his father had indeed been unfair and he could now win favour with his new subjects by reversing his father's policy, he arrogantly scorned their advice. He might have saved his kingdom had he taken more note of these verses in Proverbs, but instead he simply proved that they were true. Verse 7 told us that the fear of the Lord is

---

[6] 1 Kings 4:7–19 tells us that Solomon taxed the ten northern tribes of Israel but not the two southern tribes. 1 Kings 5:13–18 tells us that he treated the ten northern tribes like a conquered kingdom by using Israelites but not Judahites in his army of foreign slave labourers. Their sense of injustice was quite legitimate.

[7] Mockers love gushing out words as commentators rather than as players (15:2, 28). When a mocker is actually asked to play the game and make decisions, 24:7 tells us that *"he has nothing to say"*.

the beginning of knowledge, and now verse 29 responds that failure to fear the Lord is the beginning of folly and disaster.[8]

The fourth word is *kesīl* in verse 22, and this word for fool occurs forty-eight times in Proverbs and nineteen times in Ecclesiastes. It means a *stupid person*, but again one whose deficiency is not in head capacity but in heart humility.[9] Rehoboam was a *kesīl* in the sense that he had hundreds of his father's proverbs to warn him that a king must rule justly, yet he wilfully refused to listen. That's why Solomon warns in Proverbs 26:7 that a proverb is as useless as a lame man's legs to a *kesīl* unless he submits his heart to Wisdom.[10]

The fifth word is *'ātsēl* and it does not occur until 6:6, but this word for fool occurs fourteen times in Proverbs. It means a *sluggard* or a *slacker* or a *waster* – anyone whose problem isn't a lack of mental capacity but sheer laziness. He craves the same things as the wise, but he makes excuses to put off action till tomorrow, and when he finally prises himself out of bed and leaves the house he quickly complains that the road to success is too costly for him to travel.[11] He never finishes what he starts and he buries his head in the sand to problems like Rehoboam in 1 Kings 12:18. Solomon warns in verse 33 that the wise always enjoy far more ease than the sluggard in the end.

So what shall we say? Did Solomon's flight school fail because its head boy failed to pilot his life God's way? Not at all. Jesus warned in Matthew 5:22 that if we write anyone off as a fool, we are party to their murder because there is time

[8] Proverbs 14:18 tells us that no matter how much a *pethī* inherits, he will quickly squander it through folly.

[9] The normal Hebrew word for a mentally deficient fool is *nābāl*, but although this is a common word outside Proverbs it is only used in Proverbs 17:7, 17:21 and 30:22.

[10] Solomon personifies Wisdom in these verses as an Old Testament picture of Jesus the Messiah. Wisdom promises literally in verse 23 to pour out her *rūach* or *Spirit* on those who repent and turn to her. This verse corresponds to Jeremiah 33:3 as much as verse 28 states the opposite.

[11] See Proverbs 13:4; 15:19; 19:24; 21:25; 22:13; 26:14–16.

for a person to repent and listen to Wisdom's words. Whether we wear all five faces of a fool or just one or two, we can repent and walk a different path from the five-times foolish head boy Rehoboam.

Wisdom calls to us as we finish chapter 1, calling us fools with one breath and inviting us to become wise men and women with the next: *"Repent at my rebuke! Then I will pour out my thoughts to you, I will make known to you my teachings."*[12] None of us need wear the five faces of a fool like the head boy Rehoboam.[13]

[12] Since it is Jesus who speaks here as Wisdom personified, this verse uses the Hebrew word *rūach* and can be literally translated *"Repent at my rebuke! Then I will pour out my Spirit on you."*

[13] Jesus cannot be telling us never to call a person a fool, since he does so himself in Matthew 23:17 and Wisdom treats many of her listeners as fools who will reject her call in verses 24–33. He is simply warning us not to write off anyone as a fool, but to fight for each one to see sense and choose life while they still can.

Better than Money (2:1–22)

If you look for it as for silver and search for it as for hidden treasure, then you will understand the fear of the Lord and find the knowledge of God.

(Proverbs 2:4–5)

The best-paid decorator in the world got paid in something far better than money. David Choe was offered a few thousand dollars in 2005 for painting murals on the office walls of a young IT start-up company in Palo Alto. Instead of taking money, he opted to take shares in lieu of payment from the unknown company, just before Facebook became a household name around the world. Seven years later, when Facebook floated as a public company, David Choe was able to cash in the shares he earned from a few days of mural painting for a cool $200 million. It's *"some kind of happy accident"*, he celebrated on his blog. *"I get up and see my picture on the cover of the New York Times and I find out that I'm the highest paid decorator alive!"*[1]

Solomon had never heard of Facebook, but he had made his own decision to pursue something better than money. He could have chosen gold or silver or diamonds when the Lord appeared to him at the Tabernacle in 970 BC and offered to give him anything he desired. He turned them down to ask for wisdom, and now he writes that we must do the same. Because of his wisdom, we read in 1 Kings 10:27 that *"the king made silver as common in Jerusalem as stones"*. Now he urges us to acquire God's wisdom as our first and foremost passion too.

---

[1] This story was reported in newspapers around the world on 2nd February 2012.

In verse 1, he tells us to be like an ancient ruler who *stores up* vast piles of treasure. Fools may waste their lives in storing up money and possessions, but the wise store up God's wisdom in their hearts instead.[2] If we recognize that the rightness of tomorrow's decisions depends on how well we prepare our hearts today, we will be as diligent as any ancient ruler in storing up the words of Proverbs, Ecclesiastes and Song of Songs in our hearts as a precious resource for life ahead. *"Every teacher of the law who has been instructed about the kingdom of heaven is like the owner of a house who brings out of his storeroom new treasures as well as old,"* Jesus adds in Matthew 13:52. We need to store up the words of Solomon as treasures in our heart, and we need to invite Jesus to dwell in our hearts as Wisdom personified. Paul states this in New Testament language in Colossians 2:2–3, when he explains: *"My goal is that they may be encouraged in heart and united in love, so that they may have the full riches of complete understanding, in order that they may know the mystery of God, namely, Christ, in whom are hidden all the treasures of wisdom and knowledge."*

In verses 2–3, Solomon switches metaphor and invites us to join God's big conversation. He tells us to *turn our ear* to the words of Wisdom shouting in the streets, unlike the five-faced fool, and to *apply our heart* to understanding what she says. Having done that, he tells us to go one step further and *call out* and *cry aloud* to Wisdom questions of our own. There is nothing passive about acquiring God's wisdom. It means diligently listening to those wiser than ourselves, unlike the mocker, and taking time to study and apply their words, unlike the sluggard.

In verses 4–8, Solomon switches to yet another metaphor, likening the hard work of acquiring wisdom to the sweat and toil of a *miner*. This is a metaphor lifted from the first of the five books of wisdom literature in the Old Testament: Job, Psalms,

---

[2] Psalm 119:11 also uses this same Hebrew word *tsāphan* to teach us to *store up* God's Word in our hearts.

Proverbs, Ecclesiastes and Song of Songs.[3] Job 28 laments that mining for silver, gold, iron and copper is easy compared to mining for wisdom, which is far more valuable than money. It asks where wisdom can be found on land or sea or sky, which is why Solomon uses this same metaphor to answer Job's question. It can be found in Scripture and in every word which proceeds from the mouth of God. If a miner is willing to sweat and dig deep to earn mere money, we must not be so foolish as to leave the Word of God unmined. The nineteenth-century German philosopher Arthur Schopenhauer pointed out that *"If a man wants to read good books, he must make a point of avoiding bad ones: for life is short, and time and energy limited."*[4] Solomon agrees that *"Of making many books there is no end, and much study wearies the body."*[5] We therefore need to stop frittering away our reading hours on the small change of the world and to start mining deep into the Bible if we want a return on our investment like David Choe.

Perhaps Solomon suspects that we will nod at this but not do it. Perhaps he fears that we will waste our lives on chasing money when the wisdom of God is ours for the asking. Perhaps that's why he lists the three bad choices which he watched his older brothers make instead.

In verses 9–11, he warns that Adonijah pursued injustice and indiscretion because he failed to stockpile wisdom. Adonijah knew that Solomon was his father David's heir, but he lacked sound judgment and thought that he could claim the throne instead.[6]

---

[3] The Old Testament Apocrypha also contains two more books of wisdom – *The Wisdom of Solomon* and *The Wisdom of Sirach* (rather confusingly also known as *Ecclesiasticus*) – but these were written some time between 220 and 100 BC and are not included in the canon of the Old Testament.

[4] He says this in *The Art of Literature* (1891). He presumably classed this as a good book.

[5] Ecclesiastes 12:12.

[6] The Hebrew words used for *discretion* and *understanding* in verse 11 are among the ones which we saw refer to disciplined intellectual study in the chapter "Two Won't Do".

In verses 12–15, he warns that Absalom was enticed by the crooked practices of wicked men and women. The son of an Aramean princess, he had left his father's court and spent three years in his grandfather's pagan kingdom of Geshur.[7] By the time he returned, he had imbibed the teaching of *"men whose words are perverse"* and had set his heart on trying to usurp the throne before his father died.

In verses 16–18, he warns that Amnon was led astray by his sexual desire. He fooled himself that his sin would not be discovered and that it would have no long-term consequence, but Solomon remembers the death of all three brothers and warns us never to forget that sexual sin surely *"leads to death"* and to us joining *"the spirits of the dead"*.[8]

Solomon urges us not to be like his older brothers and throw away our lives so cheaply. He tells us to seek wisdom with all our hearts in order to gain *success* and *protection* and *safety* and *guidance* and *life*.[9] He promises that wisdom is far more valuable than money. It will make us inherit the earth, long after the wicked have been swept away.

So which would you rather have? A few thousand dollars in cash or $200 million in shares? The momentary riches of gold, girls and glory, or the eternal fruit of laying hold of God's wisdom? Solomon ends his second chapter by urging us to invest our lives in acquiring the thing which is far more valuable than money.[10]

---

[7] 2 Samuel 3:3 and 13:37–38. Verse 14 reminds us that Absalom didn't simply copy their ways, but *delighted in them*.

[8] Solomon speaks of common adultery here rather than of Amnon's more unusual sin of rape and incest. It doesn't matter what flavour our sexual sin may take, Solomon insists that marriage is *the covenant of our God*.

[9] Both Psalms and Proverbs use *the land* as a recurring metaphor for *eternal heavenly reward*. Jesus does the same in New Testament verses such as Matthew 5:5.

[10] This is so important that he will urge us again in Proverbs 3:13–15; 4:7; 7:1–3; 8:10–11, 18–21; 10:20 and 16:16. He may have been inspired by Psalm 119:72, 127 and 162.

The Tree of Life (3:1–35)

She is a tree of life to those who take hold of her;
those who hold her fast will be blessed.

(Proverbs 3:18)

The Tree of Life is only mentioned in three places in the Bible: in Genesis (right at the very start of the Bible), in Revelation (right at the very end of the Bible) and here in Proverbs (right in the middle of the Bible).[1] Now that's very interesting. Solomon doesn't just want to whet our appetite for wisdom. He also sheds light on the Genesis story in order to teach us how to get it.

If you have read Genesis 2 and 3, you will know that God placed two important trees at the centre of the Garden of Eden. The first one was the Tree of Life, which God created so that Adam and Eve could eat its fruit and live forever. It seems from Genesis 3:22 that they were not immortal by design but through dependency on him, and that they reaffirmed this every time they ate the first tree's fruit. They remembered that life and wisdom belong to God alone and to anyone humble enough to live as a child of God the Father. The second one was the Tree of the Knowledge of Good and Evil, which God created so that Adam and Eve could choose to rely on human wisdom as a commodity rather than on the wisdom which comes from God. The Hebrew word for *knowledge* is far more practical than its English equivalent (for example, Adam literally *knew* Eve in Genesis 4:1 and as a result she conceived a son!), so this was really the Tree of Experiencing Good and Evil. When the snake tempted Eve that *"When you eat*

[1] Genesis 2:9; 3:22, 24; Revelation 2:7; 22:2, 14, 19; Proverbs 3:18; 11:30; 13:12; 15:4.

from it your eyes will be opened, and you will be like God, knowing good and evil," she believed him. She was hoodwinked into thinking that its fruit was *"desirable for gaining wisdom"*, so she and Adam ate a fatal curse upon the human race.

Solomon picks up on this here in verses 1–18. He doesn't tell us that human reason is unhelpful – quite the contrary. Common sense should have taught Eve to believe the words of God above those of a talking snake, and Solomon reasons with us that we should choose God's wisdom because it grants us long life, peace, prosperity and a good reputation. The Spanish artist Francisco Goya was right to argue that *"The sleep of reason produces monsters,"*[2] but Solomon adds to this that reliance on human reason alone produces monsters too. *"Trust in the Lord with all your heart and lean not on your own understanding,"* he warns us in verse 5. *"There is a way that seems right to a man, but in the end it leads to death,"* he adds in 14:12 and 16:25.[3] He wants us to grasp that human wisdom can only get us so far. In the words of the French philosopher Blaise Pascal, *"The supreme function of reason is to show man that some things are beyond reason."*[4]

Solomon tells us to choose God's Tree of Life instead. He urges us to *"fear the Lord"* in verse 7, to *"honour the Lord"* in verse 9 and to view the Lord as our Father in verse 12.[5] All the other ancient books of wisdom teach their readers to find wisdom through fervent study, but Solomon is adamant that we must find it in God alone.[6] The Father is *"the only wise God"* (Romans 16:27), Jesus the Son *"has become for us wisdom from*

---

[2] Francisco Goya etched this as a proverb on the 43rd of his 80 prints known as *Los Caprichos* (1799).

[3] Solomon views this statement as so important that he lists it twice rather than just once in his Top 375.

[4] This is the 267th of Pascal's *Pensées* (1670). It ties in with the famous verse on humility in 3:34, which is quoted from its Septuagint translation in James 4:6 and 1 Peter 5:5.

[5] Verse 7 tells us what wisdom is both *positively* (fearing the Lord) and *negatively* (hating evil). Verses 11 and 12 are quoted in Hebrews 12:5–6.

[6] Solomon has already told us this in Proverbs 1:7 and 2:6.

God" (1 Corinthians 1:30) and the Holy Spirit is *"the Spirit of wisdom"* (Ephesians 1:17).[7] We must not therefore strive for human wisdom like Adam and Eve, but gain it through relationship with God. As Revelation will explain at the end of the Bible, Jesus' death and resurrection mean that we can eat once more from God's Tree of Life.

Having mentioned the Tree of Life in verse 18 for the first time since Genesis 3, Solomon proceeds to give a list of reasons why we should eat of it in verses 19–35. He reminds us that God's Spirit of Wisdom created the whole universe in just six days,[8] which should provoke us to wonder what God might do through us if we ask for the same *"hearing heart"* as Solomon did in 1 Kings 3:9. We are God's agents in the world, so if we let him fill us with his Spirit of Wisdom, we will become all that humans ought to be and fulfil our God-given calling in the world. Eve was a fool to swap her paradise for forbidden fruit, and we would be fools to fail to seek the Lord with all our hearts as the fountain of true wisdom. Yes, those around us will think us foolish for believing in God's Word, but *"the foolishness of God is wiser than human wisdom, and the weakness of God is stronger than human strength."*[9] To emphasize this, Solomon takes *kesīl* – one of his five Hebrew words for a fool – and uses it positively in verse 26, telling us literally that *"the Lord will be your foolishness and will keep your foot from being snared."* Whatever other people may think of us, if we are humble enough to eat from God's Tree of Life, verse 32 promises that he will take us into *"his secret counsel"*.[10]

---

[7] The Holy Spirit is also called *"the Spirit of Wisdom"* in Deuteronomy 34:9 and Isaiah 11:2.

[8] Genesis 1:2. John begins his gospel by telling us that Jesus is the true *Logos* – Greek for *Word* or the *Divine Reason* behind the universe – and by telling us that Jesus created the universe as the Wisdom of God.

[9] 1 Corinthians 1:25. The first section of 1 Corinthians draws heavily on this chapter, and 2 Corinthians 3:3 picks up on verse 3.

[10] David also promises this in Psalm 25:14. Job and Abraham lived it out in Job 29:4 and Genesis 18:17–33. Proverbs 3:34 teaches us that only the humble

Adam and Eve's sin destroyed the human race, and it was only because Jesus was coming that they were not destroyed straight away.[11] Jesus' life, death and resurrection are still the only reason that fools like us can avoid the curse of verse 33 and receive the favour of verse 34. God invites us to feast on the Gospel for ourselves, and then he promises to fill us with his Spirit of Wisdom and send us out as his ambassadors who proclaim it to the world.

That's why Solomon mentions the Tree of Life again in 11:30, telling us that if we live wise lives, God will turn us into little trees of life ourselves. People will taste God's wisdom through us and many of them will be saved. He mentions it again in 15:4, warning that godly lifestyle is not enough to make us trees of life. We must proclaim the Gospel with our mouths and persuade people to eat God's wisdom. He mentions it yet again in 13:12 to remind us that Gospel words must be backed up with Gospel power. Empty promises make people sick not saved, he warns, but demonstrations of the Spirit's miraculous power convince people to turn from the forbidden tree to embrace God's Tree of Life instead.[12]

So don't simply long for wisdom as an object or commodity. Seek it as the natural fruit of humble dependency on God alone. Wisdom isn't found first and foremost in the library, but in the place of prayer and intimacy with God. There he promises fools like us in James 1:5 that *"If any of you lacks wisdom, you should ask God, who gives generously to all without finding fault, and it will be given to you."*

---

can experience this, and no verse in Proverbs is quoted more often in the New Testament. James 4:6 and 1 Peter 5:5 quote it as it is amplified by the Greek Septuagint.

[11] 1 Corinthians 15:22, 45. Only Genesis 3:15 could undo Genesis 2:17.

[12] Paul teaches that this is vital to the successful advance of the Gospel in 1 Corinthians 2:4–5.

Water Supply (4:1–27)

Above all else, guard your heart, for everything you do flows from it.

(Proverbs 4:23)

Cleisthenes had a problem. He was in charge of the Greek army which was besieging the city of Kirrha in 590 BC and he knew its defences were too strong for his men. Several attempts to break into the city had ended in failure and the Greeks didn't look too kindly upon generals who failed.

Cleisthenes thought fast and it changed the face of fighting. He became the first man in history ever to use biological warfare against an enemy. He dug down until he found the pipes which channelled water into the city and added a poisonous plant called hellebore into the city's water supply. Within hours, every man and woman inside Kirrha was gripped with a debilitating case of diarrhoea. Cleisthenes ordered a final assault on the weakened city and slaughtered its entire population.[1]

Many readers struggle to understand the first nine chapters of Proverbs. They wonder why Solomon spends so long urging us to seek God's wisdom instead of cutting to the chase and beginning his list of detailed maxims for daily living.[2] They fail to grasp what Cleisthenes saw so clearly in 590 BC. Solomon keeps repeating his call for us to pursue God's wisdom with all

---

[1] The late-first-century writer Frontinus was responsible for all of Rome's aqueducts, so he makes sure to relate this event in his book of military tactics entitled *Stratagems* (3.7.6).

[2] This is the third successive chapter which lists the key benefits of pursuing wisdom: protection, honour, promotion, long life, guidance, prosperity and success. Solomon really wants us to eagerly desire wisdom.

our hearts because he knows that the heart of the human battle is the battle for the human heart. He will give us many chapters of detailed application in Proverbs 10–31, but he knows that none of it will be of any use to us unless we first grasp the message of Proverbs 1–9.

The Devil acted like Cleisthenes when he tempted Adam and Eve in the garden. He didn't tempt Eve with the symptoms of folly listed in Proverbs 10–31 – symptoms such as losing her temper, hoarding her wealth or procrastinating today's priorities. He went straight to the heart of her relationship with God because our heart is the water supply which nourishes or pollutes our entire life. *"Above all else, guard your heart, for everything you do flows from it,"* Solomon warns us here in verse 23. Eve forgot to guard her heart and lost her battle against sin. If Solomon seems to be labouring his point in lesson one of Proverbs, it's because he thinks we might do the same.

Genesis 3 tells us that the snake attacked Eve's heart through her *ears* by asking her subversively, *"Did God really say...?"* He attacked her heart through her *eyes* by promising that the forbidden fruit would help her see the world like God, and she gave in because she *"saw that the fruit of the tree was good for food and pleasing to the eye"*. Solomon wants us to grasp that what we look at and listen to has power to purify or pollute our heart. Dirty suggestions produce a dirty heart, which produces dirty thoughts, dirty words and dirty deeds. That's why Solomon is in no hurry to exchange the big-picture warnings of lesson one for the detailed application of lesson two. He doesn't want to move on until he has made our hearts a safe water supply.

Solomon gives us three ways to ensure that the wellspring of our hearts runs with pure and uncontaminated water. The first one is in verses 1–9 and is to listen to our parents. As Clint Eastwood points out in one of his westerns, *"Old people get that way by staying alive."* Even if your own father lacks the wisdom which David passed on to Solomon,[3] you can find another older person to fill your ears with wisdom and to satisfy your eyes that life works God's way.[4] Parent figures help to purify our hearts through the distilled water of their wisdom, stopping us from falling like little children for the Devil's attempts to play Cleisthenes against us. If you cannot think of any wise older person in your life, Solomon's own father David will adopt you. He still speaks to you in Psalm 1 and warns you not to *"sit in the company of mockers"* or else you will become like them. He urges you instead to become a person *"whose delight is in the law of the Lord, and who meditates on his law day and night"*.[5]

Solomon's second way in which we can protect the water supply of our hearts is to look up and see the road ahead in verses 10–19. Life is a journey and how we set out affects where we arrive. The fool sets foot on the path of the wicked in verse 14, little thinking that our sins today build momentum for tomorrow. No one can rest on that path in verse 16 because the downward pull of a polluted heart is far too strong. Listening to ungodly ideas and looking at ungodly things is like handing Cleisthenes a spade. In contrast, if we feast our eyes and ears on God's Word, we find ourselves on straight, fast roads where life's scenery just gets better and better. *"The path of the righteous is like the morning sun,"* Solomon tells us in verse 18 in deliberate contrast with the deep darkness which descends on fools, *"shining ever brighter till the full light of day"*.[6]

---

[3] David uses the same word as is used in verse 3 to describe Solomon as *tender* in 1 Chronicles 22:5 and 29:1. Bathsheba bore other sons to David (1 Chronicles 3:5) but treated him as her *only one* because he was the heir.

[4] Note the reciprocal nature of wisdom in verse 8. If we exalt wisdom, wisdom will exalt us.

[5] This is why Solomon chose wisdom over everything else when God appeared to him at the Tabernacle. He had feasted his eyes and ears on David's call here in verse 7 as much as his elder brothers had ignored it.

[6] Jesus uses a similar picture when he warns us to feast our eyes on what is good in Matthew 6:22–23. A polluted heart also leads to death in James 1:14–15, while a pure heart leads to life in Philippians 4:8–9.

Solomon's third way in which we can protect the water supply of our hearts is to see our eyes and ears as rudders to our whole body in verses 20–27. If we look and listen to the right things in verses 20 and 21, Solomon promises our entire bodies will move on a healthy course. If we fix our eyes in the right places in verse 25, he promises our thoughts and mouths and feet will be right too.[7] The New Testament appears to be looking back to verse 26 in Hebrews 12:13, and Jesus appears to be thinking of verses 23–24 when he tells us in Luke 6:45 that *"A good man brings good things out of the good stored up in his heart, and an evil man brings evil things out of the evil stored up in his heart. For the mouth speaks what the heart is full of."*[8]

Whichever of these three ways to protect the water supply of your heart comes easiest to you, one thing remains the same. Out of all of the 256 verses in lesson one, Solomon warns us that we need to remember this one *"above all else"*.[9] One smarter and more ruthless than Cleisthenes lurks outside your city walls and wants your blood. Don't let him enlist your eyes and ears as willing helpers in his plot to poison your water supply.

[7] When Solomon tells us to make level our paths in 4:26 (a verse quoted in Hebrews 12:13), the Hebrew verb he chooses is one which often describes a person using scales. Where we look affects the balance of our thoughts, which in turn affects the balance of our actions. Proverbs 5:21 uses the same verb to warn us that God then weighs our hearts by our actions.

[8] He may also have been thinking of Proverbs 10:20 which equates our *tongues* with our *hearts*.

[9] In case we still miss this in lesson one, Solomon will repeat it in 27:19 amidst the detail of lesson two.

Free Chocolate (5:1–7:27)

For the lips of the adulterous woman drip honey, and her speech is smoother than oil; but in the end she is bitter as gall, sharp as a double-edged sword.

(Proverbs 5:3–4)

I am very generous towards mice. I live in a big old house which backs onto a field full of them, so I have to be. Every time I see the tell-tale signs of small rodent intruders, I lay out pieces of free chocolate in mousetraps around my back door. The following morning I invariably find that some of them have accepted my kind offer. They have also discovered that my free chocolate has a lethal price tag.

Solomon warns us that committing adultery is an act of sheer folly, the human equivalent of taking up the offer of free chocolate in a mousetrap.[1] As the son of an adulterous couple, he remembers that it was this sin which almost wrecked his father's kingdom, and that's probably why he uses it to ground his general teaching about guarding the water supply of our hearts with three chapters of specific application. Make no mistake about it, he warns us, adultery is a perfect picture of folly in action.[2]

Sex outside marriage sounds sweet to the ears. The adulterous woman speaks such smooth and honey-coated words in 5:3 and 6:24 that *"with persuasive words she led him astray;*

---

[1] He specifically likens sin to a *trap* in 12:13, 13:14, 14:27, 22:25, 29:6 and 29:25. See also 2 Timothy 2:26.

[2] Proverbs 7:3 links back to Deuteronomy 6:8–9 and 11:18–20 and is Solomon's way of emphasizing that this is a God-inspired warning, not just his own.

she seduced him with her smooth talk."[3] Sex outside marriage also looks appealing to the eyes. Solomon warns us in 6:25, *"Do not lust in your heart after her beauty or let her captivate you with her eyes."* She dresses quite literally to kill in 7:10, with the skimpy clothing of a prostitute and with a brazen face which deliberately arouses all of his senses.[4] She is in every way the hellebore which poisoned Kirrha's water supply, and she will bear him to hell if he has no more sense than a rodent and lets her pollute his heart with her invitation to dine on folly.[5]

Solomon tells us that the way to resist chocolate in a mousetrap is to fill up on the fine food which God has already given us. He doesn't just tell us not to snack on sex outside of marriage in 5:8; he also tells us to eat our fill of sex within marriage in 5:15–20. If you are married, the best way to avoid temptation to commit adultery is to romance your wife or husband and feast your eyes on your spouse's naked body. Solomon prays for you in 5:18–19: *"May you rejoice in the wife of your youth... May her breasts satisfy you always, may you ever be intoxicated with her love."* God has given you your own pure water supply within marriage to stop you from needing to drink from the polluted pool of sexual sin.[6] If you are single, you are more like Jesus than Solomon, and Jesus will enable you to drink

[3] The adulterous woman is meant to be a parody of Lady Wisdom, since the Hebrew word which Solomon uses for her *persuasive words* in 7:21 is *leqah*, the same word he uses in Proverbs for Wisdom's *instruction*.

[4] The Hebrew word *hēk* in 5:3 means literally the *roof of her mouth*. This could either refer to her *speech* (as in 8:7) or to *passionate kissing* (as in Song of Songs 2:3). Since ordinary Hebrews could only afford to eat meat at a fellowship offering, 7:14 completes her promise to satisfy his eyes, ears, touch, taste and smell.

[5] Solomon says something similar about the sweet words of an adulteress in 22:14.

[6] Proverbs 5:19–20 tells us that getting drunk on sex at home will stop us from getting drunk on sex away from home, and Paul states something similar in 1 Corinthians 7:1–9. It is tragic that Christians are better known for negative attitudes towards unmarried sex than they are for positive celebration of married sex.

from God's river so that you can master your unfulfilled sexual longings.[7] Hebrews 4:15 tells us that Jesus *"has been tempted in every way, just as we are – yet he did not sin."* He promises to help you make a covenant with your eyes, like the one in Job 31:1, not to look lustfully at anyone while you wait for him to provide for you the kind of marriage partner described in Song of Songs.

The chocolate which I put in my mousetraps tastes sweet, but its aftertaste is the feel of metal crushing the mouse's skull. In the same way, Solomon warns us in 5:4–5 that sex outside of marriage is like bitter poison, a double-edged sword, and the harbinger of sudden death and hell.[8] It cannot satisfy like sex within marriage, since a wife binds herself to a man for life and promises to let him drink his fill of her love forever (5:15–20), whereas an adulteress merely *takes hold of him* and promises to *love him till morning* (7:10–20).[9] At least a starving man risks jail because without stolen food he will die, but a man who commits adultery pays a fatal price to snack on food he does not need and which he knows can never truly satisfy him (6:30–33).[10] He pours out his life for a woman who has pledged her life to another man. Solomon tells us in 7:27 that the promise of stolen bedroom pleasures is actually the path to bedroom slaughter.

The fool thinks he will never commit adultery. He feasts his eyes and ears on other women because he fools himself that looking and listening doesn't hurt anybody. That's why Solomon

---

[7] David was married yet fed his eyes on another man's wife (2 Samuel 11:2–3); Joseph was single but *"refused to go to bed with her or even be with her"* (Genesis 39:10). 2 Timothy 2:22 particularly addresses single people.

[8] Solomon uses the word *she'ōl* in verses 5:5 and 7:27, the normal Old Testament word for *the grave* or *hell*. His parallelism between *she'ōl* and *the pit* in 1:12 indicates that he specifically means *hell* here.

[9] Solomon uses the same Hebrew word for *getting drunk* in 5:19 and 7:18 to show that adultery is simply Folly's empty parody of the true sexual fulfilment which Wisdom grants to married couples.

[10] Thieves were commanded in Exodus 22:1–4 to pay back two to five times what they stole, and Exodus 21:30 permitted a murderer to pay a ransom to save his life. The reference to *sevenfold* repayment in 6:31 emphasizes that no amount of money can compensate for adultery (27:4). It can often even lead to murder.

warns us that the Lord sees what we lust about in secret (5:21) and that he will reveal our secret sins for all to see (5:14, 6:32–33). Nobody ever sets out to commit adultery. They just start looking, listening, thinking, flirting, fantasizing – and then suddenly the mousetrap springs shut. These three chapters warn us that secret thoughts are often the first steps on a fatal journey. They are the first steps on the *"highway to hell, leading down to the chambers of death"* (7:27).

The fool thinks he can commit adultery and not get caught. He is *"like an ox going to the slaughter, like a deer stepping into a noose... like a bird darting into a snare, little knowing it will cost him his life"*.[11] That's why Solomon asks us incredulously in 6:27–29: *"Can a man scoop fire into his lap without his clothes being burned? Can a man walk on hot coals without his feet being scorched? So is he who sleeps with another man's wife; no one who touches her will go unpunished."* Mice eat chocolate without imagining that they will ever become rodent corpses by the back door. So do fools who commit adultery.

So don't move on from these three chapters without repenting of the lust and sexual sin which the Devil wants to use to pollute your water supply. When you have done so, repent of the other subtle sins which Solomon warns against in these three chapters too: thoughtless financial decisions (6:1–5),[12] endless procrastination (6:6–11), lies and half-truths (6:12–15), and self-assertive pride (6:16–19).[13] The Devil puts all manner of temptations in his mousetraps, so don't fall for any of his bait.

Chocolate is always free in a mousetrap. But the Devil's free chocolate will cost you everything.

---

[11] Proverbs 7:22–23. The Hebrew can read *"like a fool being led to correction in the stocks"* rather than *"like a deer stepping into a noose"*. If so, it means that fools who think nothing of being caught also think nothing of repenting when they are caught.

[12] An example of someone making this kind of rash pledge can be found in Genesis 43:9 and 44:32–33.

[13] *"There are six things... seven"* is a poetic way of introducing a list of items. See also 30:15–31 and Job 5:19.

Make Tracks (6:20–24)

For this command is a lamp, this teaching is a light, and correction and instruction are the way to life.
(Proverbs 6:23)

On 10th May 1869, the final spike was hammered into the ground to complete the first transcontinental railroad in America. The Atlantic port cities of the east coast had been linked by railway to the Pacific port cities of the west coast for the first time. It had taken 2,315 days to build 1,800 miles of railway track from Nebraska to California. Every day had been difficult, but on some days the workers had been forced to cut tunnels through granite and progressed a mere six inches in a day.

Building the Overland Route was a long and painful endeavour, but travelling on it wasn't. Before the Overland Route was completed, a journey from New York to San Francisco took six months and cost $1,000. Once the rail track was laid, the same journey took only seven days and cost a mere sixty-five dollars. Laying railway track is hard work, but once we do so life gets easier. Trains travel at high speeds in the right direction because someone had the vision and discipline to lay good tracks for them to follow.

Solomon had never seen a railway line but he understood this principle. He told us in 1:5 that people become wise by building *tahbulōth* or *ropes* which prepare them to live God's way. Most English translations simply render this word *guidance*, but Solomon is saying something deeper here. Since he was a shipwright rather than a railwayman, he chose the technical word that was used for the steering ropes which held in place the rudder of a mighty sailing ship in order to guide it to its proper destination.[1] Solomon wants us to grasp that wisdom and guidance are not acquired at the moment when we need them. We develop them beforehand though studying the Scriptures and laying godly tracks in our minds which direct the way we make decisions.

Solomon had never seen the signals on a railway line, but he understood that life is full of junctions in the road. That's why he told us in 2:1 that people become wise by *creating a stockpile* of wisdom which acts as a filter to separate bad choices from good ones.[2] He used this same Hebrew word *tsāphan* again in 2:7 to promise that if we store up a stockpile of wise principles and thought patterns in our mind, God will guide us at each junction and bring us to his own stockpile of blessings at the end of the line.

Solomon had never seen the bright lights at the front of a high-speed railway train which enable its driver to see the track ahead, but he understood that we need to see what is coming up ahead of us on life's journey. That's why he uses a third picture here in 6:23, telling us that these proverbs will be *"a lamp"* and *"a light"* for us as we speed along the line. They will be friends and advisers in 6:22, not just bits of information: *"When you walk, they will guide you; when you sleep, they will watch over you; when you awake, they will speak to you."* If you want to be wise and speed through life in the right direction, you need to discipline yourself to lay wise railway tracks today.

The first way you can do this is to get up early and study the Word of God. Wisdom cries out literally in 8:17 that *"I love those who love me, and those who* ***seek me early in the day*** *will find*

[1] 1 Kings 9:26–28; 10:22. The closest we get to railway language in Proverbs is the contrast between *"the way of the sluggard"* in 15:19 and *"the highway of the upright"* in 16:17.

[2] Solomon also uses this same Hebrew verb to tell us to *create a stockpile* of wisdom in 7:1 and 10:14. See also Psalm 119:11. Proverbs 19:27 reminds us that we must keep adding to this stockpile or it will get depleted.

me."[3] If you are a night owl rather than an early riser, it doesn't matter, because she simply means that if we study Scripture in the darkness while fools sleep, we will be wise throughout the day. Solomon tells us in 3:32 that the Lord loves to reveal his *intimate thoughts* to the upright, if they will only listen.[4] Don't be discouraged if you find reading the Bible tough work, like the builders of the Overland Route who were forced to dig through granite. If you persevere, you will build a railway line of wisdom which will steer your path and guide you every day.

The second way you can lay wise railway tracks is to listen to your parents. There is a reason why the words *father, mother, son* and *child* occur thirty times in the nine chapters which make up lesson one of God's school of wisdom. If your parents are still alive, Solomon insists in 6:20–24 that one of the best ways for you to lay tracks of wisdom in your life is to listen to what they have to say. If they are no longer alive, the New Testament encourages you to find spiritual fathers and mothers who can play this role for you instead.[5] If you are a parent, these same verses urge you to help your children to start building wise railway tracks from a very early age. Solomon tells us in 22:6 to *"Start children off on the way they should go, and even when they are old they will not turn from it."*

The third way you can lay wise railways tracks is to choose your friends very carefully. Whether we like it or not, we become like our friends, because laying railway tracks is something people do together.[6] We read in 12:5 that the foolish

---

[3] I am not saying that we can "earn" wisdom through Bible study. Wisdom also uses this same Hebrew verb in 1:28 to warn that arrogant fools can get up as early as they like, but they will not find her.

[4] This same Hebrew word *sōd* is also used to promise us the same thing in Psalm 25:14 and Amos 3:7. The same word is also used to describe Job's experience of God in Job 29:4.

[5] See Romans 16:13; 1 Corinthians 4:14–15; Galatians 4:19; 1 Thessalonians 2:7, 11; Titus 1:4; Philemon 10.

[6] Other warnings against taking fools as friends can be found in 12:26, 22:24–25 and 27:17.

have their own set of *tahbulōth* or *steering ropes*, which is why Solomon warns us in 13:20 that *"He who walks with the wise grows wise, but a companion of fools suffers harm."* Put more positively, a group of wise friends can make us wiser if we listen to what they say. *Tahbulōth* is used in 11:14, 20:18 and 24:6 to encourage us to view the advice of wise friends as an extra set of steering ropes to keep us going in the right direction.[7]

The fourth way we can lay wise railway tracks in our minds is to welcome negative feedback, rebukes and criticism. None of us finds this easy – it's as painful as the hammering and blasting which was necessary to build the Overland Route – but Solomon insists in 6:23 that rebukes *"are like the road leading to life"*.[8] He refers to them as *"life-giving correction"* in 15:31, and he tells us plainly in 15:10 that *"the one who hates correction will die."* I have never liked it when people tell me what I've done wrong but, much as I find it difficult, I've never failed to benefit from it.

So don't get passive as we near the end of lesson one in God's school of wisdom. Be as diligent as the builders of the Overland Route. If you study Scripture, listen to your parents, make wise friends and listen to negative feedback, you will be rewarded. You will build a railway track which will allow you to travel wisely in the days which are to come.

---

[7] Proverbs 13:10, 15:22 and 26:12 warn that those who fail to seek advice because they think they are wise enough already are likely to make a train wreck of their lives.

[8] New English Translation. The word *mūsār* means *rebuke* or *correction*, and Solomon uses it repeatedly to emphasize the importance of criticism and negative feedback in learning wisdom. See 1:7, 8; 3:11; 4:1, 13; 5:12, 23; 8:10, 33; 10:17; 12:1; 13:1, 18, 24; 15:5, 32; 19:20, 27; 22:15.

Choose (8:1–9:18)

Wisdom has built her house... She has sent out her servants, and she calls from the highest point of the city, "Let all who are simple come to my house!"

(Proverbs 9:1–4)

Solomon is about to finish lesson one of God's school of wisdom, so he turns up the volume in these two final chapters and says it's time to choose. It's time for us to choose between two paths, two doors, two houses, two advisers, two ways of life and two destinies. It's time for us to choose between two women named Wisdom and Folly. We cannot graduate to the detailed proverbs of lesson two unless we first surrender our lives to the Lord and to his Wisdom.

Solomon tells us to surrender to God's wisdom in 8:1–21 because it is our *provider*. We saw earlier that this is Jesus speaking in Old Testament disguise,[1] so it shouldn't surprise us that Wisdom effectively promises, like Jesus in John 10:10, to give us *"life and life to the full"*. She calls out at every fork in the road in 8:2, telling us to take the path which leads to blessing as inevitably as the other path leads to death.[2] She calls out at every doorway in 8:3, promising that she will open the door

---

[1] Don't be surprised that Jesus is a female here. The Hebrew words for *wisdom* and *knowledge* are feminine so he is naturally personified as a woman. Isaiah 59:14 uses the same principle of Hebrew gender to personify Justice as a man but Righteousness, Truth and Honesty as women.

[2] Solomon's wisdom made him fabulously wealthy and powerful. However, the fact that Jesus was executed as a poor man by wicked rulers reminds us that God's definition of prosperity is often different from ours.

to *the fear of the Lord*, which she defines as *hating evil*.[3] Peter would later say to Jesus, as he watched many of his friends choose a different path, *"Lord, to whom shall we go? You have the words of eternal life."*[4] Solomon doesn't want you to move on to lesson two until you have said the same.[5]

He tells us to surrender to God's wisdom in 8:22–36 because it is our *Creator*. The fourth-century heretic Arius misunderstood verse 22 to mean that Jesus was a created being, but Solomon is actually trying to teach the opposite – that nothing exists which Jesus, the Wisdom of God, didn't partner with the Father to create.[6] They rejoiced together as they did so, which means that choosing Folly over Wisdom is like a child abandoning its parents to run off with a stranger.[7] *"Those who find me find life and receive favour from the Lord,"* Wisdom promises those she created. *"But those who fail to find me harm themselves; all who hate me love death."*

Solomon tells us to surrender to God's wisdom in 9:1–18 because it is our *saviour*. Wisdom has prepared a Gospel feast for all who listen to her: she has prepared a slaughtered sacrifice and mixed a blood-red wine to save fools from God's judgment. She sends out Gospel messengers to invite the simpleton and the mocker to her seven-pillared home so that they can receive eternal life.[8] She echoes the summary of the message of Proverbs in 1:7,

---

[3] This important exegesis of 1:7 is repeated in 16:6, Exodus 20:20, Job 28:28 and 2 Timothy 2:19.

[4] John 6:68.

[5] Note the deliberate reference back to the fruit of the Tree of Life in 8:19.

[6] Arianism used this verse and John 14:28 as its key proof texts. However, basing our Christology on the words of Wisdom in this passage is as foolish as using them to argue Jesus is a woman. Jesus is Wisdom and God is Love (1 John 4:8), but Wisdom isn't Jesus any more than Love is God.

[7] Folly pretends that life has no real meaning, but these verses stress that the Father created the world through Wisdom for great purpose, a purpose which made the angels rejoice in Job 38:7.

[8] Solomon does not define what the seven pillars are, since seven simply represents *completeness* in ancient Hebrew thought (6:31). It stresses that Wisdom's work is finished and that we simply need to come (John 19:30).

telling us that *"The fear of the Lord is the beginning of wisdom, and knowledge of the Holy One is understanding."*[9] Lesson one has not simply been a call to embrace a better lifestyle. It has been an appeal to lay hold of the Lord, who is life itself.

Meanwhile, Folly proclaims her own pathetic gospel.[10] She has no meat or wine to offer because she prefers to sit while Wisdom stands and works,[11] so she tries to convince the foolish that her bread and water are exciting and clandestine. Her lies are obvious – how can mere water taste sweet?![12] – but she knows that loud repetition is often all it takes to convince the simpleton and mocker. Arthur Schopenhauer observed that *"There is no opinion, however absurd, which men will not readily embrace as soon as they can be brought to the conviction that it is generally adopted,"*[13] and Folly places all her hope in that observation being true. She dares not throw open her door and show the world what the inside of her house is really like, because it has no pillars or table and is home to death instead of life.[14] She has no money to hire messengers because Folly seldom turns a profit. Instead, she loudly peddles forbidden fruit, knowing that mockers will always prefer to attack Wisdom's messengers than humble themselves to eat from the Tree of Life.

---

[9] Solomon says literally *"the Holy Ones"*, which is either a reference to God's People or another hint that he understood something of the Trinity.

[10] Folly's first sentence in 9:16 is exactly the same as Wisdom's first sentence in 9:4, but their messages are totally different.

[11] The Hebrew word for her seat is *kisse'*, which means literally *throne*. She uses the trappings of success to deflect attention from how little she actually has to offer.

[12] By definition, water is simply water! Job 20:12–14 tells us that even if sin does taste sweet in the mouth, it has a terrible aftertaste and feels like poison in the belly.

[13] He wrote this in his treatise *The Art of Being Right* (1831). Verses 7 and 8 warn that fools who have fallen for lies will often react very badly to the truth of the Gospel.

[14] Folly uses the word *she'ōl* in 9:18, the same Hebrew word which meant *hell* in 5:5 and 7:27. Note the parallel between this chapter and John 10:10. Jesus offers life to the full while the Devil offers death and hell.

Make no mistake about it, Solomon says you are at a crossroads as you finish lesson one of God's flight school. He says that unless you choose Wisdom over Folly, the proverbs of lesson two will be of no benefit to you. In fact, they will be harmful instead of helpful. He will warn you towards the end of lesson two in 26:7–9 that *"Like the useless legs of one who is lame is a proverb in the mouth of a fool... Like a thorn-bush in a drunkard's hand is a proverb in the mouth of a fool."*

I am no Solomon, but I do know that my life took two giant leaps forward when I responded to this call to listen to the voice of Wisdom. I was spectacularly unfruitful during my first few years in Christian ministry, but I was gripped on my thirtieth birthday by a simple phrase in Jeremiah 33:3 – *"Call to me and I will answer you and tell you great and unsearchable things you do not know."* I began to confess to God how foolish and naïve I was, and I began to do as Wisdom urges in 8:17. I began to get up an hour or two earlier than my children every morning to pore over the Scriptures and to let the Lord teach me the secrets of his wisdom.[15]

The second breakthrough came just before my thirty-fifth birthday, when I moved to Southwest London to pastor my first church. For several weeks I was gripped by the same sense of foolishness as Solomon when he told the Lord in 1 Kings 3:7–9, *"I am only a little child and do not know how to carry out my duties... So give your servant a discerning heart."* That period of renouncing Folly and choosing Wisdom made room for God to grant outstanding breakthrough and church growth. Wisdom means what she promises in these chapters.

So make an active choice of your own to renounce folly and embrace wisdom. Humble yourself before Jesus, the Wisdom of God. Only then will you be ready to move on to the detailed instruction of lesson two.

---

[15] The verb *sāhar* in 8:17 means literally *to get up early to seek* for something. Jesus promises to reveal himself to those who get up early to seek his wisdom, just as he did in Mark 1:35 and Luke 4:42. See also Job 1:5.

Lesson Two:

Live God's Way

(Proverbs 10–31)

Solomon's Toolkit (10:1–22:16)

The proverbs of Solomon...

(Proverbs 10:1)

"To the man with a hammer, everything looks like a nail," observed the American psychologist Abraham Maslow. He laughed at would-be teachers who claimed to have wide knowledge and yet proved to be experts in only one small field. Like junior apprentices, they tackled the bewildering complexities of life as if their one tool could fix everything. Maslow warned his readers not to listen to teachers who only had one overused idea at their disposal.

As we begin lesson two in God's flight school of wisdom, it is obvious that Solomon was not a one-tool tradesman. These 375 verses are his greatest hits,[1] the Top 375 which he compiled from the 3,000 proverbs that are mentioned in 1 Kings 4:32.[2] They cover diverse themes which range from friendship to farming, from marriage to moneymaking, from parenting to politics, and from idle gossip to true greatness. If you are surprised by the scope of the topics he covers, you are already making progress in the second lesson in God's school of wisdom.

[1] Since the letters that form Solomon's name have a numerical value of 375 in the Hebrew number game known as *gematria*, some readers suggest this is why he decided to limit himself to only his Top 375.

[2] 1 Kings 4:29–34 tells us that he studied widely – from music to botany to zoology – but the 375 proverbs which he selects are less about plants and animals than they are about daily human life.

Solomon's toolkit is jammed full of many different tools because God's wisdom addresses all of life's multifaceted problems.

This raises lots of questions for frustrated modern readers. The commonest question is *why are these proverbs ordered so randomly instead of being grouped by theme?* Solomon knows we would prefer a chapter on parenting, a chapter on guidance, a chapter on godly speech and a chapter on giving to the poor instead of scattered verses on each of these themes throughout these twelve and a half chapters, but instead he forces us to flit from one theme to another with breathless speed. He does so deliberately because that's the messy way in which we have to live our lives. In the words of John Lennon, *"Life is what happens to you while you're busy making other plans."*[3]

Think about it. Solomon was the builder of the Temple, one of the greatest buildings in the ancient world, so he was smart enough to know how to group his proverbs by theme if he had wanted to. He deliberately chose not to because he wanted us to understand that life simply doesn't work that way. Like the book of James, which is often called "the Proverbs of the New Testament", Solomon resists the urge to compartmentalize God's wisdom because we must not do so either. Although it's tempting to ignore the structure of Proverbs and tackle these chapters thematically, we are going to follow Solomon's structure together because doing so is actually part of his second lesson.[4]

Another question which many readers ask is *why are these proverbs so different from the rest of the Old Testament?* Unlike the books which precede it, Proverbs doesn't explicitly mention God's sovereign plan for Israel or his promise to save people

[3] Lennon used this line in his song "Beautiful Boy (Darling Boy)", from his album *Double Fantasy* (1980), but he was probably quoting from Allen Saunders in the January 1957 edition of the *Reader's Digest*.

[4] As we do so, we will discover that Solomon was far more intentional than most readers give him credit for in devising the correct order for the proverbs which comprise his Top 375.

through blood sacrifice. This makes some readers suggest that Proverbs is not a book about salvation at all, but simply a series of pithy maxims about practical day-to-day living. If you are tempted to think this yourself, you desperately need to understand the message of Proverbs. Whereas the books which precede it focus on *how* we can be saved, the book of Proverbs expands that message of salvation to encompass what God saves us *from* and what he saves us *for*. In 15:8 and 21:27, Solomon laughs at the idea that a sinner's prayer can save anyone unless they surrender their life totally to the Lord. James repeats this in the New Testament when he warns us, *"You foolish person, do you want evidence that faith without deeds is useless?... As the body without the spirit is dead, so faith without deeds is dead."*[5] Solomon's proverbs are as much about salvation as the rest of the Old Testament. They tell us that true conversion will always result in our exchanging godless folly for godly wisdom.

Still another question which many readers ask is *can we treat these proverbs as divine promises?* That's a really good question because Solomon warns in 26:9 that his proverbs are powerfully helpful when used correctly, but dangerously harmful when misunderstood and misapplied. If we treat 10:24 as a blanket promise – *"What the righteous desire will be granted"* – then we set ourselves up for a disaster, since even Jesus knew that he needed to end his prayers with *"Not as I will, but as you will."*[6] If we latch onto 16:3 – *"Commit to the Lord whatever you do, and your plans will succeed"* – and treat it as a promise of non-stop prosperity, we will be disappointed too.[7] Solomon is giving us 375 principles and guidelines, not 375 promises and guarantees, and we need to grasp this or we will run into problems. When we hear Diana Ross sing *"Ain't*

[5] James 2:20, 26.

[6] Matthew 26:39. See also 2 Corinthians 12:7–10.

[7] Righteous people *will* at times go hungry (2 Corinthians 11:27) and wicked people *will* sometimes prosper in this life. 10:27, 11:31 and 13:25 are simply teaching us that this is the exception rather than the rule.

no mountain high enough," we don't assume she is planning a mountaineering expedition because we understand pop music as a genre. We need to understand proverbs as a literary genre if we are to learn to live God's way.

The Hebrew word which is used for Solomon's proverbs in 1:1, 10:1 and 25:1 is *māshāl*, which means literally a *parable* or *comparison*.[8] These are therefore a series of brushstrokes which paint a picture of what is generally true, and two proverbs may even contradict one another to create a balanced picture of life's complex drama.[9] This picture is so important that it forms by far the longest section of Proverbs, Ecclesiastes and Song of Songs, and it therefore also forms by far the longest section of this commentary. The English thinker Samuel Johnson observed that *"Men more frequently require to be reminded than informed,"*[10] so Solomon reminds us again and again what salvation looks like in working clothes so that we will grasp how to live God's way. *Māshāl* means *victory song* in Isaiah 14:4 and a God-inspired *oracle* in Numbers 23:7 and 18, so this is a divinely inspired description of the lifestyle of anyone who truly follows the Lord.

For Solomon is no one-tool tradesman, and he has plenty of things to bring out of his toolkit of practical wisdom. This lesson is the longest because living God's way isn't easy. Let's move on from lesson one which called us to learn God's way in general, and let's explore lesson two which teaches us how to live God's way in practice.

[8] A good example of the word being used to mean a *parable* is in Ezekiel 17:2.

[9] So do English proverbs. Consider *"Many hands make light work"* and *"Too many cooks spoil the broth."*

[10] Dr Samuel Johnson wrote this in 1750 in the second section of *The Rambler*.

The Righteous and the Wicked (10:1–32)

The lips of the righteous nourish many, but fools die for lack of sense.

(Proverbs 10:21)

If I told you that *"Roses are red, violets are blue"*, you would instinctively know that I am reciting a Valentine's card poem. If I told you that *"There once was a man from Peru, who dreamed he was eating his shoe"*, you would instantly grasp that I am reciting a limerick. I wouldn't have to explain that to you. You would simply know because you are familiar with English poetry. Since Solomon wrote each of these 375 proverbs as a poetic couplet in Hebrew, we are therefore going to need to grasp a little bit about Hebrew poetry if we want to understand what he is saying.

I know there is an off-chance that the intricacies of Hebrew poetry may not be your idea of exciting reading. Don't worry. It won't take long and you will be richly rewarded for your patience in this chapter. All you need to understand is that ancient Hebrew poetry didn't rhyme (one look at their complicated verb endings and it's easy to see why). Instead it found its beauty in symmetry – either in clever acrostic poems like the one in 31:10–31, or in the poetic couplets which form the bulk of Proverbs and which Hebrew scholars refer to as *parallelisms*. Whereas proverbs in English tend to be one-liners, Solomon's Top 375 are all two-liners in which two concepts are placed in parallel with one another.

Got that? Then you are ready to delve a little deeper because there are four different types of Hebrew parallelisms.

The *synonymous parallelism* is a couplet where the second line repeats the same concept as the first line but uses different words to emphasize its message. We find one here in 10:10 when Solomon tells us that *"Whoever winks maliciously causes grief,* ***and*** *a chattering fool comes to ruin."* The tell-tale sign in a synonymous parallel is the joining word *and*, which tells us that winking is akin to chattering and grief is akin to ruin.[1]

The *antithetic parallelism* is a couplet where the second line echoes the same concept as the first line by repeating it in opposite form. The tell-tale word this time is *but*, and we find a good example straightaway in 10:1 – *"A wise son brings joy to his father,* ***but*** *a foolish son brings grief to his mother."* Interestingly, most of the parallelisms in Solomon's Top 375 are antithetic ones, including twenty-eight of the thirty-two couplets in this chapter.

The *synthetic parallelism* is a couplet where the second line adds more detail to the concept started in the first line. A tell-tale sign is often the word *for*, as we can see in 19:19 which tells us that *"A man of great wrath will pay the penalty,* ***for*** *if you deliver him, you will only have to do it again."*[2]

The *comparative parallelism* is a couplet which likens one thing to another, as we can see in 10:26 which tells us that *"**As** vinegar to the teeth and smoke to the eyes, so are sluggards to those who send them."* The tell-tale word this time is *as* or *like*, and although there aren't too many of these in this first collection of

---

[1] Since the word for *and* and *but* is the same in Hebrew, this clue is given us by the translator rather than direct from Solomon, based on the thrust of the proverb. Another synthetic parallelism can be found in 10:18.

[2] English Standard Version. The Hebrew word for *for* is not the same as the word for *and* and *but*, so this clue actually comes direct from Solomon. However, not every translator carries this little word over into English.

Solomon's proverbs in 10:1–22:16, the second collection of his proverbs is full of them in 25:1–29:27.[3]

OK. Hebrew poetry lesson over. Now let's see why understanding this is so vital if we want to grasp the meaning of the book of Proverbs.

Some people see Proverbs as a book of clever maxims rather than part of God's story of salvation. Understanding Hebrew poetry shows us that this simply isn't true. The early Old Testament writers used the word *she'ōl* to refer either to *the grave* in general (believers and unbelievers all go there in Psalm 88:3) or to *hell* in particular (unbelievers go there while believers go to heaven in Psalm 16:10–11). It was Solomon's use of a synonymous parallelism in 1:12 which told us that he equates *she'ōl* with *the pit* and therefore thinks of it as *hell* rather than simply as *the grave*. He gave us this clue early on in lesson one to warn that Proverbs is not simply a call to live a better life on earth through choosing wisdom. It is a long Gospel appeal, which urges us to lay hold of Wisdom as an Old Testament picture of God's Deliverer in order that we might be saved.[4]

Unless we grasp this, we will find chapter 10 quite bewildering. Although Solomon starts in verse 1 with the familiar contrast between the *wise man* and the *fool*, he suddenly lurches into a contrast between the *righteous* and the *wicked* instead. The word wise is used five times and the word *fool* is used six times in this chapter, but *righteous* and *wicked* are used fifteen and twelve times. We won't understand this shift in focus unless we spot the antithetic parallelism in verse 21 which contrasts the *righteous* on the one hand with *fools* on the other. Solomon wants us to grasp at the very start of lesson

[3] A variation of the comparative parallelism which occurs more frequently in the Top 375 is the type which reads *"Better x than y"*. Examples can be found in 12:9; 15:16–17; 16:8, 16, 19 and 32.

[4] I am not being anachronistic when I refer to "the Gospel" in Old Covenant Israel. Galatians 3:8 tells us that God even *preached the Gospel in advance* to Abraham.

two that he uses *wise* and *righteous* interchangeably, and *foolish* and *wicked* interchangeably too. Don't miss this and think he is changing the subject when he talks about the righteous and the wicked in this chapter. He is beginning to explain something which will be a prominent feature of this second lesson: those God makes righteous embrace wisdom, and those who embrace folly aren't truly saved.[5]

Indulge me in one final piece of Hebrew which completes what Solomon is saying in this chapter. The Hebrew word *tsadīq* can mean *righteous* (living rightly) or *justified* (treated by God as if we had lived rightly). It is the word which the rest of the Old Testament uses to refer to those who are made righteous through faith in God's blood sacrifice for sin. These first thirty-two proverbs in chapter 10 are therefore not just pithy pieces of advice. They describe the way in which God's righteous Messiah would one day live to save humankind: delighting his Father (10:1), taking the punishment deserved by fools (10:13, 16),[6] being delivered from the dead (10:2)[7] and becoming a fountain of life for all who heed wisdom's call (10:11).[8] They also describe the way he will empower those who follow him to live: no longer wicked fools but righteous men and women who are transformed by his Spirit for the glory of the God who saved them.

So don't think that lesson two of Proverbs is just a list of clever sayings which encourage us to act more like Mr Clever than Little Miss Naughty. It is a call for us to fix our eyes on the

---

[5] A form of the word *tsadīq* or *righteous* occurs 92 times in Proverbs. A form of the word *rāshā'* or *wicked* is used 83 times.

[6] Verse 16 is an Old Testament precursor to Romans 6:23, since the Hebrew word *pe'ūllāh* can mean *pay packet*. The famous promise in 10:12 that *"love covers over all wrongs"* is quoted in James 5:20 and 1 Peter 4:8.

[7] Hebrews 5:7 tells us that Jesus fulfilled verse 2 when the Father raised his Righteous One from the grave in response to his righteous life.

[8] John 4:14 and 7:37–39. We do not know how much Solomon understood about the coming Messiah, but it is unlikely that David, the writer of Psalms 22 and 110, failed to share such breathtaking insights with his son.

one who is the Wisdom of God so that we can be empowered to become his righteous people. In New Testament language, it is a call to fix our eyes on *"Christ Jesus, who has become for us wisdom from God – that is, our righteousness, holiness and redemption."*[9]

---

[9] 1 Corinthians 1:30. Paul understood what Solomon was saying in Proverbs 10. Thanks to your patient interest in the intricacies of Hebrew poetry, so can you.

God at Work (11:1)

The Lord abhors dishonest scales, but accurate weights are his delight.

(Proverbs 11:1)[1]

As the builder of God's magnificent Temple in Jerusalem, we might have expected Solomon to talk a lot about it in Proverbs. But he doesn't. Not even once. There's no mention of the Temple, of priests, of Levites, of the altar, or of any of the trappings of the Temple. He only mentions sacrifices three times, and each time it is to tell us God detests them unless our lifestyle matches up with our spiritual façade.[2] The builder of the Temple deliberately shifts our gaze away from religious buildings in order to focus us on the day-to-day religion which James also emphasizes in the "Proverbs of the New Testament": *"Those who consider themselves religious and yet do not keep a tight rein on their tongues deceive themselves, and their religion is worthless. Religion that God our Father accepts as pure and faultless is this: to look after orphans and widows in their distress and to keep oneself from being polluted by the world."*[3]

It is therefore no coincidence that Solomon moves on from a chapter about the righteous and the wicked straight into a verse about our righteousness being seen by how we act in the workplace. It was common practice in the ancient world for

---

[1] Translators struggle to interpret the Hebrew in Proverbs more than most other books in the Old Testament. Therefore I quote from both the 1984 and 2011 editions of the NIV, since they sometimes differ.

[2] Proverbs 15:8; 21:3; 21:27. Solomon makes a reference to the Temple later in Ecclesiastes 5:6, but never in the book of Proverbs.

[3] James 1:26–27.

traders to carry two sets of weights in their bags in order to fiddle business transactions in their favour. They would carry one set of weights which was heavier than stated so that when they purchased items they could measure out more than they had paid for, and they would carry a second set of lighter weights so that when they sold items they could give away less product than had actually been purchased. The Lord had forbidden his People to act this way in Leviticus 19:35–36, and David had tried to enforce the prohibition in 2 Samuel 14:26, but despite his best efforts it had remained an ingrained feature of Israel's business community.[4] Everybody did it and expected others to do the same, regarding anyone who didn't do so as naïve. Nevertheless, Solomon warns us in 11:1: *"The Lord detests dishonest scales, but accurate weights find favour with him."*

The ancient Israelites were not alone in thinking God was interested in what they did at the Temple but not in their working lives. Ray Kroc, the founder of the McDonald's chain of fast-food restaurants, spoke for many modern Christians when he joked that *"I believe in God, family, and McDonald's – and in the office, that order is reversed."*[5] The atheist German philosopher Ludwig Feuerbach wasn't completely wrong when he complained that *"Nature, the world, has no value, no interest for Christians. The Christian thinks only of himself and the salvation of his soul."*[6] We find it as easy as Solomon's original readers to split our lives into watertight "spiritual" and "secular" compartments, and to convince ourselves that God is interested in church and family and leisure time but not in what we do at work. We need to recover Solomon's emphasis on what it means to live as a believer in Yahweh – in the marketplace, on the farm, at political meetings, at college and in the home. Note that Wisdom cries out in the street and in the marketplace in Proverbs, not from inside the Temple. We need to grasp what

[4] See Amos 8:5–6; Micah 6:10–11.

[5] Ray Kroc in his book *Grinding It Out: The Making of McDonald's* (1977).

[6] Ludwig Feuerbach in *The Essence of Christianity* (1841).

the Dutch prime minister Abraham Kuyper did when he stated, *"There is not a square inch in the whole domain of our human existence over which Christ, who is Sovereign over all, does not cry: 'Mine!'"*[7]

I lead a church so it's not an easy thing for me to say, but church leaders can actually be the worst offenders in this area. We can get more excited that a church member leads a Bible study for a dozen people on a Tuesday evening than we do that they also manage a hundred factory workers from Monday to Friday. We can give more profile to the student who goes on a three-week mission to work with street children in Brazil than we give to someone who works for the rest of the year teaching thirty children at the school just around the corner. We need to remind ourselves that the Reformation restored the Church to Solomon's view of the world as well as to Solomon's Gospel. Martin Luther wrote in the early days of the German revival that

> *However sacred and lofty the works of monks and priests may be, they do not differ one whit in the sight of God from the works of the rustic labourer in his field or the woman attending to her household tasks. All works are measured before God by faith alone... Very often, in fact, the common work of a servant or maid is more acceptable to God than all the fasting and religious works of a monk or priest, if they are done without faith.*[8]

To help church leaders and church members, Solomon uses a Hebrew word in this verse which ought to shock us into action. He tells us that unrighteous lifestyle in the workplace is a

[7] Kuyper was prime minister of the Netherlands from 1901 to 1905. He said this in his inaugural address at the opening of the Free University of Amsterdam in 1880.

[8] Luther wrote this in 1520 in a treatise entitled *The Babylonian Captivity of the Church*.

tō'ēbah, a *detestable abomination*. This is the same word which is used to describe how God views executing the innocent in 17:15, murdering children in Jeremiah 32:35, worshipping idols in Deuteronomy 7:25, and homosexual sex in Leviticus 18:22 and 20:13.[9] It doesn't matter that everybody else in your workplace does it. Solomon insists that if your righteousness has not affected the person you are from Monday to Friday, what you claim to be on Sunday morning is a lie.

I used to work at a senior level in business so I'm not naïve about how difficult this teaching is to apply. I worked for a company which routinely short-filled the jars and bottles produced in its factories in order to make a little more profit from the unsuspecting consumer. I worked in a sales team which had such bullish targets that its standards of integrity and honest persuasion were often compromised.[10] I know how difficult it can be if you work for an insurance company which promises full cover in large print but withholds it in the small print, or for a medical team where the line between protecting and terminating human life is often blurred, or for a news team where the truth isn't allowed to get in the way of a good story. So does Solomon, one of the greatest merchants of the ancient world,[11] which is why he refuses to let you turn a deaf ear to God's demand to be Lord of every single aspect of your life.[12]

Every minute of every hour of every day of your life matters to God. If you embrace his wisdom and ask him to make you righteous, he tells you bluntly that you must let him make you

---

[9] In case we still fail to grasp how seriously God views unrighteousness in the workplace, Solomon repeats that this is a *detestable abomination* in 20:10 and 20:23.

[10] Solomon challenges the way people routinely lie in business negotiations in 20:14.

[11] 1 Kings 10:11, 14–15, 22, 28–29. Solomon was a practitioner and not just a theoretician.

[12] To help you, Solomon follows up this proverb with 10 more in 11:2–11 which urge you to trust that dishonesty is career suicide and that integrity brings greater prosperity and promotion in the long run.

righteous in your whole life or else he won't make you righteous at all. If your work colleagues and those who do business with you can't tell that you are saved, Solomon warns you that you may not actually be saved at all.

Money Talks (11:16–28)

Those who trust in their riches will fall, but the righteous will thrive like a green leaf.

(Proverbs 11:28)

An English proverb tells us that the quickest way to a man's heart is through his stomach. Solomon disagrees. He tells us that the easiest way to discover what is in a man's heart is through his wallet. It doesn't matter what he says he believes; what he truly believes is proved by how he spends his money. His true statement of faith is his bank statement, which is why Solomon follows up his teaching on how the righteous act at work with further teaching about what they do with the pay packet they bring home.

Yet again it pays to know a little bit about Hebrew poetry. Verse 28 is the key which unlocks the meaning of the dozen proverbs which precede it. It is an "antithetic parallelism" which contrasts the statement *"Those who trust in their riches will fall"* with a second statement *"but the righteous will thrive like a green leaf"*. It's fairly obvious that a thriving green leaf is the opposite of a dead autumnal leaf which falls from the tree, but Solomon tells us it is equally true that being righteous is the opposite of trusting in money. This insight stops 11:16–28 from being a mere series of reminders to give generously, and it turns it into a warning that how generously we give reveals whether or not we are truly saved. Only wicked fools place their trust in the fading power of money. Robert J. McCracken understood this when he said, *"Get to know two things about a man. How he earns his money, and how he spends it. You will then have a clue to his character. You will have a searchlight that shows up the inner recesses of his soul. You know all you need to know about his standards, his motives, his driving desires, his real religion."*

Solomon wants to shock us in verse 16 when he dismisses wealth as *"only money"*. In a world which worships Money as a god, this is meant to snap us to attention.[1] Solomon grabs our full attention so that he can tell us in verses 18–19 that Money is a deceptive idol which promises much but delivers little, and that the wages of worshipping Money is death while the wages of worshipping the Lord is life.[2] The way we use our money doesn't make us righteous or wicked; it simply reveals the true state of our hearts. As Solomon explains later in 21:26: *"The righteous give without sparing."*

Jesus demonstrated this in Luke 19 when he invited himself to the home of a wicked money-worshipper named Zacchaeus. Jericho's chief tax collector was a dirty, dishonest, grasping little man who looked so much like the wicked man described in Proverbs that the crowds were shocked that Jesus would even eat with him. But when Zacchaeus saw that Jesus cared for a man like him, he believed the Gospel promise that wicked people can be made righteous through God's Messiah. He stood up and declared, *"Look, Lord! Here and now I give half of my possessions to the poor, and if I have cheated anybody out of anything, I will pay back four times the amount."* Jesus turned to the crowd and echoed Solomon's teaching in these verses when he declared that *"Today salvation has come to this house."* Zacchaeus had climbed a sycamore-fig tree that morning, and he had come down from the tree looking like the green leaf of Proverbs 11:28. His financial generosity had proved his conversion to be genuine. The wicked man of Jericho had become the righteous man of Proverbs.

---

[1] Jesus did the same in Matthew 6:24 and Luke 16:13 by referring to wealth as *Mammon*, the personification of money as an idol. Most modern English translators express this by rendering it *Money* with a capital "M".

[2] These verses are another Old Testament precursor to Romans 6:23.

Solomon wants to persuade us that being generous with our money is the path to true prosperity. He doesn't promise that if we give away our riches, we will get even richer, but he does promise that we will find something which is far more valuable than *"only money"*. He tells us in verses 24–27 that hanging onto our money results in poverty, curses and trouble, but that giving till it hurts always results in blessing.[3] It makes us like God the Father, who gives sunshine, rain and crops freely to those who hate him. It makes us like Jesus the Son who poured out his blood for a world that hated him and who cried out as he died, *"Father, forgive them."*[4] It makes us like God the Holy Spirit, who is poured out on God's People without limit.[5] Followers of the Righteous One will always show their righteousness by their generosity. Money talks and an unconverted wallet shouts about its unconverted owner.

Giovanni Francesco di Bernardone understood these verses. Born in 1182, he was the son of a wealthy Italian cloth merchant, and he lived the medieval high life as a privileged teenager and as a dashing young cavalryman. He was wealthy, well-connected and poised for greatness, but he read verses such as these ones and concluded that the reality of our faith is seen by what we do, not by what we say. He refused to become like the corrupt Italian church whose grasping love of money made it stink like a locked up and stagnant canal which is too full to receive any fresh water. He turned his back on the loud and pompous worship of his peers in order to listen to the voice of Wisdom telling him that true righteousness will always touch our wallet.

---

[3] The reference to hoarding food in 11:26 should alarm you if, like me, you are a European. In 2007, the European Union hoarded 13,476,812 tonnes of cereal, rice, sugar and milk products in order to protect prices. The financial reasons for doing so have to be weighed up against these verses and 28:27.

[4] Luke 23:34. Paul encourages us in 2 Corinthians 8:9 that Jesus' great act of generosity will always motivate his true followers to give generously too.

[5] John 3:34.

He sold the contents of his father's warehouse and gave away the proceeds. When his furious father dragged him to court for theft and threatened to disinherit him of his massive fortune except for the clothes that he was wearing, he stripped off in the courtroom and walked barefoot in his underwear into the snowy street outside. Giovanni Francesco di Bernardone – we now know him better as Francis of Assisi – said goodbye to his father, telling the judge that *"From now onwards I can turn to God and call him my Father in heaven."*[6] His father is now forgotten along with all the cloth he treasured in his warehouse. Francis of Assisi still inspires millions of people around the world today.

Francis of Assisi is easier to admire than he is to copy. So is Zacchaeus. So is Jesus. So is anyone who listens to the voice of Wisdom in these verses. Yet Solomon insists that wealth is *"only money"*, and that how we use it reveals quite clearly whether we have truly repented of the idols of this world and been made righteous by the God who didn't count the cost of providing us with a perfect blood sacrifice.

Jesus held nothing back for you. Now he calls you to be wise by holding nothing back for him.

---

[6] For a good biography of Francis, try *Francis of Assisi: A Revolutionary Life* by Adrian House (2000).

Wisdom is Contagious (11:30)

The fruit of the righteous is a tree of life, and the one who is wise saves lives.

(Proverbs 11:30)

The same people who tell you that Proverbs isn't a book about salvation will also tell you that it isn't about spreading the news about salvation either. We have already discovered the message of God's salvation running through the book of Proverbs. Now it is time to discover his call to share that message too.

Solomon couldn't make it any plainer. He talks about the Tree of Life again as a clue for anyone who is willing to listen. He tells us that the righteous person isn't just *"like a green leaf"* in 11:28. They are also like the Tree of Life in 11:30, bearing godly fruit through sharing their wisdom with fools. This verse is a "synonymous parallelism" which tells us that the fruit of our being wise and righteous is always saving other lives. God's wisdom is contagious. We become trees which produce fruit which produces more trees like ourselves. Wise believers will always share the message of God's wisdom in a way which produces more believers.

Solomon tells us throughout Proverbs that wise people always *live like Jesus*. When this particular proverb inspired the great English preacher Charles Spurgeon to publish one of his best-loved books, entitled *The Soulwinner*, he commented that *"'The fruit of the righteous' – that is to say, his life – is not a thing fastened upon him, but it grows out of him. It is not a garment which he puts off and on, but it is inseparable from himself."* If

Proverbs focuses more on the righteous character of believers than it does on methodologies of evangelism, it is because actions speak louder than words and Wisdom is proved right by her children's lifestyle.[1] Spurgeon continues: *"Remember, the righteous man would not be righteous unless God had made him righteous, and the fruit of righteousness would never come from him unless the divine sap within him had produced that acceptable fruit."*[2] There is no such thing as a fruitless believer. If we are truly wise, our wisdom will draw those around us to follow Jesus too.[3]

Solomon also tells us throughout Proverbs that wise people always *love like Jesus.* If we are honest, one of the reasons why we bear so little Gospel fruit is that we would rather devour the Gospel ourselves behind the safety of our church doors than go out to share its fruit like the shepherd in Jesus' parable who left the flock behind to go and seek the one sheep which was lost. Solomon tells us in 18:1 that *"An unfriendly man pursues selfish ends; he defies all sound judgment,"* because wise people are as generous with their time and their hearts as they are with their money. They are like Jesus, who was criticized for being *"a friend of tax collectors and sinners"*.[4]

Solomon also tells us throughout Proverbs that wise people *ask questions like Jesus.* If you tend to think of sharing your faith in terms of speaking while other people shut up and listen, this is a very important principle for you to grasp. *"If you find honey, eat just enough – too much of it, and you will vomit,"* Solomon warns us graphically in 25:16. Forcing people to listen to a Gospel monologue is more likely to repel them than it is to win

---

[1] Jesus told his critics in Luke 7:35 that *"Wisdom is proved right by all her children."*

[2] Charles Spurgeon published *The Soulwinner* in 1895 after preaching it to his trainee church leaders.

[3] Mark 1:17; John 15:16; Matthew 7:20. Retreating ever deeper into the Christian subculture is not a mark of spiritual maturity. Ephesians 4:11–13 says that we need to be sent out by evangelists in order to be mature.

[4] Matthew 11:19; Luke 7:34; 15:1–7. See also Proverbs 10:21.

them, but asking questions which create an eager desire to hear more will make them want to eat from God's Tree of Life. *"The purposes of a person's heart are deep waters, but one who has insight draws them out,"* he explains in 20:5. Questions are the bucket which we use to draw out the deep waters of a person's thoughts in order to share the Gospel in a manner which makes them instantly see its relevance to their lives. Since Jesus chose to ask questions rather than preach on his visit to Jerusalem in Luke 2:46–47, it's pretty clear that we also need to learn to do the same.

Solomon tells us throughout Proverbs that wise people *share like Jesus.* He warns in 24:24 that *"Whoever says to the guilty, 'You are innocent,' will be cursed by peoples and denounced by nations."* We must confront people with their sin so that they turn from Folly to the Wisdom of God revealed in Jesus, because 28:23 promises that *"Whoever rebukes a person will in the end gain favour rather than one who has a flattering tongue."*[5] We need to challenge the arrogant in the same way that Jesus challenged the Pharisees, and we need to help the humble in the same way that Jesus welcomed the prostitutes, the tax collectors and the lepers. *"The wise in heart are called discerning, and make their lips persuasive,"* Solomon adds in 16:23.[6] If we listen to the voice of Wisdom and let her words transform us from the inside out, Solomon promises that we will attract unbelievers to the fruit of our lives as much as blossom attracts bees to an apple tree.

Solomon tells us throughout Proverbs that wise people *persevere like Jesus.* Fools are not won over to wisdom without a fight, so soul-winning often takes a lot of time. The foolish believer gets discouraged by the delay and stops sharing the

---

[5] Solomon made 11:31 come after 11:30 for a reason. 1 Peter 4:18 quotes it as a reference to God's judgment.

[6] This is the NIV footnote reading. The meaning of Hebrew poetry is not as clear as Hebrew prose, so there is often more than one valid way of translating Solomon's proverbs.

Gospel, which is why 20:4 warns that *"Sluggards do not plough in season; so at harvest time they look but find nothing."* Neglecting our duty to share the Gospel makes us partners with Satan in the destruction of human souls, since 18:9 tells us that *"One who is slack in his work is brother to one who is a Master Destroyer."*[7] If we refuse to give up and we resist the temptation to sleep at harvest time (10:5), Solomon promises we will reap an abundant harvest in the end (14:4).

So let's not rush over Proverbs 11:30 and miss this verse's reference to the Tree of Life and its promise that God's wisdom is contagious. Solomon does not want us to be mere consumers of wisdom, when God has called us to be ambassadors of his wisdom too. If we accept this proverb, he will teach us to pull down strongholds of wrong thinking (21:22) because it only takes one wise man or woman to save a city or a nation (Ecclesiastes 9:14–15). As we eat from the Tree of Life, we must become trees of life which bear the fruit of God's wisdom: human souls. Charles Spurgeon continues:

> *A fruit becomes a tree! A tree of life! Wonderful result this! Christ in the Christian produces a character which becomes a tree of life... Jesus alone is* **the** *Tree of Life, but... may we every one of us be made like our Lord, and may His fruit be found upon our boughs!... Oh, if you have any humanity, let alone Christianity, if you have found the remedy, tell the diseased about it! If you have found life, proclaim it to the dead; if you have found liberty, publish it to the captives; if you have found Christ, tell of Him to others.*

[7] This is one of the literal translations of the Hebrew text of 18:9.

Strong on the Inside (12:4)

A wife of noble character is her husband's crown, but a disgraceful wife is like decay in his bones.

(Proverbs 12:4)

The world contains a lot of concrete. There is more concrete in the world than any other man-made material. An extra seven billion cubic metres of the stuff is produced each year – that's an extra cubic metre for every person on the planet every 365 days – so if it feels like it's a concrete jungle out there, you're not wrong. But here's the really strange thing: concrete isn't actually all that strong. The load-bearing strength of concrete is less than that of very average wood. It's what the concrete has on the inside which makes it strong.

In 1849 a Frenchman named Joseph Monier invented reinforced concrete. He overcame the load-bearing weakness of concrete by putting steel bars inside the concrete to create a product strong enough to build bridges, buildings, reservoirs and skyscrapers. In doing so, he revolutionized the face of modern cities.

Solomon lived too early to use reinforced concrete in his building projects, but he understood the principle behind it when he looked at the issue of marriage. He told us in 11:15 that who we bind our life to is a make-or-break decision, and he stresses this throughout Proverbs because he doesn't want his son Rehoboam to make the same mistakes as he did. Although he focuses on men looking for a wife, this is equally true for women looking for a husband. To use the language of Joseph Monier, 12:4 tells us that a good spouse is like the steel bar which makes weak concrete strong, but a bad spouse is like an old and rusty bar which crumbles into powder and shatters the concrete it should have protected.

One of my friends recently bought a house which has a cesspit capped with very poor quality reinforced concrete. The steel inside has rusted and it has shattered the concrete so completely that his little daughter could fall through the hole into the cesspit. That's a good picture of what Solomon is saying about the importance of who we marry. *"The wise woman builds her house, but with her own hands the foolish one tears hers down,"* he warns in 14:1, because who we marry doesn't just shape our own character for good (13:20; 27:17) or ill (12:26; 22:24–25). It also shapes the character of our children and sets them off on the path of life or on the highway to hell.[1] Your spouse will share your bank account,[2] represent you outside the home and be a large part of your destiny. No wonder the final chapter of Proverbs is a mother's plea for her son to understand that a good wife is worth far more than a massive fortune.

Solomon therefore warns us not to marry for looks alone. It doesn't matter how pretty concrete looks on the outside, what matters is the strength of the steel girder on the inside. *"Like a gold ring in a pig's snout is a beautiful woman who shows no discretion,"* he says in 11:22, warning us that some girls who catch our eye will foul up our life if we take them into our home.[3] A wise woman adds in 31:30 that *"Charm is deceptive, and beauty is fleeting; but a woman who fears the Lord is to be praised."* She is echoed by 1 Peter 3:3–4, which tells us that true beauty doesn't lie in gold jewellery, fine clothing or well-groomed hair, but in

[1] Proverbs 14:26 tells us that a father's wisdom – including who he chooses to marry – protects his children from harm.

[2] This is one of the applications of Solomon's repeated warning for us not to strike hands in pledge to bind our life to another person lightly in 6:1–5, 11:15 and 17:18.

[3] Solomon says literally that she lacks *taste*, meaning *the ability to distinguish right from wrong*. He uses the same word which David used in 1 Samuel 25:33 to praise the *good judgment* of his soon-to-be wife Abigail.

the *"inner self, the unfading beauty of a gentle and quiet spirit, which is of great worth in God's sight"*. A handsome husband or a gorgeous wife can be very ugly on the inside.

Solomon knows enough about romance to know that you and I are going to need a little bit more persuading. Love is blind, so he lays on this message thicker and thicker as he progresses through his Top 375. He warns in 19:13 that living with a bad wife is a nightmare because *"a quarrelsome wife is like the constant dripping of a leaky roof"*. By the time he reaches 27:15, he takes this a step further to tell us that *"a quarrelsome wife is like the dripping of a leaky roof* ***in a rainstorm****"*! She makes her husband long to live on the corner of the roof or in the arid desert under the baking hot sun just to get away from her constant nagging (21:9, 19; 25:24).[4] If we marry in haste, we will repent at our leisure. Better to wait for the right marriage partner whom God says in 18:22 and 19:14 he will provide for us.[5]

If it feels as though Solomon labours this point a little strongly throughout Proverbs, remember that he had made this mistake himself. 1 Kings tells us he married the daughter of the Egyptian Pharaoh in order to forge a political alliance (3:1), even though he knew he shouldn't marry an unbeliever (11:1–2),[6] and that Solomon's kingdom was destroyed by the cancerous effect which she and his other pagan wives had on his character

---

[4] Very few of Solomon's proverbs are repeated in his Top 375 in 10:1–22:16 or in the new Top 125 in 25:1–29:27. The fact that this proverb is repeated is a warning that we ignore it at our own extreme peril.

[5] Since these proverbs are general principles rather than hard-and-fast promises, it may be that God's plan is for you to remain unmarried like his Son who died a 33-year-old virgin. However, Genesis 2:18 implies that most of us can expect these verses to apply to us.

[6] 2 Chronicles 8:11 makes it clear that he knew this deep down but chose not to listen to his heart of wisdom. The New Testament warns us not to marry a non-Christian in 1 Corinthians 7:39 and 2 Corinthians 6:14–18, but it also promises in 1 Corinthians 7:12–17 that if you are already married to an unbeliever, God can give you grace for the extra challenges it entails.

(11:1–13). Ironically, his marriage to Pharaoh's daughter actually had the opposite effect to the one he intended anyway, since her father's dynasty ended midway through Solomon's reign and this made the new Pharaoh view him as an enemy and rival (11:40; 14:25–26).[7] Many of Rehoboam's failings were due to his mother being another, equally unsuitable foreign wife of his father (14:21). Solomon stresses the importance of who we marry because he knows from bitter experience that a bad wife is like an enemy deep at the heart of her husband's operations, actually making him weaker than he would have been if he had never married at all.

The Country singer Amy Dalley sang that *"Shoes don't stretch and men don't change,"* and Solomon wants you to know that it is true. No matter how much the shop assistant tells you the shoes will stretch, and no matter how much your excited heart tries to persuade you that he or she will change, that's just wishful thinking. *"Restraining her is like restraining the wind or grasping oil with the hand,"* Solomon despairs in 27:16 as he looks at his own home life and hopes for better things in yours. Learn from Joseph Monier to choose a husband or wife who will make you strong on the inside like a steel girder. Don't marry a good-looking person who makes you weak on the inside.

---

[7] Even while his father-in-law was still alive, he refused to extradite Solomon's arch-enemy Hadad to Israel because Hadad was his brother-in-law (1 Kings 11:14–22).

The Strongest Muscle (12:6–13:3)

The words of the reckless pierce like swords, but the tongue of the wise brings healing.

(Proverbs 12:18)

Gerald Ratner was doing so well. He had started out in the jewellery trade at the tender age of seventeen and had worked like a slave for twenty-five years to turn his Ratner's chain of jewellers into one of Britain's most successful high street retailers. Hailed as the man with the Midas touch, he now travelled between his many luxury homes by helicopter or by classic Bentley. Then he accepted an invitation to dinner.

The leading company directors of London had recognized his success by inviting him to speak at their annual luncheon at a stunning venue on the same road as Buckingham Palace. Buoyed by the occasion, he joked in his speech that he sold jewellery at such fantastic prices *"because it's total crap... It's cheaper than a Marks and Spencer prawn sandwich and it probably won't last as long."* He was smiling as he said it but nobody else was laughing. When his speech was broadcast on the evening news, shocked customers boycotted his stores and turned his lunchtime meeting into the most expensive meal in modern history. The value of the Ratner's chain of jewellers plummeted by £500 million and he was fired as its CEO. Warren Buffet later observed: *"It takes 20 years to build a reputation and five minutes to ruin it. If you think about that, you'll do things differently."*[1]

---

[1] Ratner gave this disastrous speech in 1991, as recorded in Stephen Weir's book *History's Worst Decisions: And the People Who Made Them* (2008). This

Solomon was even smarter than Warren Buffet so he spends much of Proverbs warning us not to underestimate the massive power of the human tongue. Whatever the medical facts, the tongue is without a doubt the strongest muscle in the human body.[2] *"The tongue has the power of life and death,"* he warns in 18:21. *"Those who guard their mouths and their tongues keep themselves from calamity,"* he adds in 21:23. In addition to littering the whole of Proverbs with warnings for us to guard how we use our tongues, Solomon gives us an entire chapter of teaching on the power of the tongue here in 12:6 to 13:3.

First, Solomon tells us to *be honest*. He told us in 6:16–19 that the Lord detests both liars and their lying tongues, and he repeats in 12:22 that *"The Lord detests lying lips, but he delights in people who are trustworthy."* To tell the truth is to be wise and righteous, and it provokes the Lord to bless us.[3] To tell lies is to be wicked and foolish, and it provokes the Lord to judge us. Our lies may fool people in the short term (12:19), but God will soon expose the truth (12:9) so that we become the only people fooled by our fantasies (12:11). Solomon warns us that those who set out to deceive others will ultimately deceive their own hearts (12:20) like Arthur Dimmesdale, the lying clergyman in Nathaniel Hawthorne's classic novel *The Scarlet Letter*, who mourns: *"No man can wear one face to himself and another to the multitude without finally getting bewildered as to which may be true."*[4] Lying will bring us misery but truthfulness will bring us joy.

Next, Solomon tells us to *be calm*. Words spoken in anger may sound clever but they are very rarely wise. *"Fools show their annoyance at once, but the prudent overlook an insult,"* he

---

is also the source for Ratner's statement later in this chapter.

[2] Technically the tongue comprises eight muscles, but this doesn't alter Solomon's basic argument that the tongue can do more good or harm than any other muscle in our body.

[3] Although 12:17 appears quite obvious, it is actually making a vital point. If you lie, you are a liar, whatever you may argue to the contrary.

[4] Nathaniel Hawthorne, *The Scarlet Letter* (1850).

explains in 12:16, and he follows this up even more strongly in 15:1 by telling us that *"A gentle answer turns away wrath, but a harsh word stirs up anger."* However trifling an angry riposte may seem at the time, it is *"like a scorching fire"* (16:27) and acts like the spark which starts a forest fire. *"Consider what a great forest is set on fire by a small spark,"* James 3:5–6 exclaims as part of its New Testament echo of the book of Proverbs. *"The tongue also is a fire, a world of evil among the parts of the body. It corrupts the whole body, sets the whole course of one's life on fire, and is itself set on fire by hell."* The way we use our tongues couldn't be more important.

That's why Solomon tells us to *be thoughtful.* Fools blurt out words without thinking and come to ruin in 12:23 and 13:3,[5] but the wise set up a security perimeter between their lips and their lives by thinking before they speak.[6] Unlike most of the muscles in the human body, the tongue is only attached at one end, so we must fasten it at the other end to wisdom. *"The words of the reckless pierce like swords,"* Solomon warns in 12:18, and Gerald Ratner reflected thirteen years after his costly luncheon that this warning is true: *"It was a total nightmare. One day I was on top of the world, Mr. Big Shot flying on the Concorde... The next, I was a complete laughingstock. It was such a seismic event. It's like BC – before crap and afterwards."*

More positively, Solomon encourages us to *be expectant.* If the tongue has power to do great harm, it also has equal power to do great good. Our words can rescue the dying (12:6), make our lives fruitful (12:14; 13:2), and bring healing to the hurting (12:18). They can bring joy to the Lord (12:22), hope to the helpless (12:25) and life to a dying world (12:28). Note the

---

[5] The Hebrew word used for *opening wide* our mouth rashly in 13:3 is only used in one other place in the Old Testament. In Ezekiel 16:25 it refers to a prostitute opening her legs wide to passers-by. This should shock us into treating foolish talk as seriously as God does.

[6] The fool failed to reflect between *hearing and doing* in 7:21–23, and here he fails to reflect between *thinking and speaking* too. See also 29:20.

deliberate reference in 12:14 to God using our tongues to make us little trees of life. In case we miss it, Solomon tells us more explicitly in 15:4 that *"The tongue that brings healing is a tree of life."* Careless words can be destructive but that is only half the story. The other half is a wonderful promise that God can use our tongues to change the world.

Jesus modelled the lesson of this chapter for us perfectly. The New Testament tells us that

> *Christ suffered for you, leaving you an example, that you should follow in his steps. "He committed no sin, and no deceit was found in his mouth." When they hurled their insults at him, he did not retaliate; when he suffered, he made no threats... For, "Whoever would love life and see good days must keep their tongue from evil and their lips from deceitful speech."*[7]

So let's not gloss over Solomon's chapter of instruction on how to use our tongues. Let's not ignore his claim that how we speak reveals whether we are truly wise or foolish, truly righteous or wicked. Let's not ignore the echo of these words in James 1:26 and 3:2 which warn that if we fail to keep our tongue in check, we may not be followers of Jesus after all, and which promise that if we can tame our tongues by Jesus' strength, we will be able to follow him in every other area too.[8] Let's learn from Solomon that, if wisely used, our tongues are far more valuable than all of Gerald Ratner's jewellery put together. He tells us in 25:11: *"The right word at the right time is like precious gold set in silver."*[9]

---

[7] 1 Peter 2:21–23; 3:10.

[8] James 3:9–12 also states that how we use our tongue reveals whether or not we have truly been saved. No one can tame their tongue by human strength alone, but all those who are saved by Jesus are empowered through the Holy Spirit to tame their tongue by his divine strength.

[9] Contemporary English Version.

The Sluggard (13:4)

The sluggard craves and gets nothing, but the desires of the diligent are fully satisfied.

(Proverbs 13:4)

If you travel on the London Underground, you are bound to see the posters: *"Spotting a ticket inspector is easy – they look just like you."* Most of us have the same problem with the sluggard in the book of Proverbs. He sounds like he should be very easy to spot – perhaps sleeping in a hammock while his house is on fire – but Solomon warns us that he looks just like us. Sluggards aren't idle in masking their laziness, so the first place that Solomon warns us to look for one is in the bathroom mirror.

The sluggard *wants success* as much as a wise person. Solomon tells us in 13:4 that *"the sluggard craves and gets nothing"* and in 21:25 that *"the sluggard's craving* [not laziness] *will be the death of him"*. The Hebrew verb *'āwāh* is a strong word which can be translated *to long for, to lust after* or *to sigh with desire*. Don't imagine that the sluggard is easy to spot because he has no ambition or goals. He looks just like us.

The sluggard *plans for success* as much as a wise person. Solomon tells us that he is full of ideas, and he classes him among *"those who chase fantasies"* in 12:11 and 28:19. Sluggards even put some of their plans into action: catching game (12:27), planting crops (10:5) and putting their hand to cooking a great dinner (19:24; 26:15). The issue isn't that the sluggard fails to talk about success, plan for success or start out on the road to success. The sluggard is harder to spot than we tend to imagine. He looks just like us.

The sluggard's problem is that he fools himself that wanting, talking, planning and beginning are the same thing as actually doing. He doesn't grasp what Solomon tells us in 14:23 – that *"hard work brings a profit, but mere talk leads only to poverty"*. He plans great harvests for his farm but doesn't get around to ploughing his fields at the crucial time and therefore harvests nothing (20:4). Even when he does manage to plough and plant, he fails to weed and tend the crops he plants and therefore still misses out on harvest (24:30–34).[1] When he plans lavish dinners he is better at shopping for ingredients than at cooking (12:27), and he loses interest in what he cooks before he has a chance to eat it (19:24). The way to spot a sluggard is to see if he perseveres and finishes what he starts. At the start of a task he looks just like us.

So don't try to spot a sluggard by looking for someone who is not doing anything, because the sluggard's tell-tale cry is always *"I'm so busy!"* He is usually so worn out from chasing fantasies and from the hard work of procrastination that he has no energy left to do the tasks which would turn his pipedreams into reality (21:25). He is so exhausted by worry and his list of fruitless activities that he genuinely feels that he deserves to indulge himself with all the time he spends relaxing and in bed. He thinks it is only *"a little sleep, a little slumber, a little folding of the hands to rest"* (6:10; 24:33) when a truer verdict is that *"As a door turns on its hinges, so a sluggard turns on his bed"* (26:14).

Don't try to spot a sluggard by looking for someone who says he doesn't like to work, because the sluggard works very hard to find plausible excuses. His other tell-tale cry is *"I can't because..."*, and he has convinced himself that real obstacles prevent him from pushing himself any harder (15:19). However much Solomon may tell us to laugh at his excuses (22:13; 26:13), the sluggard has truly convinced himself that his trumped up

---

[1] Proverbs 24:33–34 repeats 6:10–11 in order to emphasize that this is a particularly important lesson for us to learn.

fears make it too dangerous to proceed. He sounds very wise in meetings as he pokes holes in other people's plans, but don't be fooled. The sluggard looks just like us.

He looks like the teenager who doesn't study hard, unaware that laziness at school leads to harder labour throughout our working lives (12:24).[2] He looks like the young man who spends his money on gadgets and toys yet can't afford to move out of his parents' home. He looks like the young woman who hates being single but won't give internet dating a try because it sounds far riskier than waiting for God to make the perfect man fall into her lap. He looks like the middle-aged woman who settles for a mundane marriage and a dead-end job because she is too scared to tell her husband or her boss what she is really looking for. He looks like the man in his sixties who cannot afford to retire because he spent his money instead of saving it in his younger years.[3]

He looks like the Christian who rarely starts spiritual conversations with unbelievers yet shares his frustration that none of his friends seems very interested in Jesus or in church (20:4). He looks like the believer who seldom reads the Bible or spends time in prayer, completely unaware that his hobbies, TV watching and computer games are entertaining him to death.[4] He looks like the church member who is too busy to lead a spiritual discussion group for non-Christians or to disciple a new believer. He looks like the jaded former leader who takes

---

[2] That's the irony of the sluggard. The comforts of the palace come to people who are willing to work hard, but lazy people end up working harder than they would have if they had only stirred themselves to action!

[3] In 6:6–8, Solomon tells people who make no provision for their old age to learn from the ants who save up their winter food supply in summer. Even tiny insects think ahead more than a sluggard.

[4] We have grown so used to mind-numbing pleasures that we do not see them as major discipleship issues. However, Solomon uses an antithetic parallelism in 15:19 to tell us that a sluggard is the opposite of an upright person. A synonymous parallelism in 24:30 also tells us that a sluggard *"has no sense"*.

a back seat, forgetting that *"He who gathers crops in summer is a prudent son, but he who sleeps during harvest is a disgraceful son"* (10:5).

He looks like the church leader who complains that reaching people with the Gospel is very difficult in his town, failing to notice that nobody anywhere else seems to have it any easier. He is a sluggard because his actions show he thinks that Jesus was fooling around when he told his followers to go and make disciples of all nations. He forgets that evangelism isn't difficult; it's impossible. It always has been and it always will be. Jesus tells us that *"I am sending you out like lambs among wolves,"* but then promises that *"surely I am with you always, to the very end of the age"*.[5]

So let's not pretend that when Solomon talks about sluggards in Proverbs that he is talking about people who are obviously lazy. Let's learn from the London Underground posters and take a long look in the mirror. It is easy to spot a sluggard – they look just like you and me.

---

[5] Luke 10:3; Matthew 28:20.

Two Ears, One Mouth (13:10–20)

Where there is strife, there is pride, but wisdom is found in those who take advice.

(Proverbs 13:10)

Solomon was one of the foremost biologists of his day. 1 Kings 4:33 tells us he was a pioneer of botany, zoology, ornithology, herpetology and ichthyology. But you don't need a PhD in biology to grasp his main conclusion from his studies. He tells us God gave human beings two ears and one mouth, and that wise people will use them in that proportion.

We saw at the start of Proverbs that Solomon uses five main Hebrew words to describe the fool. One of them was *lēts*, which means *mocker* or *scoffer* and describes the fool who adamantly refuses to listen to advice. God has given him two ears but all he wants to do is use his mouth. He criticizes everybody's opinion but his own, and he is cynical about every thought except for those which he concocts in his proud heart. Having warned us not to misuse our tongues in the previous chapter, Solomon continues in these verses with a warning not to underuse our ears.

He tells us in 13:1 that a mocker will not listen to his *parents*. As a father who compiled the book of Proverbs for his son, Solomon treats this as the pinnacle of stupidity. A nation of mockers treats children as the pride of their parents, but Solomon turns this on its head in 17:6 by telling us that *"parents are the pride of their children"*. We don't need Solomon's grasp of zoology to spot that God has designed human children to stay with their parents longer than the young of any animal because he wants the human race to grow wiser with each succeeding generation. If we listen to our parents, we can spend our lifetime building on the wisdom of preceding generations, but if we start from scratch, Solomon tells us in 20:20 that our generation will be one of *"pitch darkness"*.[1] The Roman orator Cicero warned that *"To be ignorant of what happened before you were born is to remain a child always."*[2] The mocker's failure to use his ears more than his mouth means that he never matures into the grown-up wisdom described in Proverbs.

Solomon tells us in 13:10 and 13:13–14 that a mocker will not listen to his *teachers*. Although *"the teaching of the wise is a fountain of life, turning a person from the snares of death"*, the mocker is far too proud to listen to what his teachers have to say. Solomon uses a parallelism in verse 10 to emphasize that the mocker's unwillingness to take advice is rooted in plain old pride.[3] The problem is not that he has no thirst for wisdom (14:6) but that he thinks he is already wise and therefore looks for those who echo back more foolish thinking like his own (3:7; 26:12). James 1:19 summarizes these verses when it warns us, *"My dear brothers and sisters, take note of this: Everyone should be quick to listen, slow to speak."* The mocker is like a little child who will not listen to her piano teacher because she too busy thumping on the piano keys, and yet who blames the piano teacher for the fact that she fails her exam.

Solomon adds in 13:20 that a mocker refuses to listen to *wise friends*. He hates the path of wisdom so intensely that he rejects the company of those who dare to challenge him about his sin (9:7–8 and 15:12).[4] He has no time for the old church leader's advice that we should *"Get a friend to tell you your faults,*

---

1 See also 15:20 and 19:26.

2 Marcus Tullius Cicero said this in 46 BC in his *Orator ad M. Brutum*.

3 He states this even more explicitly in 21:24.

4 Proverbs 24:9 tells us that the wise eventually reject his company too, since his mocking cynicism becomes as repulsive to them as it is to God.

or, better still, welcome an enemy who will watch you keenly and sting you savagely. What a blessing such an irritating critic will be to a wise man, what an intolerable nuisance to a fool!"[5] Instead, he gathers friends who are as foolish as he is, and he makes a pact with them to pursue ever-increasing foolishness together (1:11–14). Solomon warns us throughout Proverbs that we become like the people we choose as friends,[6] so this spells disaster for the mocker. He has nobody to make him hungry to eat from the Tree of Life (13:12) or thirsty to drink from the Fountain of Life (13:14),[7] so he reaps poverty, shame and harm (13:18, 20) along the way to being snared by death and hell (13:14–15).

Even though God graciously intervenes and disciplines him in his folly, Solomon tells us in 13:18 that a mocker will not even listen to *life experience*. He tells us in 17:10 that a wise person responds to verbal feedback in an instant, but that a mocker shrugs off a hundred bad experiences without learning anything. He compares the mocker to a street dog which eats poisonous food and vomits in 26:11, yet which returns to make a fresh meal of the poisonous food its stomach has just rejected![8] Aldous Huxley observed that *"Experience is not what happens to a man; it is what a man does with what happens to him."*[9] The mocker is too busy talking to listen to what happens to him, so the years which pass leave him none the wiser than he was before.

Ultimately, Solomon tells us that a mocker will not even listen to *God*. He tells us in 13:15 that the root of the mocker's problem is not that he is foolish but that he is *unfaithful* –

[5] Charles Spurgeon in his *Lectures to My Students* (1890).

[6] Proverbs 12:26; 13:20; 14:7; 17:12; 22:24–25; 25:4–5; 27:17.

[7] Note the way that 13:19 repeats some of the same wording as 13:12 in order to contrast the Tree of Life with the Tree of the Experience of Good and Evil.

[8] The New Testament quotes Proverbs 26:11 and applies it to fools within the Church in 2 Peter 2:22.

[9] Aldous Huxley in the introduction to his essay *Texts and Pretexts* (1932).

the Hebrew word means literally that he is *a traitor*. He is in rebellion against the God who made him and his refusal to listen to anyone else is simply the fruit of his trying to be a little god himself. That's why Solomon used a parallelism in 9:7 to equate the *mocker* with the *wicked*, just as elsewhere he equates the humble listener with the wise. If we omit to listen to God, we commit sin against God.

Most readers (especially mockers!) assume that Solomon is talking about someone other than themselves, so let's apply these words to Christians. We can be cynical too; we simply dress our mocking up in Christian clothes. We find it easy to despise our parents *(what's the point of these outdated spiritual traditions?)*, to despise theologians *(what do they know in their ivory towers?)*, to despise church leaders *(what do they know about the real world?)*, to despise fellow church members *(you run your life and let me run mine!)*, to despise experience *(how can God let me down like this?)*[10] and even to despise God himself *(surely the Bible can't actually mean that?!)*.[11]

But to Christians as well as non-Christians, Solomon insists his biology research is true: God has given us two ears and one mouth, and he expects us to use them in that proportion.

[10] Solomon tells us in 19:3 that this is the normal reaction of a fool to God's loving discipline.

[11] Paul warns us that churches will be full of such foolish mockers in 2 Timothy 4:1–4.

A Hearing Heart (14:12)

There is a way that seems right to a man, but in the end it leads to death.

(Proverbs 14:12)

It must have been hard for Solomon to choose just 375 proverbs out of his massive back collection of 3,000. Every choice to include one was a choice to leave out seven more. So we mustn't miss the importance of the fact that he chose to include one of his proverbs twice. Proverbs 14:12 is identical to 16:25 because he wants to emphasize that this is one of the most important proverbs of them all. Having talked about using our tongues properly and about using our ears sufficiently, he wants to round off this theme by warning us what will happen if we fail to listen to the Lord. He tells us twice in his Top 375 that *"There is a way that seems right to a man, but in the end it leads to death."*

Solomon had seen first hand as a teenager that choices can seem logical and yet be terribly unwise. It had made sense for his brother Absalom not to go into battle with David until he had mustered a massive army in 2 Samuel 17:1–14, yet that decision proved to be the turning point which doomed his rebellion to fail. It had made sense for his father David to count the fighting men of Israel in 2 Samuel 24, yet doing so had caused the death of 70,000 Israelites in three terrible, plague-filled days. Solomon is not advocating thoughtlessness in this proverb – he clarifies in 14:15 that *"the prudent give thought to their steps"* – but he is saying that human logic is not enough to save our lives. For that, we must develop a hearing heart which listens to the Lord.

Solomon's observations as a teenager convinced him to

ask the Lord in 1 Kings 3:9 for *"a hearing heart"* himself. Like an untrained pilot trying to fly a plane, he knew he needed to hear the control tower. In response, the Lord didn't give him a blueprint for how to rule as king of Israel. Instead, he gave him his Spirit of Wisdom so that the ears of his heart would be opened to hear divine instructions every day.[1] The reason Solomon repeats this proverb in 14:12 and 16:25 is that he knows it lies at the heart of his own experience of God. He knows that it will also mean the difference between life and death for his readers.

Solomon unpacks the meaning of this proverb in the verses which surround it. He tells us in 14:26 that a hearing heart will protect us from disaster. Life is full of forks in the road and we need to hear God's wisdom at each one of them, just as Solomon promised in 8:2 that God would help us to. Jesus did not promise *"I am the Map"* but *"I am the Way"*, so he promises to guide us at every fork in the road.[2] Proverbs 14:12 simply states negatively what 3:5–6 told us positively: *"Trust in the Lord with all your heart and lean not on your own understanding; in all your ways submit to him, and he will direct your paths."* If we tremble at God's Word and listen carefully for his guidance at every turn, this fear of the Lord will be a fortress to protect us and our families from harm.

Solomon explains the meaning of this proverb further in 14:9 and 14. He warns that *"fools mock at making amends for sin"*, little realizing that *"the faithless will be fully repaid for their ways"*.[3] Because they do not have a hearing heart, they rely on human logic and compare their lives with one another.

[1] Although Paul talks about the *eyes* rather than the *ears* of our hearts in Ephesians 1:17–18, he essentially promises that God will give us the same hearing heart which he gave to Solomon.

[2] John 14:6. We can watch Paul living out Proverbs 14:12 in Acts 16:6–10 and 2 Corinthians 1:12–2:13.

[3] The Hebrew used in 14:14 is different from the Hebrew which was used to refer to *"the unfaithful"* in 13:15. Here it means literally *"the backslider in heart"*.

They conclude that they are fine upstanding citizens and fail to realize that God's Word says they have fallen short of being citizens of heaven. Paul explains in Romans 3:19–20 that God has given us his Word *"so that every mouth may be silenced and the whole world held accountable to God. Therefore no one will be declared righteous in God's sight by the works of the law; rather, through the law we become conscious of our sin."* Without a hearing heart, we will assume that the way of life which pleases men and women also pleases God. We need a hearing heart to grasp that the path of human respectability leads to death too. Solomon included this proverb twice in his Top 375 so that you and I would turn our ears to God and be convicted of our sin.

Solomon then leads us to 14:27, which is one of the great Gospel verses in the book of Proverbs: *"The fear of the Lord is a fountain of life, turning a person from the snares of death."* This verse is strikingly similar to 13:14, except that this time it is *"the fear of the Lord"* rather than *"the teaching of the wise"* which is a fountain of life, because fear of the Lord means being willing to listen to what God says. The Fountain of Life here and in 13:14 is closely linked to the Tree of Life in 13:12, and Jesus explains in John 4:10–14 that it refers to the salvation which comes through the Holy Spirit.[4] A hearing heart will not simply teach us that we are sinners under God's judgment. It will also teach us how to come to God through his Messiah and receive forgiveness through the Gospel.[5]

As a result, Solomon promises in 14:32 that *"The wicked will be cast out in their wickedness, but the righteous have hope in their death."*[6] Since the wicked do not take refuge in God's

[4] Solomon refers to *"the Fountain of Life"* in 10:11, 13:14, 14:27 and 16:22. John makes it clear in Revelation 21:6 and 22:1–2 that the Fountain of Life and the Tree of Life go hand in hand together.

[5] It is unclear how much Solomon understood of what he prophesied, but Proverbs 16:14 can be translated literally as *"The King's wrath is like angels of death, but the Wise One will appease it."*

[6] This is my own literal translation of the Hebrew. Jesus was thinking of verses like this one when he told the early believers in Luke 24:25–27 and 45–47 that

Word, they know nothing of their sin and nothing of God's remedy for it. They follow the normal human path which seems so right but leads to death, whereas the wise have hearing hearts which convict them that they need to lay hold of God's path to resurrection and to salvation from hell to heaven. Solomon chose to repeat this proverb in 14:12 and 16:25 in order to prevent us from mistaking this book of the Bible for a set of moral principles instead of a call to receive the Gospel.

A couple of years ago, when I first moved to London, I was coming back from the north of England in the early hours of the morning and decided to cross the city to my home which is south of the river. I didn't know my way around London so I switched on my satnav and simply followed its directions. I had been driving for over an hour when I suddenly realized that there was a glitch in the software and it had been sending me round in circles. Unless I switched off the satnav and started looking out for road signs, I would never make it home. That's what Solomon wants us to understand through this proverb. If we follow the crowd, we will perish alongside them, but if we switch off our autopilot and cry out to God for a hearing heart, he will guide us. He will save us from the path which leads to death and guide us along the path which leads to wisdom and to everlasting life.

the whole of the Old Testament predicted his work of salvation.

God in Disguise (14:20–31)

Whoever oppresses the poor shows contempt for their Maker, but whoever is kind to the needy honours God.

(Proverbs 14:31)

There is a famous story about a rich old lady whose sole surviving grandson stood to inherit her fortune when she died. He visited her weekly and was attentive to her needs, but she knew that those visits didn't show what kind of man he was. Who wouldn't be loving and attentive to a dying grandmother who stood to leave him millions? She longed for a way to peel away his self-interest and to peer into the true state of his heart. She decided to disguise herself as a beggar and wait in the street outside his house.

When the grandson returned home from work that evening, he found a bag lady sleeping on the doorstep of his home. He was furious and woke her to tell her she was trespassing on his property. When she refused to listen, he stepped over her frail body and slammed the front door behind him. When she knocked a little later to ask for something hot to drink to keep herself warm, he warned her to take her noisy coughing elsewhere or he would call the police. His rude answer was successful because the bag lady had disappeared by the time he opened his door in the morning. His pleasure was short-lived, however. When his grandmother died a few months later, her new will told him what she had learned about his true character that night. It also left him nothing.

Solomon tells us that we are all like that grandson and

that God keeps coming to us in disguise. He tells us that the way we treat the poor who can offer us nothing in return reveals whether we are truly wise or truly foolish, truly righteous or truly wicked.[1] One of the great themes of Proverbs is that wise people love justice and feel a responsibility towards the poor, while the wicked simply care about themselves.[2]

In 14:20–21, Solomon describes the way that fools treat people who are in need. They are like Danny DeVito's character in the movie *Other People's Money*, who states his philosophy as *"Make as much as you can. For as long as you can. Whoever has the most when he dies, wins."*[3] They charm the rich because they hope to get something in return, but they despise the poor and therefore sin against the Lord.[4]

In 14:31, Solomon explains why. Since God created even the filthiest beggar in his own image, we honour their Maker when we show them human kindness and we despise their Maker when we refuse.[5] It is an offence under English law to deface a banknote which bears the Queen's image, and it is an offence under heaven's law to despise the image of God in a fellow human being, no matter how heavily disguised that image might be. Solomon states the positive flip side to this in 19:17 when he promises us that *"Whoever is kind to the poor lends to the Lord, and he will reward them,"* and this was one of the verses which stirred the English cricket legend C.T. Studd to

---

[1] Jesus picks up on Solomon's teaching to tell us a parable with a similar message in Matthew 25:31–46. He tells us that we only love him as much or as little as we show love towards those who are in need.

[2] Some of the clearest verses which say this are Proverbs 1:3, 2:9, 8:15, 11:1, 18:5 and 29:7.

[3] Danny DeVito says this as the arch-capitalist Larry Garfield in *Other People's Money* (Warner Brothers, 1991).

[4] The teaching of Proverbs 19:6 has to be understood alongside the teaching of Proverbs 22:16.

[5] Job states this principle in Job 31:15 as *"Did not he who made me in the womb make them? Did not the same one form us both within our mothers?"* Solomon also states it in 17:5, 22:2 and 29:13.

give away his fame and fortune in Victorian Britain in order to go and spend his life helping the poor and dying multitudes of China. He wrote,

> *I cannot tell you what joy it gave me to bring the first soul to the Lord Jesus Christ. I have tasted almost all the pleasures that this world can give. I do not suppose there is one that I have not experienced, but I can tell you that those pleasures were as nothing compared to the joy that the saving of that one soul gave me.*[6]

The rewards may be high, but in 14:22–23 Solomon warns us that helping those in need is never easy. He tells us in 14:22 that we will need to plan our good deeds as meticulously as wicked people plan their evil deeds. It isn't enough for us to deal with need as we chance upon it, because most poverty tends to be tucked away behind closed doors.[7] Nor is it enough to talk about helping those in need, since 14:23 reminds us that fine-sounding plans are merely empty chatter unless they lead to action. That's why Solomon spurs us on in 14:22 with a reminder that God will pour out his love and faithfulness on anyone who acts to help the poor.[8]

It's also why Solomon spends the rest of these verses helping us to decide how much we should give to help those in need. There is nothing intrinsically wrong with our being rich (14:24), but there is if our money makes us trust in riches and miss out on the true security which the generous find by trusting in the Lord (14:26). If we forget that the people around us matter far more than our money (14:28), our wealth becomes a cancer which eats away at us on the inside (14:30).

---

[6] Quoted by Norman Grubb in his biography *C.T. Studd: Cricketer and Pioneer* (1933).

[7] Proverbs 24:11–12 warns that being ignorant of poverty and need does not make us innocent.

[8] See also Proverbs 22:9, 16 and 22–23.

"Complete possession is proved only by giving. All you are unable to give possesses you," warned the French author André Gide, and Solomon agrees.[9] He told us in 10:22 that all our money is a gift from the Lord, and in 11:24–28 that how we steward it dictates how much more the Lord can entrust into our hands.[10] Solomon doesn't mention tithing or focus on how much we should give; instead he challenges us to consider how much we ought to have left over.[11]

If all of this sounds costly, that's precisely because it is. It cost Jesus all his blood, not just 10 per cent of it, to save us. We can't twist 14:23 to argue that the poor are lazy and undeserving, because we are just as undeserving of the blood which Jesus shed for us. We can't use 16:26 to complain that the poor may abuse our generosity, because we have all abused Jesus' far greater generosity towards us. Put simply, the way we care or don't care for those in need is a true mark of whether or not we have truly grasped the Gospel. God comes to us in disguise. Those who fail to recognize him are wicked fools.

The nineteenth-century Scottish preacher Robert Murray M'Cheyne exclaimed in the middle of one of his sermons:

> *Ah! my dear friends! I am concerned for the poor; but more for you... I fear there are many hearing me who may know well that they are not Christians, because they do not love to give. To give largely and liberally, not grudging at all, requires a new heart; an old heart would rather part with its life-blood than its money. Oh, my friends! enjoy your money; make the most of it; give*

[9] André Gide in *New Fruits of the Earth* (1935).

[10] Proverbs 3:9–10 and 2 Corinthians 9:10–11 also tell us that God is looking for people he can entrust with wealth so that they will channel it to those who are in need.

[11] Jesus echoes Solomon's teaching by saying something similar in Luke 21:1–4 and by teaching in Matthew 5:20 and 23:23 that *"justice, mercy and faithfulness"* will stir believers to give far more than 10 per cent.

none away; enjoy it quickly; for I can tell you, you will be beggars throughout eternity.[12]

So let's not be like the foolish grandson who lost a fortune. Let's show our love for the Lord by loving the poorest, the neediest and the least deserving people he has made. *"Whoever oppresses the poor shows contempt for their Maker, but whoever is kind to the needy honours God."*

[12] Robert Murray M'Cheyne preached this sermon at Dundee in Scotland on 4th February 1838.

Beads and Trinkets (15:16–17)

Better a little with the fear of the Lord than great wealth with turmoil. Better a small serving of vegetables with love than a fattened calf with hatred.
(Proverbs 15:16–17)

Peter Minuit bought an island in May 1626. It cost him a collection of beads and trinkets worth less than $1,000 in today's money.[1] The Native Americans went back happily to their tepees with their trinkets, but the better end of the bargain had been the Dutchman's. That island, which the Native Americans had named Manhattan, would become one of the most expensive parcels of real estate in the world. In 2011 a single home on the Upper East Side of the island went on sale for $90 million. Peter Minuit had exchanged the superficial glitter of his beads and trinkets to obtain something far better.

Solomon faced his own Manhattan moment when the Lord appeared to him at the Tabernacle at the start of his reign and offered to give him anything he wanted. He must have been tempted to choose great riches because ancient rulers believed that money bought peace and safety from their enemies, the love of many women, countless friends and favour with the gods. Yet long before The Beatles sang that money "Can't Buy Me Love", Janet Jackson sang "The Best Things in Life Are Free", and Jessie J sang "It's Not About the Money", Solomon sang a similar song at the Tabernacle. He saw past the beads and

---

1 The collection was valued at $24 in the nineteenth century.

trinkets which captivate the foolish world and asked the Lord to give him wisdom instead. Like Peter Minuit, he exchanged the baubles of this world for something far better. Having told us to use our wealth to help the poor and needy, he now attacks the love of money even further by telling us to be like Peter Minuit and sacrifice what is good to get what is even better.

Money can never buy true peace and security. In fact, 13:8 warns that it often takes them both away. *"Better a little with the fear of the Lord than great wealth with turmoil,"* Solomon warns us here in 15:16, and he repeats his warning again in 17:1: *"Better a dry crust with peace and quiet than a house full of feasting, with strife."* Over a dozen times in his Top 375 he uses a particular kind of comparative parallelism to warn us *better this than that,* and it is normally to warn us about the deceptive lure of money. Money itself is not evil but the love of money can quickly become an idol, and a weak idol at that. Although *"the wealth of the rich is their fortified city; they imagine it a wall too high to scale"*, Solomon warns us that it deserts its worshippers when they need it most.[2] He urges us to choose wisdom and the fear of the Lord instead of money, promising us in 2:11 that *"Discretion will protect you, and understanding will guard you."*

Money can never buy true love either. Wealthy rulers may assemble harems and take their pick of beautiful women, but they cannot overrule the fact that true love is never bought but only given. *"Better a small serving of vegetables with love than a fattened calf with hatred,"* Solomon warns us here in 15:17, and we will do well to listen to one who knew the ups and downs of marriage like no other. *"Many waters cannot quench love; rivers cannot sweep it away,"* he concludes in Song of Songs 8:7. *"If one were to give all the wealth of one's house for love, it would be utterly scorned."* Money is mere beads and trinkets in the marketplace of love. Solomon didn't choose money at

[2] He contrasts the false fortress of Money in 18:11 with the true fortress of God in 18:10. Solomon's friends tell us in 23:4–5 that only a fool would strive for something which flies away just when we need it.

the Tabernacle because he knew that God's wisdom produces marriages which money just can't buy.

Nor can money ever buy true friendship. Its trappings may attract a host of fickle acquaintances in 19:4–7, but Solomon warns in 17:17 and 18:24 that a true *"friend loves at all times"* and that *"one who has unreliable friends soon comes to ruin"*. He wasn't interested at the Tabernacle in the fickle popularity of men and women, but in the wisdom which breeds true friendship with the Lord and with other believers. There is no greater friend than Jesus, the embodiment of God's wisdom, which is why Solomon tells us in 18:24 that *"there is a friend who sticks closer than a brother"*. He is our true peace, our true security, our true Lover and our true Friend. He gives us the wisdom upon which all true and lasting friendship must be built.[3] Solomon didn't ask for the beads and trinkets of popularity because he had seen something far better.

Nor can money ever buy us favour with the Lord. God condemns in 17:23 and 29:4 earthly judges and earthly kings who are won over by bribes, so we should not imagine that the Lord can ever be bribed to ignore our sin.[4] *"Better a little with righteousness than much gain with injustice,"* Solomon warns us in 16:8. Vaults of gold bullion are mere beads and trinkets before God the Judge, since only he can make us righteous and he doesn't need our money. Solomon warns us not to waste our lives pursuing wealth when God's wisdom is what really matters.

The American steel magnate Andrew Carnegie understood this principle early on in his career. He resolved when he was thirty-three that

> *The amassing of wealth is one of the worst species of idolatry – no idol more debasing than the worship of*

[3] Solomon's friends tell us in 22:11 that choosing wisdom will make us even count kings among our friends.

[4] Solomon reminds us that God will never take a bribe in 15:27.

money... To continue much longer overwhelmed by business cares and with most of my thoughts wholly upon the way to make more money in the shortest time, must degrade me beyond hope of permanent recovery. I will resign business at thirty-five.[5]

That sounds wise but the fact is that Andrew Carnegie didn't retire from business at thirty-five at all. He retired in his late sixties and believed he could fix the world's problems through the money he had earned. Although he is remembered fondly as a great philanthropist, he failed to learn what Solomon teaches in these verses and played with his large pile of beads and trinkets until he died. He even published a book in 1889 entitled *The Gospel of Wealth*, in which he hoped that money *"is destined... to bring 'Peace on earth, among men Good Will.'"*

So, having told us in chapter 14 not to be like the miser Ebenezer Scrooge, Solomon tells us in chapter 15 not to be like the generous philanthropist Andrew Carnegie either. He wants us to grasp that wisdom means more than simply giving to the poor and needy; it also means not relying on what we have left over.[6] He wants to free us from the love of money and to help us to see worldly wealth as mere beads and trinkets. He wants to teach us to do what Andrew Carnegie knew he ought to do but failed. He wants to teach us to make the same choice he made at the Tabernacle, urging us in 16:16:

How much better to get wisdom than gold, to get insight rather than silver!

[5] He resolved this in a letter which he wrote to himself while staying in New York City in December 1868. It is footnoted in the 2009 reprint of his autobiography, first published a year after his death in 1920.

[6] The love of money which Paul warns against in 1 Timothy 6:9–11, 17–19 expresses itself as much in Andrew Carnegie's self-confident philanthropy as it does in Ebenezer Scrooge's self-centred misanthropy. The political Right tends to make the same mistake as Scrooge and the Left the same mistake as Carnegie.

How to Make God Hate You (16:1–19)

> *The Lord detests all the proud of heart. Be sure of this: They will not go unpunished.*
>
> (Proverbs 16:5)

"The God that holds you over the pit of hell, much as one holds a spider or some loathsome insect over the fire, abhors you and is dreadfully provoked," Jonathan Edwards warned the townspeople of Enfield, Connecticut, in his famous sermon "Sinners in the Hands of an Angry God".

> *His wrath towards you burns like fire; he looks upon you as worthy of nothing else but to be cast into the fire; he is of purer eyes than to bear to have you in his sight; you are ten thousand times so abominable in his eyes as the most hateful venomous serpent is in ours. You have offended him infinitely more than ever a stubborn rebel did his prince: and yet 'tis nothing but his hand that holds you from falling into the fire every moment... You hang by a slender thread with the flames of divine wrath flashing about it, and ready every moment to singe it and burn it asunder; and you have no interest in any mediator and nothing to lay hold of to save yourself, nothing to keep off the flames of wrath, nothing of your own, nothing that you ever have done, nothing that you can do, to induce God to spare you one moment.*[1]

---

[1] Although the Great Awakening had already begun across New England, it only reached Enfield when Jonathan Edwards preached this sermon there on 8th July 1741.

Such was the language which marked the Great Awakening, the revival which swept across America in the middle of the eighteenth century, but it jars with us today. We have had our fill of fire-and-brimstone sermons and prefer our preachers to be humorous and winsome. We tend to react against the idea of an angry God altogether. Rob Bell warns against *"a distorted understanding of God... that God is angry, demanding, a slave driver... so that God's religion becomes a system of sin management, constantly working and angling to avoid what surely must be the coming wrath that lurks behind every corner, thought, and sin"*.[2] It's easy for us to dismiss Jonathan Edwards and his friends as simply the products of their culture. That's why Solomon warns us that we are products of our own.

Solomon warns us in verse 5 that the Lord hates sinners and not just their sin. Writing 2,700 years before Jonathan Edwards stood up to preach at Enfield, he tells us that we can make God hate us. It isn't just that God hates the actions of sinners (6:16–19), the thoughts of sinners (15:29), the lifestyle of sinners (15:9) and the religion of sinners (15:8) – Solomon tells us plainly in verse 5 that *"The Lord detests all the proud of heart. Be sure of this: They will not go unpunished."* If this surprises you, you can also find the same teaching in 3:32 and 11:20.[3] One of the reasons why Jonathan Edwards and his friends saw great revival is that they preached the message of Proverbs.

Solomon knows that this requires some explanation, so he also tells us in verse 5 what the problem is. Although God hates people lying (8:7), cheating (11:1), play-acting (21:27) and refusing to listen (28:9), he hates those sins as symptoms of an underlying sin which makes him detest sinners themselves. Each of those sins is an expression of *human pride*, an arrogant desire to sit on the Lord's Throne and act like little gods ourselves. It

---

[2] Rob Bell in his book *Love Wins* (2011).

[3] We can also read literally in 13:5 that the wicked *stink* or *are odious* to God.

shouldn't surprise us to read in 3:34 that such vile blasphemy and rebellion turns the Lord from friend into foe.[4] Nor should it surprise us that he repeats this warning here in verse 18, telling us that *"pride goes before destruction"*.[5]

It gets worse. Solomon doesn't want us to think that he is talking about other people, so he makes it clear that God will hate us too unless we repent of our pride. When we make plans as if we were the masters of our own souls (verse 1); when we claim we are innocent and forget that God weighs the tainted motives of our hearts (verse 2); when we fool ourselves that God will turn a blind eye to those scales of justice (verses 10–11), we despise our Maker and turn him into our enemy.[6] That's why Solomon warns us in verse 4 about the day of final judgment and warns us in verse 5 not to fool ourselves that we will escape it without a Saviour. He wants us to think back to 15:11, where he used the two main Hebrew words for hell – *she'ōl* which means *hell* and *abaddōn* which means *Place of Destruction* – and where he warned us that God sees deep inside every human heart.[7] Solomon doesn't just tell us that what Jonathan Edwards said was true; he also tells us that it is the message which we ourselves most need to hear.

Charles Finney, who led the Second Great Awakening which revived America again about a century after Edwards, warns us that *"Evermore the Law must prepare the way for the Gospel. To*

[4] No verse in Proverbs is quoted more often in the New Testament than 3:34. James 4:6 and 1 Peter 5:5 both quote it in the Greek Septuagint's amplified form.

[5] Solomon's proverb has become a common English proverb in its contracted form – *pride goes before a fall* – but pride remains as big an issue for us today as it was for Solomon's original readers.

[6] In fact, 17:15 uses the same Hebrew word as 16:5 and 12 to emphasize that God *detests* the belief that he will acquit the guilty as much as he *detests* the sinner and their sin.

[7] This verse tells us that hell is not where Satan rules in spite of God, but where Satan and his followers are punished by the just decree of God. *Abaddōn* is only used in the Wisdom Books (in Job 26:6; 28:22; 31:12; Psalm 88:11; Proverbs 15:11; 27:20). *She'ōl* is used 65 times throughout the Old Testament.

overlook this in instructing souls is almost certain to result in false hope, the introduction of a false standard of Christian experience, and to fill the church with spurious converts. Time will make this plain."[8] This explains why Solomon has drawn so many proverbs together in chapter 16 which speak of God's hatred of sinners and of the certainty of God's judgment. He did so because he wants to lead us to forgiveness through the Gospel.

God hates sinners, but he doesn't just hate sinners. He loves them too, which is why he promised Solomon's father David that he would send his Messiah to deal with the problem of our sin so that we could be forgiven. Solomon promises in verse 6 that the Lord will atone for our sin through his *hēsēd*, or *covenant love*, which forms a deliberate contrast with God's fierce hatred in the previous verse. Jesus was humble and faithful wherever we have been proud and failed. He *"did not consider equality with God something to be used to his own advantage"*,[9] so he did nothing to deserve the punishment David prophesied would come upon him in Psalm 22. Solomon's proverb in verse 14 can even be translated as a prophecy about Jesus' death at Calvary: *"The King's wrath is an angel of death, but the Wise One will appease it."* A wise person knows how to appease the anger of an earthly ruler, but the true Wise One has appeased for us the righteous anger and hatred of the King of kings. No wonder Solomon continues in verse 15 with a celebration of the life-giving favour which the Gospel message brings.

This is the message which saved the townspeople of Enfield. It is the message which still saves proud people today. The Wise One bore God's wrath towards sinners so that we might know his love.

---

[8] Finney wrote this in a pamphlet entitled *How to Win Souls*, first published in 1871.

[9] Philippians 2:6. Adam was a man who lusted to be God. Jesus is God yet he deigned to become a man.

How Not to Help the Poor (16:26)

The labourer's appetite works for him; his hunger drives him on.

(Proverbs 16:26)

Solomon thinks we have finally got it. He thinks we have grasped that wise and righteous people always help the poor. He hasn't placed any caveats so far on his call to generous giving in case we use them to deflect the firmness of his message, but now he thinks we are ready to hear him explore the subject more. He warns us that unthinking generosity and misapplied charity can actually harm the very people we intend to help. He warns us not to empty our pockets naïvely, but to spend time thinking about the ways we shouldn't help the poor before we do.

Solomon tells us in 16:26 that we should never help people in a way that sabotages their need to take responsibility for their own lives. *"The labourer's appetite works for him; his hunger drives him on,"* he warns. Proverbs tells us repeatedly not to act like sluggards, so we must not give in a way that turns the needy into sluggards. A well-fed stomach promotes laziness unless it comes with an opportunity to work hard for even more. We can kill people with our kindness if we give in a way that robs them of a sense of their own responsibility and which lessens their resolve to tackle the underlying problems behind their poverty.

One of the words Proverbs uses to describe the poor and needy is *'āni*, which means *oppressed* or *ravaged*. Victims of injustice need our help because their poverty is brought on them by others. We need to help them to fight unfair wages, high-interest loans,[1] con artists and a society which favours the rich at the expense of the poor. But another word which Proverbs uses to describe the poor and needy is *'ātsēl*, which means *sluggard*, because some people are victims of their own folly and weak character. The word *sluggard* occurs twice as often as *oppressed* in Proverbs because Solomon wants us to be wise in the way we help the poor. Similarly, 1 Timothy 5:3 makes a clear distinction between those *"who are really in need"* and those whose greater need is to receive some discipline which forces them to address the underlying issue.

Can you see why Solomon has saved this teaching about poverty until relatively late in his Top 375? He knows that some of us would have grasped at this as an excuse not to give to the poor at all. The political Right has a tendency to expect those in need to pull themselves up by their own boot straps, so Solomon warns that it is the duty of those who are not in need to lift up those who are.[2] By far the commonest Hebrew word for *poor* in Proverbs is the neutral word *rūsh* because God wants us to grasp that we are all undeserving sinners and that we must therefore help the so-called undeserving poor as well. The political Left has a tendency to treat sluggards in the same way as they do the oppressed, so Solomon points out several principles in the later chapters of Proverbs that teach us to help the poor without harming them through well-intentioned but foolish acts of kindness.

First, he tells us not to give in a way that protects a person from feeling God's discipline because of their sin. He tells us in 19:19 that *"A hot-tempered man must pay the penalty; if you*

---

[1] Solomon addresses the issue of debt when he warns us that money gained too easily is usually spent too easily (13:11 and 20:21). He therefore tells us to pay off any money we owe as quickly as possible (3:28 and 22:7), and that God will judge anyone who oppresses the poor through giving them high-interest loans (28:8).

[2] He particularly warns the successful in 18:23 not to answer the poor harshly because of their own success.

rescue him, you will have to do it again." People who become poor through a gambling addiction or through chasing get-rich-quick schemes instead of knuckling down to hard work need to feel the pain of their wrong decisions. Otherwise, the bail-out will simply set them free to repeat the same mistake again. This happens whenever parents pay off their children's debts without teaching them that their income must determine their standard of living,[3] and it happens whenever governments bail out businesses without forcing them to make fundamental changes to address what has gone wrong.[4]

Second, Solomon tells us not to give in a way which reduces a person's sense of urgency to resolve their own problems. He explains why there were no unconditional welfare handouts in his kingdom by telling us in 27:7 that *"He who is full loathes honey, but to the hungry even what is bitter tastes sweet."*[5] The hungry able-bodied person will take any job, no matter how unattractive it is, so if our generosity encourages them to stay at home, we may not have helped them at all. Better to give accommodation to a friend or family member at a discounted rent with an agreement that the rent will rise each month so that it becomes increasingly attractive for them to move out and stand back on their own two feet again. Wise givers agree clear goals with those they help financially, helping while also insisting that steps are taken to resolve the underlying issues. Paul taught this when he insisted that the church at Ephesus should not help poor believers in a way that allowed church members to neglect their own family obligations, and when he told the church not to add anybody to its formal list of those

---

[3] Proverbs 19:19 deliberately follows on from 19:18 for this reason. See also 21:17.

[4] Proverbs 21:17 and 23:21 remind us that the greed which promotes excessive spending is as much a cause of poverty as having insufficient income.

[5] This is the Hebrew equivalent of the English proverb *"Beggars can't be choosers."* Those we help need to continue to feel some pain if it is in their own power to fix the underlying causes of their poverty.

who received financial help unless some underlying character issues were addressed as well.[6]

Third, he tells us not to give in a way which deals with the symptoms of a person's problems instead of with the root cause. *"One who is slack in his work is brother to one who destroys,"* he warns in 18:9, so financial aid should be given in a way which teaches the recipients to work. We serve the God who gave the Israelites manna but told them to go out and gather it in baskets, who told the Israelites to help the poor by leaving grain unharvested in the fields, and who told the Church to help the needy by providing good deeds for them to do.[7] There were no needy people in the Early Church because money was given via church leaders rather than directly to individuals, and because church leaders sent those who were able to work to help those who weren't as the condition for receiving financial aid.[8] The early Christians were not simply provided for because the rest of the church were generous, but because the church leaders had read Proverbs and had graduated from God's flight school of wisdom.

So give generously, as God has given generously to you, but as you do so make sure you give in a manner which promotes the godliness which is worth far more than money. That is true mercy, true generosity and true wisdom. If we give wisely as well as generously, we will really help the poor.

---

[6] Paul wrote these instructions for the church at Ephesus in 1 Timothy 5:3–16.

[7] Exodus 16:15–18; Leviticus 19:9–10. 1 Timothy 5:9–10 seems to describe a similar group of working widows to the one we find in Acts 9:36–41. Poor widows received help as they helped others themselves.

[8] Acts 4:34–35.

Two Big Brothers (17:15)

Acquitting the guilty and condemning the innocent – the Lord detests them both.

(Proverbs 17:15)

Solomon had two big brothers who died as fools. One was like Catherine the Great of Russia and the other was like the stand-up comedian Emo Philips. Perhaps that's why Solomon refuses to move on without restating his warning in the previous chapter about God's judgment. He knows how easy it is for both unbelievers and believers to fool themselves that God's judgment day isn't coming.

Solomon's big brother Absalom was like Catherine the Great. The Russian ruler boasted famously, *"I am a dictator: that's my job. And the good Lord will forgive me: that's his job."* Even though she despised the Christian faith and merely used it as a clever way to manipulate her peasant subjects, even though she usurped the throne as part of a violent coup against her husband, and even though she took a long string of illicit lovers, she still convinced herself that God's judgment day was for other people and not for her. Absalom had the same attitude when he pretended to worship Yahweh in order to conceal his plans to use violence to usurp the throne and to bed his father's harem in broad daylight.[1] Even though he had blood on his hands, he dared the royal executioner to prove *"if I am guilty of anything"*, and he mistook his own low standards and short memory for a clear conscience towards God.[2] He only learned how wrong

---

[1] 2 Samuel 15:7–10; 16:20–22.

[2] 2 Samuel 14:32. Joab executed his judgment on Absalom in 2 Samuel 18:9–15.

his self-assessment had been on the day that the executioner ignored his belated pleas for mercy and drove a spear into his sinful heart.

Many non-Christians view God's judgment day like Absalom. If there is a God, they reason, he will not judge people like themselves. The German poet Heinrich Heine echoed Absalom and Catherine the Great on his deathbed in 1856, insisting with his final breath that *"Of course God will forgive me: that's his job."*[3] Absalom's name meant *My Father Is Peace*, and as such he represents all those who fool themselves that God will turn a blind eye to their sin and grant them peace instead of judgment. That's why Solomon follows up his warning that God hates sinners in 16:5 with a fresh warning which uses the exact same Hebrew word in 17:15: *"Acquitting the guilty and condemning the innocent – the Lord detests them both."*[4] God doesn't just detest it when bad things happen to good people who don't deserve it. He also hates it when bad things don't happen to bad people who do deserve it![5] Solomon's big brother Absalom learned too late that God doesn't indulge sin, so he includes this proverb in his Top 375 to stop us making a similar error of judgment.

But Solomon knows that most of his readers will not be unbelievers. If you are one of the few non-Christians who bother to read his words of wisdom, then well done for reading this far, and make sure you don't ignore the coming judgment day like Absalom. But if you belong to the majority of readers who are Christians, your bigger danger is to act like Adonijah, another one of Solomon's big brothers. Adonijah means *My Lord*

---

[3] Quoted by Sigmund Freud in his book *The Joke and Its Relation to the Unconscious* (1905).

[4] Solomon says that the idea of letting unrepentant sinners go unpunished is a *tō'ēbah* to God, which means a *detestable thing* or *an abomination*.

[5] Solomon stresses this again in 18:5, telling us that if God ignored a person's sin, he would actually be unjust towards those who were affected by their sins.

Is Yahweh, and as such he represents all those who claim to be believers yet fool themselves that cheap confession of sin is the same thing as conversion. Adonijah was like Emo Philips, the American stand-up comedian who joked that *"When I was a kid I used to pray every night for a new bicycle. Then I realised that the Lord doesn't work that way so I stole a bicycle and asked him to forgive me."*[6]

Adonijah looked like a sincere follower of Yahweh. He had sided with his father David during Absalom's rebellion, and when he launched his own bid for the throne he was supported by the high priest Abiathar and by the man who had executed Absalom. He proclaimed himself king as part of a great religious celebration in which the high priest sacrificed many animals to the Lord, and when his plot to seize the throne was thwarted he rushed to the Tabernacle and laid hold of the horns of the Lord's altar. He convinced himself that he could escape judgment simply by making a quick confession for his sin, because he thought God was a sucker who could not resist a person who said sorry. The newly crowned King Solomon was not convinced and sent him home with a warning that *"If he shows himself to be worthy, not a hair of his head will fall to the ground; but if evil is found in him, he will die."*[7] Adonijah's subsequent actions quickly proved that his confession of sin was superficial, so Solomon sent the royal executioner to his house to tell him that his judgment day had come.

That's why Solomon's biggest warning is not for unbelievers like Absalom but for false believers like Adonijah. This proverb serves as an Old Testament precursor to Jesus' warning in Matthew 7:21–23 that *"Not everyone who says to me, 'Lord, Lord,' will enter the kingdom of heaven, but only the one who does the will of my Father who is in heaven. Many will say to*

---

[6] Emo Philips wrote this in the British newspaper *The Guardian* on 29th September 2005.

[7] 1 Kings 1:52. Solomon makes it clear in Proverbs 17:11 that Adonijah was a rebel against God and that the fate he experienced was God's judgment day.

me on that day, 'Lord, Lord,'... Then I will tell them plainly, 'I never knew you. Away from me, you evildoers!'"

Solomon wants you to understand that God never ignores sin. He always punishes it in the sinner or in the Messiah's sacrifice for sin. If you ignore the Gospel like Absalom, you will discover that God finds your self-confidence detestable. If you lay hold of the Gospel half-heartedly like Adonijah, confessing your sin but not truly repenting of it, you will discover that God hates the idea that he will acquit the guilty as much as the idea that he would ever condemn the innocent.

Dietrich Bonhoeffer, a Christian leader in the German opposition to Adolf Hitler, wrote a similar warning a few years before he died in a Nazi prison:

> *Cheap grace is the deadly enemy of our Church... Cheap grace is the grace we bestow on ourselves. Cheap grace is the preaching of forgiveness without requiring repentance... Cheap grace is grace without discipleship, grace without the cross, grace without Jesus Christ, living and incarnate. Costly grace is the treasure hidden in the field; for the sake of it a man will gladly go and sell all that he has. It is the pearl of great price to buy which the merchant will sell all his goods... Such grace is costly because it calls us to follow, and it is grace because it calls us to follow Jesus Christ. It is costly because it costs a man his life, and it is grace because it gives a man the only true life. It is costly because it condemns sin, and grace because it justifies the sinner. Above all, it is costly because it cost God the life of his Son... and what has cost God much cannot be cheap for us.*[8]

[8] Dietrich Bonhoeffer in *The Cost of Discipleship* (1937). Bonhoeffer was hanged by the unrepentant Nazis in April 1945.

Omission (18:9)

One who is slack in his work is brother to one who destroys.

(Proverbs 18:9)

On the evening of 6th March 1987, a ferry named *The Herald of Free Enterprise* sank within moments of leaving the Belgian port of Zeebrugge: 193 passengers and crew members lost their lives in the freezing water, and an inquest discovered what had caused the great disaster. The answer was very simple: somebody had forgotten to close the bow doors before leaving harbour. It was the job of assistant boatswain Mark Stanley, but he had been asleep in his cabin. It was the job of first officer Leslie Sabel to check he did it, but he had left his post to attend to other tasks. The last man on deck who might have closed the doors was boatswain Terence Ayling, but he told the judge he didn't think it was his job to do so. The court ruled that the owners and crew of the ferry were *"infected with the disease of sloppiness".*[1] It ruled that they were fools like the ones which Solomon describes in Proverbs 18:9.

Religion tends to talk a lot about sins of commission – the things we do but shouldn't do. It tells us not to steal, not to lie, not to blaspheme and not to hurt others – all the acts of folly which Solomon addresses throughout the book of Proverbs. He warns us in 28:24 that committing such sins makes us *"partner to the one who destroys"*, or more literally *"an accomplice of*

---

[1] This was the verdict of the final *Report of Court No. 8074*. In fairness to these men, the report not only criticized their negligence but also praised their courageous action once they saw their error.

the Destroyer". Through our active sins, we aid and abet the Devil in his plans to destroy people who are made in the Lord's image. The founders of the world's great religions all warn their followers against sins of commission. For example, the Chinese philosopher Confucius told his followers, *"Do not do to others what you would not want them to do to you."*[2]

Solomon therefore expects all of his readers to understand about sins of commission, but he adds this proverb to remind us that the Lord is not like pagan idols. He doesn't just judge sins of commission because he alone can see the secrets of every human heart (16:2). He also judges sins of omission: the good things we should do but often don't. Solomon has worked hard in these few chapters of Proverbs to convince us that God always judges sin and that we need to repent and receive forgiveness through the Gospel. Now he makes sure we grasp the full extent of our sin by telling us literally that *"the one who is slack in his work is brother to the Master Destroyer".* Sins of omission couldn't be more serious. Solomon tells us they make us look like Satan's brother.

Most of us find it easier to point the finger at neglectful ferrymen than we do to admit our own sins of omission. Paul needed to encourage the Romans to admit that *"I do not do the good I want to do,"* and James had to write to the early Christians with a warning that *"Anyone who knows the good he ought to do and doesn't do it, sins."*[3] They were simply unpacking the message of Proverbs 14:31 that those who fail to help the poor actually help the Devil to destroy them, and they were simply expanding on what Jesus taught through the Parable of the Good Samaritan in Luke 10. The priest and the Levite didn't need to punch and rob the traveller to sin against God on the road to Jericho. All they had to do was cross the road and fail to do the good which

[2] Confucius as quoted by his disciples shortly after 500 BC in *The Analects* (15.24).

[3] Romans 7:19; James 4:17. It is remarkable how often James' short letter echoes the themes of Proverbs.

they might have done. Don't miss the fact that Jesus performs a massive upgrade on Confucius' teaching when he tells us that *"In everything, do to others what you would have them do to you, for this sums up the Law and the Prophets."*[4] Unlike Confucianism and the other world religions, the Lord calls his followers to do more than avoid sins of commission. He warns them that sins of omission are deadly too.

Think about it. Religion is fundamentally self-centred; it hopes that doing good will impress God enough to earn salvation. It therefore focuses on sins of commission, as Paul points out in Colossians 2:21–22: *"'Do not handle! Do not taste! Do not touch!' These rules... are based on merely human commands and teachings."* Christianity, however, is not self-centred but God-centred. It calls us to surrender to God and to die with Christ in order to be raised by the Spirit for works of service. Jesus rebuked the Jewish leaders for thinking that the Old Testament was only focused on sins of commission by summarizing the Law in a way which focused primarily on sins of omission. He repeated Solomon's warning that thoughtless neglect can make us just as much accomplices of Satan as outright disobedience and rebellion.

In Matthew 22:37, Jesus says that the greatest commandment in the Old Testament is to *"Love the Lord your God with all your heart and with all your soul and with all your mind."*[5] Note how much this focuses on what we don't do as well as what we do. Passive neglect of prayer is therefore just as sinful as active blasphemy, and failure to worship the Lord as he deserves is as great a sin as denying him to others.[6] Failure to love the Church, give money to the Church, serve in the Church and lay down our lives for the Church is as serious

---

[4] Matthew 7:12; Luke 6:31.

[5] Jesus is quoting from Deuteronomy 6:5. See also Luke 10:27.

[6] Once again it is James who echoes this statement that sins of omission are as serious as sins of commission. See James 2:10.

in God's sight as standing outside and throwing bricks at the windows of the Church.

Jesus continues by telling us in Matthew 22:39 that the second greatest commandment is very similar: *"Love your neighbour as yourself."*[7] Failure to rebuke a fool and to warn him that judgment day is coming therefore makes us an accomplice to his murder.[8] Failure to share our possessions with those in need makes us as guilty as those who break into their homes to steal, as Basil of Caesarea pointed out to his congregation during the great famine of 368 AD:

> *When someone steals a man's clothes, we call him a thief, so shouldn't we give the same name to one who could clothe the naked and does not? The bread in your cupboard belongs to the hungry, the coat in your wardrobe belongs to the naked, the shoes you let rot belong to the barefoot, the money in your vaults belongs to the poor. You do wrong to all those you could help but do not.*[9]

But if this discourages you, you haven't understood the message of Proverbs. Solomon doesn't tell us this to depress us but to deliver us. He includes this proverb because he knew that God's perfect Messiah would one day come and live the perfect life we could not live, and would bear the judgment we deserve both for our sins of commission and our sins of omission. He wants us to admit we are far guiltier than we imagined. Let's pray and receive the forgiveness which is ours through the Wise and Righteous One who neglected none of God's commands.

---

[7] Jesus is quoting from Leviticus 19:18. See also Romans 13:9–10, Galatians 5:14 and James 2:8. This was the verse which Jesus sought to illustrate through the Parable of the Good Samaritan in Luke 10:25–37.

[8] Proverbs 29:5; Ezekiel 3:16–21; 33:1–9.

[9] Basil preached this in his sermon "On the Rich Fool" from Luke 12:13–21.

Swimming with Sharks (18:10–11)

The name of the Lord is a fortified tower; the righteous run to it and are safe.

(Proverbs 18:10)

If anybody tries to tell you that Proverbs is a random collection of sayings pieced together in no particular order, simply take them to these verses in chapter 18. It isn't simply that the next verse after Solomon's warning against sins of omission is an encouragement to pray, the very thing which believers feel most conscious of neglecting. It's also that he deliberately places two proverbs next to one another in verses 10 and 11 which expose why we don't pray and encourage us that prayer is always rewarded. In these two verses Solomon contrasts two different types of fortified tower.

The reason why most of us pray less than we ought is the same as the reason why people swim off the coast of Australia and South Africa. Although some of the world's most dangerous sharks are known to inhabit those waters, the locals have long become accustomed to the danger. In the same way, verse 11 warns us that *"The wealth of the rich is their fortified city; they imagine it a wall too high to scale."* The reason we pray as little as we do is that we fool ourselves that the dangerous waters of life are safe enough for us to swim in on our own. That's the pride which Solomon warns against in verse 12, telling us that pride always comes before a fall. We demonstrate our humility when we speak out our reliance upon God, but it would be safer for us to swim in shark-infested waters than to try to go it alone without prayer.

Human strength looks more impressive than humble prayer – like a *city* in verse 11 compared to a mere *tower* in verse 10 – but for all it looks impressive human strength crumbles when life gets rough. Ronald Reagan lived in the ultimate fortified city when he served two terms in the White House as president of the United States. He wielded supreme executive power every day from the Oval Office, but in his autobiography he remembers the moment when he realized that human strength is not enough. When his wife Nancy was diagnosed with breast cancer, he was forced to his knees in the Oval Office as he learned to rely on the true strength which comes through the name of the Lord in prayer. He writes that *"For all the powers of the president of the United States, there were some situations that made me feel helpless and very humble. All I could do was pray – and I did a lot of praying for Nancy during the next few weeks."*[1]

Prayer may not look very impressive to the unbelieving world, but Solomon tells us it is stronger than any shark-proof cage. *"The name of the Lord is a fortified tower; the righteous run to it and are safe,"* he promises us from his own experience in prayer. There is no need for us to panic or get discouraged when the waters of life get dangerous (verse 14), because God's People can always quickly run to prayer. It doesn't matter how long the problems of life may besiege us like an army or circle us like sharks, the Lord will answer our prayers with the words of Psalm 91:14: *"I will protect him, for he acknowledges my name."* Solomon is simply passing on to us the very lesson which his own father David taught him in Psalm 20 as the secret to a successful reign: *"May the name of the God of Jacob protect you... May the Lord grant all your requests... Some trust in chariots and some in horses, but we trust in the name of the Lord our God."*

---

[1] He recalls this humbling period in *Ronald Reagan: An American Life* (1990).

Ronald Reagan was able to run into the strong tower of God's name during his wife's cancer by laying hold of the Lord as *Yahweh Rophek*, or *The Lord Who Heals You*, in Exodus 15:26. Solomon was able to run into the strong tower of God's name when two of his subjects presented him with an impossible decision in 1 Kings 3:16–28 by laying hold of the Lord as *The God Who Searches Minds and Hearts* in Psalm 7:9.[2] You can do exactly the same with the sharks which encircle you today. Do you need provision? Then God is *Yahweh Yireh, The Lord Who Provides* for you (Genesis 22:14). Do you feel alone and afraid? Then God is *Yahweh Shammah, The Lord Who Is There* with you (Ezekiel 48:35). Do you need forgiveness in light of all that Solomon has said about judgment day? Then God is *Yahweh Tsidkenu, The Lord Our Righteousness* (Jeremiah 33:16). Do you need guidance for some difficult decisions ahead? Then God is *Yahweh Rohi, The Lord My Shepherd* (Psalm 23:1). Whatever your situation and whatever sharks may snap at your heels, Solomon promises that the Lord's name is strong enough to protect you, just so long as you run to the place of prayer.

Let me suggest three things for us to do today in order to apply what Solomon is teaching us about prayer. First, let's not be afraid to swim the waters of life and let's not shrink back from taking risks through fear. The fact that we are protected by the shark-proof cage of God's name should make us bold to grab all that God has promised us through faith. *"The neglect of prayer is the fearful token of dead spiritual desires,"* warns E.M. Bounds.[3] Let's allow the scale of protection to dictate the scope of our spiritual desires.

Second, let's pray to God in a manner which expects that he will answer. Far from offending God with our presumption, we

---

[2] Solomon's father had also taught him this name in 1 Chronicles 28:9 and 29:17, and Solomon made it the basis for his prayers again later in 1 Kings 8:39.

[3] E.M. Bounds wrote this in an article in his *Christian Advocate* magazine on 4th October 1890.

will delight him with our faith if we stop treating his promises as spiritual niceties and start viewing them as gifts which usher us into the presence of Almighty God to receive what he has promised (verse 16). Charles Spurgeon challenged his congregation that

> *I believe in business prayers: I mean, prayers in which you take to God one of the many precious promises which he has given us in his Word, and expect it to be fulfilled as certainly as we look for the money to be given to us when we go to the bank to cash a cheque or note. We should not think of going there, lolling over the counter, chatting with the clerks upon every conceivable subject except the one thing for which we had gone to the bank... We should seek out the promise which applies to that particular case, plead it before the Lord in faith, expect to have the blessing to which it relates, and then, having received it, let us proceed to the next duty devolving upon us.*[4]

Third, let's not stop praying until we have received what the Lord has promised and what we know must be ours as we look down from the ramparts of our position in Jesus' name. We might be turned away from the White House or the Kremlin or Ten Downing Street with a petition which contains a million names, but we will never be turned away by God when we come to him with a petition in Jesus' name.

So let's not be fooled by the brash but weak fortified city which human strength pretends to be. Let's devote ourselves to prayer as the fortified tower which enables us to swim through the shark-infested waters of life and not be harmed.

---

[4] Charles Spurgeon said this at one of his prayer meetings, recorded in *Only A Prayer Meeting* (2010).

Christmas 1914 (18:17)

The first to present his case seems right, till another comes forward and questions him.

(Proverbs 18:17)

Maybe you think that Solomon had it easy. It's all right for him to tell us in 29:5 that if we fail to share the Gospel with those around us, we are guilty of their murder. But who wouldn't respond positively to an invitation from King Solomon to come and worship the Lord at the magnificent Temple he had built? For the rest of us, sadly, sharing the Gospel simply isn't all that easy. Unbelievers don't want to listen, they dig in their heels and they often seem more entrenched in their views after we share with them than they were before we started. If that's how you are tempted to feel, you are going to love this proverb. Solomon reveals the secret of how any believer can get a good hearing for the Gospel.

Actually, Solomon found it just as difficult as we do to challenge the deep-seated views of unbelievers. In 1 Kings 4:34 and 10:1–13 we are told that pagans came to Jerusalem from every nation and that Solomon spent much of his time talking to them about the Lord. His reputation won him a positive hearing, but we shouldn't imagine that his visitors were easily persuaded. We are told that the Queen of Sheba *"came to test Solomon with hard questions"*, and that she told him frankly that she had heard about his worship of the Lord but that she *"did not believe these things"*.[1] Solomon had to use all of the wisdom

[1] *Sheba* was modern-day Yemen, so she was presumably queen of the pagans of southern Arabia.

God had given him to share the Gospel effectively with people from other religious backgrounds. He learned that sharing foolishly entrenches unbelievers in their folly, but that sharing in the right way converted the Queen of Sheba and will convert those we share with too.

Imagine you are in the World War One trenches in December 1914. The British and the Germans have been fighting for over four months now, but there is stalemate and neither side is yielding any ground. Every day they fire shells at one another but all they do is make the other side dig themselves even deeper into their entrenched position – just like us when we lecture people and criticize their views. But now imagine you are in those same trenches on 25th December 1914. On that famous Christmas Day, some British soldiers brought a football out into no-man's-land and invited the German soldiers to leave their weapons behind to play a friendly game of football together.[2] Men who had shot at one another only hours before now swapped souvenirs and chatted with one another. That's what happens when, instead of arguing and debating, we ask questions which draw unbelievers out of their entrenched position to discuss spiritual matters as friends together in no-man's-land. Solomon tells us in 18:17 that unbelievers don't want to listen to us because they are convinced that they are right. What they really need is a friend who cares enough to ask them questions.

Asking questions *draws out what people currently believe,* which has to happen before people can change their minds. Solomon tells us in 20:5 that *"A person's thoughts are like water in a deep well, but someone with insight can draw them out."*[3]

---

[2] Multiple matches were played all along no-man's-land. Since there is no record of the final score, it is probably safe to assume that, as usual, the Germans won on penalties.

[3] Good News Bible. The Hebrew word *dālāh* in 20:5 is the same word which is used in Exodus 2:16 and 19 to describe people *drawing* water out of a deep well with a bucket.

Solomon used questions like a bucket to draw out what his pagan visitors believed, and 1 Kings 10:2 tells us that as a result the Queen of Sheba *"talked with him about all that she had on her mind"*. Because he honoured her by listening and got her to lay her views out on the table, he created a fertile no-man's-land for a positive discussion in which he could challenge her in places where her thinking was weakest. *"The first to present his case seems right, till another comes forward and questions him."* It's far more effective than firing missiles at pagan trenches.

Asking questions *helps people to admit where they are wrong*. Solomon tells us in 27:14 that the right words spoken in the wrong way will be taken as hostility instead of love, but he also tells us in 16:24 that *"pleasant words are a honeycomb"* which unbelievers find *"sweet to the soul and healing to the bones"*. If Solomon had simply told his pagan visitors that they were wrong and that they needed to shut up and listen to his wisdom, they would never have confessed to him their sin. As it was, 1 Kings 10:7 tells us that the Queen of Sheba admitted her former scepticism and started worshipping the Lord as a result of his helping her to change her mind.[4]

Asking questions *stirs people's interest so that they ask us questions too*. In my early days as a Christian, I thought evangelism meant delivering a lengthy Gospel presentation to people without letting them get a word in edgeways.[5] I hadn't learned the lesson which Solomon teaches in 27:7: *"One who is full loathes honey from the comb, but to the hungry even what is bitter tastes sweet."* Lecturing people results in their feeling full quickly, no matter how sweet the truth we share, whereas questions whet people's appetites to want to hear more of what we have to say. Sure enough, after Solomon had asked the Queen of Sheba lots of questions, we read in 1 Kings 10:3 that *"Solomon answered all her questions; nothing was too hard*

[4] Proverbs 19:3 is an example of how unbelievers can delude themselves spiritually. Asking questions is the answer.

[5] I was zealous but I had not learned the lesson of Proverbs 19:2.

for the king to explain to her." He was like the twelve-year-old Jesus in Luke 2:45–47, who was discovered *"sitting among the teachers, listening to them and asking them questions"*. Because he coaxed them out into no-man's-land, they were very soon listening to *"his understanding and his answers"*.[6] If you find that people don't want to listen to what you have to say, try listening a little more yourself.[7] You will be surprised how much they imitate you.

Lastly, asking questions *enables you to challenge people to respond to the Gospel.* Solomon learned from the many dignitaries who visited him that giving the wrong kind of appeal can actually drive an unbeliever away (25:20).[8] He learned to ask questions to discover where his visitors most needed God to intervene in their lives and discovered that *"through patience a ruler can be persuaded, and a gentle tongue can break a bone"* (25:15). As an example of Solomon's persuasiveness, we read in 1 Kings 10 that the Queen of Sheba *"was overwhelmed"* and exclaimed *"Praise be to the Lord your God."* Because Solomon invited her out of the trenches of her pagan thinking and into no-man's-land through his friendly questions, she felt able to respond to the Gospel and was saved.[9]

So, enough of firing missiles at non-Christians in their trenches! Let's learn from Solomon and use questions to invite them into no-man's-land where we can come alongside them as one saved sinner offering directions to another soon-to-be-saved sinner.

---

[6] If even Jesus, the greatest preacher in history, chose to ask questions instead of simply preaching, we had better learn the vital lesson of this proverb ourselves.

[7] This is what Solomon tries to teach us here in 18:13, and he is echoed by James 1:19.

[8] That's why the early Christians always asked questions to discover what particular spiritual questions a person was asking before they brought a tailored Gospel challenge. See Acts 8:30, 35 and 17:22–23.

[9] Jesus makes it clear she was converted in Matthew 12:42 and Luke 11:31.

How to Murder Your Child (19:18–19)

Discipline your children, for in that there is hope; do not be a willing party to their death.

(Proverbs 19:18)

Because he endured racism in his youth, Nelson Mandela strove to put an end to apartheid as an adult. Because he stuttered as a child, Winston Churchill studied oratory and learned to deliver the speeches which would later inspire his nation to win a war. Because he was blinded by a childhood accident, Louis Braille devoted the rest of his life to inventing a way for blind people to read. And because Solomon watched three of his older brothers die through their father's foolish failure to discipline them, he resolved not to let parents who read Proverbs murder their children through misplaced kindness. *"Discipline your children,"* he urges us here in 19:18. *"Do not be a willing party to their death."*

This is not a message which many twenty-first-century parents want to hear. Like Solomon's father David, we lead such busy lives that we like our time with our children to be non-stop fun and friendship, unspoilt by conflict and confrontation.[1] We give in quickly to their demands, afraid to quash their creativity and confident that they will grow out of their childish ways in the course of time without the need for a parental showdown. The Duke of Windsor famously joked that *"The thing that impresses*

[1] 1 Chronicles 27:32 tells us that the busy David hired a man named Jehiel to do his childcare for him. Perhaps this is why Solomon speaks specifically about *"children left to themselves"* in 29:15.

me most about America is the way parents obey their children,"[2] but Solomon tells us this is by no means a modern American problem. Scripture tells us that David caused the death of his son Amnon by getting angry about his sin but doing nothing; that he caused the death of his son Absalom by giving him the silent treatment instead of straightforward discipline; and that he caused the death of his son Adonijah by failing to confront him with his sin.[3] This is what Solomon is remembering when he tells us in 13:24: *"Whoever spares the rod hates their children, but the one who loves their children is careful to discipline them."*[4]

Solomon therefore tells us throughout Proverbs *not to assume that children are born wiser than they really are.* Whereas most paperback literature on parenting focuses on how to bring the best out of little children, Solomon warns that the real question is how to drive the worst out of them in their early days![5] He encourages us in 22:15 that *"Folly is bound up in the heart of a child, but the rod of discipline will drive it far away."*

Solomon warns us throughout Proverbs *not to assume that we have longer to teach our children wisdom than we really do.* Any experienced parent will tell you that childhood days fly by with rapid speed, so Solomon warns that what happens in those first few formative years often determines what happens for the remainder of the child's life. *"Start children off on the way they should go, and even when they are old they will not turn from it,"* he encourages us in 22:6. If you do not have children

[2] The former King Edward VIII said this in the 5th March 1957 edition of *Look* magazine.

[3] 2 Samuel 13:21; 14:24, 28; 1 Kings 1:6. We read literally in 2 Samuel 13:27 that *"Absalom broke past him"* when they had a disagreement with one another.

[4] Proverbs 23:12–14 links this to the earlier chapter "Make Tracks". If we resent God's *mūsār* or *correction* (23:12), we will not give our children the *correction* which they require either (23:13–14). Verses 13 and 14 also tell us that parents who fail to discipline their children are accomplices to their murder.

[5] Solomon is echoing earlier Scriptures such as Genesis 8:21 and Psalm 51:5 and 58:3.

of your own, these verses are still very relevant to you as you disciple spiritual newborns. A golf ball struck only slightly wrong on the tee will end up in a very wrong place further down the fairway.

Solomon warns us throughout Proverbs *not to assume that verbal discipline is more effective than it really is.* He is the first to encourage parents to talk about wisdom (1:8) and to praise wise actions (12:18), but he warns us not to think that words alone can dislodge folly from a child's heart. Folly is "bound up" in the hearts of our children and there will be times when it needs to be displaced by force. If even Jesus in Hebrews 5:8 *"learned obedience from what he suffered"*, making our children cry does not make us bad parents. Perhaps that's why Solomon follows up 19:18 with a further warning in 19:19 that unless fools feel the consequences of their folly they will simply repeat it. Solomon warns us to let our children taste the fruit of folly at a young age if we want them to love wisdom all their lives. The actress Bette Davis observed that *"If you have never been hated by your child, you have never been a parent."*

Perhaps most controversially for our culture, Solomon tells us to use physical discipline with our children. We can debate what he means by *"the rod"* (and I have yet to meet any parent who actually uses a rod!), but we mustn't miss the fact that Proverbs tells parents seven times to use one.[6] The Hebrew word *shebet* is the same word that is used for a shepherd's *staff* or a king's *sceptre*, so it speaks of daring to use physical force to assert our God-given authority as shepherds to our children. Don't let the horrible misuse of force by foolish parents stop you from using appropriate force, or you will produce foolish children instead. The reformer John Knox told Mary Queen of Scots that *"I can scarcely well abide the tears of my own boys, whom my own hand corrects... But I must sustain, albeit*

---

[6] Proverbs 10:13; 13:24; 22:15; 23:13, 14; 26:3; 29:15. Note that two of these references to *"the rod"* are by Solomon's friends, which reminds us that this is Scripture talking and not just Solomon.

unwillingly."[7] So must we. If a sculptor needs to use a chisel to form a beautiful statue out of stone, we must not be surprised that smacked hands are a necessary part of forming beautiful adults out of foolish children.[8]

That's why Solomon promises us throughout Proverbs that *disciplining our children will result in true happiness for us and them.* It is easy to see why he tells us in 10:1 and 17:21 that whether a child is wise or foolish determines whether a parent is happy or miserable,[9] but he also insists that whether a parent is wise or foolish in using discipline determines whether a child is happy or miserable too. Solomon tells us in 17:6 that such *"parents are the pride of their children"* because they make them ready to live life to the full, and he promises in 28:23 that they also make their children love them more in the end because *"Whoever rebukes a person will in the end gain favour rather than one who has a flattering tongue."* Tony Campolo comments on this from his work with American families: *"Children are somewhat ambivalent about power. On the one hand, they are tempted to secure it... On the other hand, children feel insecure when they are able to dominate their parents. They lose confidence in their parents and become afraid of being in charge... When control was taken away from them, they were relieved."*[10]

So don't murder your children with acts of foolish kindness, like David. They are more foolish than you think and you have less time than you think to teach them wisdom. If you discipline them, both with words and with force, you will teach

[7] John Knox said this when confronting Mary with her sin at Holyrood Palace, Edinburgh, on 24th June 1563. Mary wept at his rebuke, but he told her he had learned enough wisdom as a parent not to relent.

[8] Solomon will state even more clearly in 26:3 and 29:19 that words are not enough to discipline a foolish child. He will add in Ecclesiastes 8:11 that discipline also has to be carried out swiftly.

[9] Solomon also stresses this in verses such as 15:20, 17:6, 17:25, 19:13, 19:26, 27:11, 28:7 and 29:17. His friends agree in 23:24–25 and 30:17.

[10] Tony Campolo in *Choose Love Not Power* (2009).

them wisdom and make them proud to be your children. They will bring you joy because you taught them how to be wise men and women.

Kindness to Fools (19:25, 29)

Flog a mocker, and the simple will learn prudence.
(Proverbs 19:25)

If you don't have children, you might have assumed that Solomon's teaching on daring to discipline wasn't intended for you. Think again. He broadens his teaching at the end of chapter 19 because weak parenting is simply one specific symptom of a larger, more general folly. Whether we have children or not, Solomon wants us to grasp that pain in general is one of the great ways in which God showers kindness on fools.

There was no pain in the world before Adam and Eve ate from the Tree of the Knowledge of Good and Evil. God was merciful and drove them out of Paradise because if they had stayed there they might never have woken up to their sin. As he drove them away from the garden and its Tree of Life, the Lord promised Adam *"painful toil"* and Eve *"painful labour"*.[1] These would be his wake-up call to warn them not to fall again for the four foolish lies which had caused them to eat the forbidden fruit.

Adam and Eve had fooled themselves that *they could act like little gods*. That view has been at the root of all sin and folly ever since. One of the reasons we hesitate to discipline our children is that we are so used to acting like little gods ourselves that we indulge sin when we see it mirrored back to us in them. When Solomon tells us in 20:30 that *"Blows*

---

[1] Genesis 3:16–19.

and wounds scrub away evil, and beatings purge the inmost being," he uses a word which is only used in one other place in the Bible: three times for Esther's intense cleansing process which prepared her to stand before King Xerxes.[2] Although it is painful to discover through God's discipline that the world revolves around him and not us, it cleanses our hearts of the self-worship which we have inherited from Adam and Eve. 19:25 tells us that those who are wise enough to grasp this from Scripture and verbal rebuke alone spare themselves a lot of pain, but that otherwise God loves us enough to alert us to this truth through painful discipline.[3]

Adam and Eve fooled themselves that *they could define what is right and wrong*. They fell for the snake's suggestion that the Lord might have got his definitions wrong, and they ate the fruit so that they could experience good and evil for themselves. Ever since then, their descendants have tried to drown out the twin voices of conscience and Scripture. The US magicians Penn and Teller summed up the sentiment of our own generation when they told viewers, *"Whatever you do, don't read the Bible for a moral code... Read it because we need more atheists, and nothing will get you there faster than reading the Bible."*[4] God is kind enough when we break his commandments to let us feel the pain of breaking ourselves on his commandments. Like the burning smell I noticed this morning while trying to fix my power shower, God lets us taste his discipline as a warning that our attempts to rewire our consciences have gone wrong.

Adam and Eve fooled themselves that *they could sin and still escape God's judgment*. They believed the snake's lie that the

---

[2] The Hebrew word is *tamṙiq* and it only occurs in Proverbs 20:30 and Esther 2:3, 9 and 12.

[3] Once more we see Solomon's wisdom in ordering his Top 375 at the end of chapter 20. If we refuse the gentle challenge of 20:27, we receive the heavy discipline of 20:30.

[4] Penn Jillette said this as part of their show on 6th May 2004 in a feature entitled "The Bible: Fact or Fiction?"

Lord had not really said he would punish them, and they rushed headlong out of Paradise and down the Devil's highway to hell. That's why Solomon emphasizes here in 19:29 that *"Penalties are prepared for mockers, and beatings for the backs of fools."* Every time we threaten to punish our children but fail to follow through, we murder them with kindness by teaching them that God may be like us and the snake's lie may be true.[5] Every time the police leave crime unpunished they encourage people to think that God is like the weak and indulgent law courts of their land.[6] On the other hand, Solomon promises us in 19:25 that every time a child is punished, his brothers and sisters learn wisdom by watching it, and that every time a criminal is punished, a nation learns to fear God too.[7]

Adam and Eve fooled themselves that *the here and now is all that matters*. They were so consumed by desire for the quick pleasures of the moment that they exchanged a future in Paradise for a tasty mouthful now. It's no coincidence that the nations where life is most comfortable are also the nations where faith in heaven and hell is rarest. Go to nations where God has expressed his kindness through letting people feel the great pain caused by human sin, and you will find people who think and talk a lot about the age to come. Pain is for them like the hot sun which drives a person to the shadow of a big rock, or like the storm which drives a ship into safe harbour. Paul responded to God's discipline by telling his converts that *"Our light and momentary troubles are achieving for us an eternal glory that far outweighs them all. So we fix our eyes not on what*

---

[5] Jesus is pictured wielding a *rod* in Psalm 2:9. If parents do not use *"the rod"*, they convince their children that Jesus will not dare to do so either.

[6] Solomon will go on to state this even more explicitly in Ecclesiastes 8:11. Although our culture instinctively resists Solomon's teaching on discipline, our crime statistics suggest that Solomon is right, not us.

[7] We have already seen that Solomon uses at least five words for five different kinds of fool. It is therefore significant that he uses different words in 19:25 to tell us that punishing a *mocker* will teach the *simple* wisdom. See also 21:11, 15.

is seen, but on what is unseen, since what is seen is temporary, but what is unseen is eternal."[8]

So it doesn't matter if you are not a parent. The principle of daring to discipline is a general principle for us all. Whether you are a teacher, a church leader, a policeman, a football coach or simply a good friend, don't be afraid to rebuke and discipline those the Lord has given you to care for. Be like the Lord who *"disciplines those he loves, as a father the son he delights in"* (3:11–12). Be like Solomon who tells us that *"Better is open rebuke than hidden love. Wounds from a friend can be trusted, but an enemy multiplies kisses"* (27:5–6).

And when you find yourself on the receiving end of discipline, don't be like a fool and resent the kindness of God (12:1). Learn from Hebrews 12:5–11, which quotes from Proverbs 3:11–12 and puts them in a New Testament context:

> *"Do not make light of the Lord's discipline, and do not lose heart when he rebukes you, because the Lord disciplines the one he loves, and he chastens everyone he accepts as his son." Endure hardship as discipline; God is treating you as his children... We have all had human fathers who disciplined us and we respected them for it. How much more should we submit to the Father of spirits and live! They disciplined us for a little while as they thought best; but God disciplines us for our good, in order that we may share in his holiness.*

---

[8] 2 Corinthians 4:17–18.

Get Out of God's Way (20:22)

Do not say, "I'll pay you back for this wrong!" Wait for the Lord, and he will avenge you.

(Proverbs 20:22)

Only four years apart but two very different matches. Consider two historic moments in the career of David Beckham.

The first was during the match between England and Argentina in the 1998 World Cup. The match had turned nasty and the Argentinians were goading the young David Beckham by jostling and fouling him whenever he got the ball. One foul from Diego Simeone proved too much for Beckham's patience and he reacted by kicking the Argentinian in revenge. If you follow World Cup football, you will know what happened next. David Beckham was sent off and the ten-man England went on to lose the match and crash out of the competition. Beckham learned the hard way not to take matters into his own hands and seek revenge.[1]

Now fast-forward four years to the 2002 World Cup, where England and Argentina played each other once again. The match was as nasty as the one before, and Diego Simeone and his team mates committed a similar cynical foul on an England player. This time, however, David Beckham had learned that it is always self-destructive to take revenge. He left room for the referee

[1] Although Beckham is a magnificent sportsman, this incident also proved Proverbs 16:32 – *"Better a patient man than a warrior, a man who controls his temper than one who takes a city."* (See also 12:16; 14:17, 29; 17:14; 19:11; 20:3; 25:28.)

to decide how Argentina should be punished, and the referee awarded a penalty to England. Unlike four years earlier when his folly sent England home early from the competition, David Beckham scored the penalty and this time sent the Argentinians home instead.

Hold that thought and now read Proverbs 20:22. What it says is so important that Solomon's friends say something similar in 24:29 and the apostle Paul makes reference to it when he teaches something similar in Romans 12.[2] Solomon tells us that we can make our lives miserable through taking revenge, like David Beckham did in 1998. He also promises that if we get out of God's way, he will avenge us and vindicate us as much as David Beckham was vindicated in 2002. *"Do not say, 'I'll pay you back for this wrong!' Wait for the Lord, and he will avenge you."*[3]

Solomon is not saying that we should let evil go unpunished. He is clear that life can be far nastier than a match between England and Argentina. He uses the Hebrew word *ra'* to describe the fouls of life as *evil* or as *wickedness* because he isn't trying to minimize the seriousness of sin. He is simply telling us that taking matters into our own hands and seeking revenge is a self-destructive way to try to tackle evil. Instead of lashing out like David Beckham and deflecting God's wrath away from those who wrong us, we should get out of God's way and let him be the referee. It's precisely because there is so much evil in the world that we mustn't get in the way of God the Judge.

Solomon is telling us that letting God be God is part and parcel of our salvation. The Hebrew word in this verse which some English translators render as *to avenge* is *yāsha'*, the normal Hebrew word for *to save*. He wants us to understand

---

[2] Paul actually quotes from Proverbs 25:21–22, but his comments in Romans 12:19 are very similar to 20:22.

[3] Revenge says *"I will do to you what you have done to me"*, but Jesus teaches us in Matthew 7:12 and Luke 6:31 to say *"I will do to you what I wish you had done to me."*

that God saving and God avenging are two sides of the same coin when it comes to the Gospel. His father David had already made it clear in Psalm 19:14 that the Lord is our *Kinsman-Redeemer*, who fulfils what was prophesied through Boaz the *kinsman-redeemer* in Ruth 3:9. Proverbs 23:11 follows this up by telling us that the Lord is our *Kinsman-Avenger* who fulfils what was prophesied through the *kinsman-avenger* described in Numbers 35:19–21.[4] The sin which other people commit against us is just as serious as the sin which we ourselves commit, but it is dealt with through the same Gospel message. The one who promises to be our Redeemer when we sin also promises to be our Avenger when other people sin against us.

Don't be shocked by this. It is exactly what Paul teaches in Romans 12:17–21. He makes reference to this proverb and then quotes God's words in Deuteronomy 32:35 – *"Do not take revenge, my dear friends, but leave room for God's wrath, for it is written: 'It is mine to avenge; I will repay, says the Lord.'"* Refusing to retaliate and take revenge is not pretending evil doesn't matter. It is simply recognizing that we are sinners ourselves and that we have no right to play judge over others. It is obeying Jesus' command in Matthew 5:39 to turn the other cheek, and learning David Beckham's lesson against Argentina. Our petty acts of revenge actually get in the way of the far greater judgment which we can entrust to God the great Judge and Avenger.[5]

Miroslav Volf is a Yale professor of theology who experienced the bitter civil war in Yugoslavia firsthand in the early 1990s. He watched Serbs commit acts of genocide, watched his fellow Croatians swear to get even, and watched a whole nation destroy itself through bitterness and revenge.

---

[4] The same Hebrew word *gō'ēl* is used to mean *kinsman-redeemer* and *kinsman-avenger* in these four verses. It is also used in Joshua 20:5 and Deuteronomy 19:6.

[5] 24:17–18 tells us not even to gloat when our enemy falls because our petty act of gloating will get in the way of God's wrath and deflect his judgment away from them.

He celebrates Solomon's wisdom in this proverb as the only true path to peace between feuding individuals or warring factions: *"If God were not angry at injustice and deception and did not make the final end to violence God would not be worthy of our worship... Violence thrives, secretly nourished by belief in a God who refuses to wield the sword... The practice of non-violence requires a belief in divine vengeance."*[6] He told his fellow Croatians that they would only find peace in their nation if they got out of God's way and let him be their Avenger.

This should reassure you if you are currently being wronged by others, because it promises that God will bring justice down on those who persecute you if you get out of his way. It should also alarm you if you are doing wrong to others, because God will take your victims' side and become God the Avenger against you if you continue to oppress them (22:22–23; 23:11). It should fill us all with hope, since 25:21–22 tells us that our refusal to take vengeance into our own hands is likely to make those who hurt us repent when they see us forgiving them as God has forgiven us.[7] Even if they don't repent, it should fill us with reassurance that if we get out of God's way, he will take far better vengeance on them.

Take it from Solomon and take it from David Beckham: revenge is a self-destructive act of folly, but getting out of God's way is the wisest vengeance of them all.

---

6 Miroslav Volf in *Exclusion and Embrace* (1996).

7 Proverbs 25:21–22 is one of only eight direct quotations from Proverbs in the New Testament. *Heaping burning coals on his head* seems to link with Psalm 140:10 and suggests that the best revenge on people is to convert them!

The Last Word (21:30–31)

The horse is made ready for the day of battle, but victory rests with the Lord.

(Proverbs 21:31)

If you have ever played the children's game "Snakes and Ladders", you will understand what Solomon wants to tell us as he reaches the end of his Top 375. If you have ever rolled a one and landed on a large snake when you were on the brink of victory, or if you have ever rolled a six and landed at the bottom of a long ladder which brought you from behind to win the game, you will understand what Solomon means. He wants to teach you to view life a bit like "Snakes and Ladders". We make our plans and roll the dice, but God always gets to have the last word.

Naïve fools deny this. They are convinced they can control the outcome of their own lives. They are like the gullible rookies in a casino who haven't yet grasped that the dice are loaded against them and that the house always wins in the end. They plot and plan and scheme, but Solomon warns them in 21:30 that *"There is no wisdom, no insight, no plan that can succeed against the Lord."* However much they convince themselves the odds are stacked in their favour, the Lord warns them that they are only one roll of the dice away from disaster.

Sluggards also deny this, but they do so because they are convinced that nobody controls the outcome of their lives. They live in fear that they will land on a snake and so they minimize risk to the point of attempting nothing. Solomon creates a comic stereotype of their excuse-making in 22:13, telling us that *"The sluggard says, 'There's a lion outside! I'll be killed in the public square!'"* They need to see the ladders of life as well as the snakes, and to view it as very good news that the Lord is in control of every roll of the dice. Solomon sees it as a cause for celebration when he tells us in 16:33 that *"The lot is cast into the lap, but its every decision is from the Lord."*

Mockers deny this because they have convinced themselves that they can play the game of life by their own rules. They convince themselves that all ahead is ladders and that even if there are snakes, they are too intelligent to land on one. The author H.G. Wells epitomized the mocking confidence of early twentieth-century Europe and America when he ended his *Short History of the World* with an arrogant boast:

> *Man is still only adolescent... We are hardly in the earliest dawn of human greatness... Can we doubt that presently our race will more than realise our boldest imaginations, that it will achieve unity and peace... going on from strength to strength in an ever widening circle of adventure and achievement? What man has done, the little triumphs of his present state, and all this history we have told, form but the prelude to the things that man has yet to do.*[1]

It took twenty-five years, the Great Depression, a World War and a Holocaust to convince him that God is in control of life's snakes as well as life's ladders. He was a broken man when he wrote just before he died that *"The cold-blooded massacres of the defenceless, the return of deliberate and organised torture, mental torment, and fear to a world from which such things had seemed well-nigh banished – has come near to breaking my spirit*

[1] H.G. Wells published *A Short History of the World* in 1922. It begins with the world starting by chance 2,000 million years ago and it ends with humankind as the masters of chance and of the universe.

altogether… 'Homo Sapiens', as he has been pleased to call himself, is played out."[2]

Wicked fools deny that God is in control because they think they can thwart his agenda through their lies. They laugh at the idea that God controls the dice rolls because they have no intention of moving the number of spaces he tells them to anyway. They see God as a neutral spectator who is either too bored or too busy to pay them any attention, so they plot and plan to do whatever they choose. They forget that no verse in Proverbs is more quoted in the New Testament than the one which tells us that *"God opposes the proud but gives grace to the humble."*[3] They also forget that Solomon uses active verbs to tell us that the Lord *"thwarts the craving of the wicked"* (10:3) and *"tears down the house of the proud"* (15:25). God holds the dice and he employs the might of heaven to ensure that wicked fools land on snakes again and again. They make their schemes but the Lord has the last word.

At the other end of the scale, the wise draw great comfort from the fact that God is in control of their lives. They work hard in the knowledge that diligence brings wealth and promotion (10:4 and 22:29), but they know that gaining those things depends on what God does with their trust in him and not on how hard they work and scheme (10:22). They get organized because prior planning prevents poor performance (19:2 and 21:5), but they hold their plans lightly because they believe Solomon when he warns that *"To man belong the plans of the heart, but from the Lord comes the reply of the tongue"* (16:1). The most gifted candidate doesn't always get the job. The strongest army doesn't always win the battle. Time and chance

---

[2] He wrote this in *Mind at the End of its Tether* (1945). He died the following year.

[3] James 4:6 and 1 Peter 5:5 both quote 3:34 from the Greek Septuagint which amplifies the Hebrew reading.

are massive factors and they are in the hand of the Lord.[4] If you are wise, you will find it tremendously encouraging that Solomon promises us in 21:31 that *"The horse is made ready for the day of battle, but victory rests with the Lord."*

So let's not talk about luck or chance or coincidences. Let's not fear the snakes or fool ourselves that we can force our way up ladders.[5] Instead, let's throw off the arrogant pride which is the distinguishing mark of wicked fools (21:4), and let's remember that *"In their hearts humans plan their course, but the Lord establishes their steps"* (16:9). Let's be glad that life is like a game of "Snakes and Ladders" and that the Lord decides the outcome of every single dice roll in the game.

As Solomon draws his Top 375 to an end with a reminder that the last word always belongs to God, he wants us to remember that we have something better to roll than dice anyway. He used the Hebrew word *gālal* or *to roll* in 16:3 to urge us literally to *"Roll whatever you do onto the Lord and he will establish your plans."*[6] It would be wonderful enough simply to know that the Lord is sovereign over each dice roll in our lives, but it is even better that he promises that if we roll our actions onto him, he will make the dice land on the right numbers for us.

We have reached the end of Solomon's Top 375, so it is fitting that he tells us here that the last word always belongs to the Lord.

---

[4] Solomon points this out to us very clearly in Ecclesiastes 9:11. See also Proverbs 19:21.

[5] Wise people fear God too much to strive to push themselves forward for promotion, since any platform we scale in our own strength is simply a greater height from which we will fall. We can rely on the Lord to let our gifting open doors for us in the proper way and at the proper time (18:16).

[6] This is the same Hebrew word which is used in Psalm 22:8 to describe the Messiah *rolling his trust* onto his Father, and in David's exhortation in Psalm 37:5 for us to *roll our trust* onto the Lord.

Solomon's Friends (22:17–24:22)

Pay attention and turn your ear to the sayings of the wise.

(Proverbs 22:17)

Solomon has finished his Top 375, but he was not the only writer of wisdom literature. Job wrote the first book of biblical wisdom literature nine hundred years before him, and the ancient Akkadians and Egyptians followed suit with their own pagan writings. The most famous of them today is perhaps *The Instruction of Amenemope,* which was written by an Egyptian almost 300 years before Solomon and which is similar in places to Proverbs 22:17–24:22.[1] We have reached the end of Solomon's first batch of proverbs and have now reached the thirty sayings of his wise friends, which he added as an appendage to his own Top 375.[2]

Solomon doesn't tell us exactly who these wise friends were. 1 Kings 4:31 suggests they may have been the psalmists Ethan and Heman, perhaps helped by Heman's two wise relatives Kalkol and Darda. Whoever they were, it is clear they

---

[1] The structure of the 30-chaptered *Instruction of Amenemope* helps us to know that the ambiguous Hebrew text of 22:20 should read *"thirty sayings"*. However, in my opinion many scholars have massively overplayed the parallels between the two.

[2] We can tell that Solomon included these extra sayings rather than later editors because, unlike 30:1 and 31:1, he introduces the 30 sayings personally. The NIV headings break 22:17–24:22 down into its constituent 30 sayings, although I personally see 22:17–21 as an introduction and 24:10 and 24:11–12 as separate sayings.

were Hebrew worshippers of Yahweh and that Solomon was inspired by the Holy Spirit to include their proverbs as a God-inspired supplement to his own.[3]

Perhaps God inspired Solomon to include their thirty sayings in order to convince us that the Top 375 is not simply the perspective of one wise man. Solomon's friends have a very different style from him – his Top 375 are all two-liners while their Top 30 are each anywhere up to a dozen lines long – and yet the wisdom which they teach us is very similar in content to his because both are the inspired Word of God. The wise friends repeat Solomon's call for us to search for wisdom (24:3–4 and 24:13–14),[4] to listen to our parents (23:22–25) and to choose a wise group of friends to act as counsellors (22:24–27; 24:5–6). They repeat Solomon's warnings against adultery (23:26–28), against the lure of money (23:1–7), against the short-term gain of sin (23:17–18; 24:1–2, 19–20) and against getting in God's way by taking revenge on those who hurt us (24:17–18).[5] They repeat Solomon's call to work hard (22:29), to submit to rulers (24:21–22),[6] to discipline our children (23:13–16)[7] and to care for the poor (22:22–23; 24:11–12).[8] As such, they remind us

---

[3] 2 Timothy 3:16–17.

[4] Proverbs 24:13 is a good example of why we need to understand the context of each proverb to determine its meaning. Placed next to 24:14, it emphasizes that wisdom is sweet, but on its own it would simply tell us to put honey on our toast instead of jam!

[5] For other Old Testament warnings not to gloat over our enemies, see Job 31:29 and Obadiah 11–16.

[6] Although it is not a direct quotation, it appears that this verse was the Old Testament inspiration for the charge in 1 Peter 2:17 to *"Fear God and honour the king."*

[7] Note the deliberate way that 23:12 and 23:13–14 go together. If we apply our own hearts to *mūsār* or *correction* in verse 12, we will not withhold *mūsār* from our children in verse 13. Solomon's friends say that the main reason we fail to discipline our children is that we have first failed to discipline ourselves.

[8] Paul quotes from 24:12 in Romans 2:6 and uses it as a key text which teaches that God will judge each person according to their works.

that we must treat the words of Solomon as we would any other Scripture.[9]

But these thirty sayings also do something more than reinforce the words of Solomon. They also highlight three important themes which Solomon didn't include in his Top 375 but which supplement his teaching. These three new themes are also part of the flight school of wisdom and they will keep us flying straight as we learn to live God's way.

First, these thirty sayings warn us *not to act as if the world belongs to us*. Solomon's friends think moving ancient boundary stones is so serious that they devote not just one but two of their thirty sayings to the matter. Boundary stones were the ancient equivalent of hedges which marked the division between fields, and Job 24:2 tells us that the rich and powerful tended to steal land from their weaker neighbours by moving the markers when they weren't looking. If we move garden fences to steal part of our neighbour's garden or if we twist facts to take advantage of weaker colleagues, God says it is a very serious matter.[10] In saying this, 22:28 also reminds us that we should respect decisions made by previous generations and not overturn their traditions without thinking. 23:10–11 also reminds us that God is the Kinsman-Avenger of the poor, and that if we take advantage of them, we will recruit him as our enemy.

Second, these thirty sayings warn us *not to drink too much alcohol*. Solomon touched on this briefly in 20:1 but his friends devote two of their thirty sayings to a much more detailed warning about the dangers.[11] They point out in 23:19–21 that drunkenness leads to poverty, and they devote their longest saying in 23:29–35 to the underlying dangers of drinking. The Devil hates humans made in the image of God and so he loves

[9] This is the main point of 22:19.

[10] See also Deuteronomy 19:14; 27:17; Hosea 5:10. Solomon also hinted at this in Proverbs 15:25.

[11] Interestingly, the other section of Proverbs which was not written by Solomon also warns against the dangers of alcohol in 31:4–7.

to use alcohol to deface God's image in us by making us behave like brute animals. Wine may look and taste as lovely as the forbidden fruit which Eve ate in the garden, but *"in the end it bites like a snake and poisons like a viper"*. Solomon's friends aren't telling us to abstain from alcohol completely – that would be impossible to square with verses such as Psalm 104:14–15 and 1 Timothy 5:23 – but they are warning us to drink it very carefully. Since too much alcohol will cause us *woe* and *sorrow* and *strife* and *needless bruises* and *bloodshot eyes,* we must not be like the fool in 23:35 who never learns but always rushes back to buy another drink. Wisdom means thinking before we act, and alcohol can prevent us from doing so. Paul repeats this warning in New Testament language in Ephesians 5:18 when he tells us, *"Do not get drunk on wine, which leads to debauchery. Instead, be filled with the Spirit."*

Third, these thirty sayings warn us *to get ready for times of trial*. Solomon was right to tell us that the righteous are often spared from the trouble which comes upon the wicked, but his friends are also right to add in 24:16 that we need to brace ourselves for the trials which are sure to come. They tell us in 24:10 that the true strength of our character is seen in times of trial rather than in times of ease, and that we can comfort ourselves when trouble comes because it will reveal the work which God has done inside us.

Solomon's friends want to convince you that Proverbs is far more than a list of one wise man's observations. They add their own voices to his so that you can be equipped by all the teachers in the flight school of wisdom in how to live God's way.

First Things First (24:23–34)

Put your outdoor work in order and get your fields ready; after that, build your house.

(Proverbs 24:27)

There is a famous story about a man who was asked to give a lecture to a group of high-flying business achievers. He started with a quiz, taking a gallon jar and starting to fill it with rocks the size of tennis balls. When no more rocks would fit into the jar, he asked the group of high achievers, *"Is the jar full?"* When they said yes, he reached under the table and pulled out a bag of gravel which he poured into the jar until it filled the gaps between the rocks. *"Is the jar full now?"* he asked before reaching for a second time under the table and bringing out a bag of sand. When he had poured the sand into the jar so that it filled all of the little spaces between the rocks and the gravel, he asked the audience a third time, *"Is the jar full now?"* He reached yet again under the table and brought out a jug of water which he poured into the jar to fill the tiny gaps between the grains of sand.

"Now, what is the important lesson I have taught you today?" he asked. One of the keenest young executives raised his hand: *"I know. You've shown us that it doesn't matter how busy our lives are, we can always squeeze more into them."* The lecturer looked at the ambitious businessman and gravely shook his head. *"No, that's not the point at all. I have taught you that if you don't get the big rocks into your life first then you will never get them in at all."*

Solomon wants to teach us a similar lesson in the final verses of chapter 24. Having given us the thirty sayings of the wise in 22:17–24:22, he now adds five more of his favourite proverbs from the various writings of his friends. The first, second and fourth proverbs are all to do with honesty, and they underline Solomon's warning for us not to take revenge because God is just and will never acquit the guilty.[1] The third and fifth proverbs are the equivalent of the lesson of the gallon jar. Solomon wants us to look at our lives and make sure that we are putting the big rocks in first.

Solomon's friends lived in an agricultural society, which makes the importance of priority setting very obvious. Who can't see the wisdom in their command in verse 27 to *"Put your outdoor work in order and get your fields ready; after that, build your house"*? Who can't see the folly of a person working on the internal decoration of their house while their fields lie unploughed and unsown outside at the height of planting season? Who can't see the folly of the sluggard in verses 30–34, who does the hard work of planting a vineyard and building a wall around it but then sleeps all summer while the thorns and weeds choke the life out of his vines? It is so obvious, and yet Solomon included these two proverbs because it is often so obvious that we miss it. It's even harder for us to prioritize wisely in an urban society than it was in Solomon's day.

If you are a Christian, you know that time with God needs to be the first rock in your gallon jar. Our first priority should be reading the Bible, praying and worshipping, but I've yet to meet a Christian who doesn't struggle to keep these first things first. While Jesus spent hours alone in Scripture meditation and in prayer, and asked his parents incredulously, *"Didn't you know I had to be in my Father's house?"*,[2] we tend to be much more like Homer Simpson. When Marge tells him to get ready

---

[1] If anything, Solomon's friends are even more straightforward about this in 24:23–25 than he was in 17:15. The New Testament backs up their statement in Colossians 3:25, telling us that *"Anyone who does wrong will be repaid for his wrong, and there is no favouritism."*

[2] Matthew 14:23; Mark 1:35; 14:32–39; Luke 2:49; 5:16; 6:12.

for church because *"The Lord only asks for an hour a week,"* even her scaled-down demands prove too much for her husband. *"In that case he should have made the week an hour longer,"* Homer complains.[3] Don't be a Christian sluggard and let the thorns and weeds choke the life out of your walk with God.[4]

The second rock in your gallon jar needs to be your family. The great American preacher D.L. Moody understood the lesson of these two proverbs and told his hearers, *"I believe the family was established long before the church, and my duty is to my family first; I am not to neglect my family."* Let's not be like Solomon's father David who neglected his children and sowed the seeds for Solomon's own personal failures later. Let's not be like Randolph Churchill, who barely spoke to his young son Winston because he was too busy working for the British government, little knowing that time spent with his son would have served the future British government far more. If you aren't married or don't have children, prioritize your parents, siblings and friends, as well as making time to meet the man or woman God has prepared for you. Solomon told us in 19:14 that God wants to bring along the perfect partner for you, but if you are too busy with other priorities, you may miss that partner when they come.

The third rock in your gallon jar needs to be the Church. Most English translators assume that the Hebrew text of 9:10 should read that *"knowledge of the Holy One is understanding"*, but a more literal reading is that *"knowledge of the **holy ones** is understanding"*. Solomon placed this statement as a synonymous parallelism with *"the fear of the Lord is the beginning of wisdom"* because, put simply, wise people don't just love God, they also love his People. They don't just treat their wisdom as a personal plaything, but as something to share with others in the Church as they play their role in advancing the Church's mission. Jesus

[3] *The Simpsons*, Season 4, Episode 3 – "Homer the Heretic" (1992).

[4] Jesus may have been thinking back to 24:30–34 when he told the parable in Matthew 13:22.

told Peter in John 21:15–17 that to love him is to love his Church. He says the same to you and me.

The fourth rock in your gallon jar needs to be your work. For some this is paid work and for others it is unpaid, but whether you are a full-time parent, a retired volunteer or a busy factory worker, the importance of your work remains the same. Remember the words of Solomon in 18:9: *"One who is slack in his work is brother to one who destroys."*

Then and only then is it time to put the pieces of gravel into the jar. Hobbies, leisure, sport and relaxation are all good so long as we have put first things first and have not fallen into the foolish trap which Solomon's friends warn against here.[5]

Harry Emerson Fosdick, spiritual adviser to the billionaire philanthropist J.D. Rockefeller, listened to the advice of Solomon's friends, and he urges us to do the same: *"No steam or gas drives anything until it is confined. No Niagara is ever turned into light and power until it is tunnelled. No life ever grows great until it is focused, dedicated, disciplined."*[6]

[5] All of these things are good but the fool spends so much time and money on them (21:17, 20) that he has nothing left for the things which really matter (23:21).

[6] Fosdick wrote this in his book *Living Under Tension* (1941).

Solomon's Missing Tools (25:1–29:27)

These are more proverbs of Solomon, compiled by the men of Hezekiah king of Judah.

(Proverbs 25:1)

On 18th November 2008, the NASA astronaut Heidemarie Stefanyshyn-Piper lost her toolkit. She was spacewalking outside the Space Shuttle Endeavour in order to make some essential repairs, when she lost hold of her backpack-sized tool bag and helplessly watched it float away. Astronomers back home were excited that they could see her missing toolkit with their telescopes as it floated out of view in the weeks which followed. NASA was rather less excited, however. $100,000 worth of vital tools had now been lost in space.

Solomon's toolkit of 375 proverbs had also been lost shortly after he wrote them, and it proved far more costly to Israel than any missing toolkit could be to NASA. Rehoboam had largely ignored the book his father dedicated to him, and he had lost most of his father's kingdom through his failure to listen to what it said. Subsequent kings of Judah had also ignored Solomon's toolkit and had brought decades of misery on their nation. One of them had even married the daughter of the wicked King Ahab and Queen Jezebel of the northern kingdom of Israel, and it nearly resulted in the destruction of David and Solomon's dynasty. Another king tried to play priest and was struck down with leprosy, while still another worshipped Edom's gods and brought God's judgment on the land. One of them even told the people of Judah to sacrifice their babies in the fire to the false god Molek. By the time that Hezekiah came to the throne in 715 BC, Solomon's toolkit had been as good as lost in space for over 200 years.

But Hezekiah was different. On his very first day as king he reopened the doors of Solomon's Temple, removed the idols from its courtyards and reconsecrated Judah to the Lord. He led the southern kingdom in repentance and revival which was so sincere that even the survivors of the exiled northern kingdom were converted back to worshipping Yahweh too.[1] 2 Chronicles 30:26 recounts that *"There was great joy in Jerusalem, for since the days of Solomon son of David king of Israel there had been nothing like this in Jerusalem."* As part of the revival, 2 Chronicles 29:30 informs us that they rediscovered *"the words of David and of Asaph the seer"*. Solomon's missing toolkit was finally found. Along with most of Psalms, Hezekiah's servants also rediscovered Proverbs 1–24.

Proverbs 25:1 tells us that the five chapters which follow *"are more proverbs of Solomon, compiled by the men of Hezekiah king of Judah"*. Hezekiah had rededicated Judah to the Lord and his servants were hungry for Solomon's writings and for their claim that "Life Works God's Way". They read Proverbs 1–9 and responded to its charge to "Learn God's Way" by devouring Proverbs 10–24 and learning how to "Live God's Way". They then pored over the other proverbs which Solomon had written but had not included in his Top 375, and they found many more which they felt should form part of God's flight school for a new generation. Under the inspiration of the same Holy Spirit who had given Solomon his wisdom, they compiled an additional Top 125 which would bring the total number of Solomon's proverbs which were preserved up to 500. They were determined that God's People would never lose Solomon's toolkit again. They were determined that this new and even bigger toolkit would

[1] A full account of this revival is found in 2 Kings 18:1–12 and 2 Chronicles 29–31.

contain all of the tools which a new generation of believers would need to live God's way.

This new Top 125 in Proverbs 25–29 is very similar to Solomon's original Top 375 in Proverbs 10–22. Some of the proverbs are even repeats because Hezekiah's servants saw them as such essential lessons in God's flight school.[2]

Nevertheless, there are some significant differences in this new collection of Solomon's proverbs. Some of them are obvious: for example, the fact that all of Solomon's Top 375 are two-liners while some of the Top 125 are four-liners. Some of them are structural since, unlike Solomon, the servants of Hezekiah decided to group their Top 125 much more by theme than is the case with the Top 375. Perhaps most important of all, there are several new themes which the servants of Hezekiah include from Solomon's back collection in reaction to two centuries of Israelite history while his toolkit was missing. Chapters 25–29 concentrate much more on the duty of a king to dispense wisdom and of his subjects to hold him accountable to God in doing so. They stress that the wise must be active as messengers of God to bring wisdom where there is folly for the sake of their nation. They address the problems of greed and of spiritual hypocrisy which had ruined the life of Israel and Judah because they had not been shaped by Solomon's missing tools.

Hezekiah practised what he preached and lived out the book of Proverbs. He presided over one of the Old Testament's greatest miracles when his prayers delivered Jerusalem from an Assyrian siege which was about to spell the end of God's chosen nation. 2 Kings 18:5 tells us that *"Hezekiah trusted in the Lord, the God of Israel. There was no one like him among all the kings of Judah, either before him or after him."* That's a glowing verse of praise from God for Hezekiah, but it's also a hint about what happened once he died.

---

[2] For example, 25:24 repeats 21:9, 26:22 repeats 18:8, 27:12 repeats 22:3, 27:13 repeats 20:16, 28:6 repeats 19:1, and 28:19 repeats 12:11.

Sadly, the revival of Judah proved to be short-lived. Hezekiah's successors were even more evil than the kings who had gone before him. They included kings like Manasseh who slaughtered the prophets of the Lord, like Amon who led Israel into idolatry, and like Jehoiakim who cut up and burnt the Word of God.[3] Perhaps the wise men of Hezekiah predicted this would happen, because the last verses of their Top 125 point to a better Messianic King who would come and save Israel from their sins. While Jesus hides in the shadows in Solomon's Top 375, he steps out of the shadows at the end of this Top 125. One king finally listened to the message of Proverbs, brought revival to his nation, and presented Solomon's missing toolkit to God's People along with 125 more missing tools. A better King would come 700 years later and fulfil the message of Proverbs to the letter.

We are followers of King Jesus, the one who is greater than Solomon and Hezekiah.[4] So let's not fail God's flight school like the generations of Israelites between Solomon and Hezekiah, or like the generations between Hezekiah and the exile. Let's read these chapters and devote ourselves to following the true Wise One, the true Righteous One, the true hope of Israel. Let's not allow Solomon's toolkit to get lost in space, for the glory of Jesus our great King.

[3] 2 Kings 21:16; 24:3–4; 2 Chronicles 33:21–23; Jeremiah 36:1–32.

[4] Matthew 12:42; Luke 11:31. Jeremiah 21:1–23:8 makes it clear that Jesus would succeed as king where all of Hezekiah's successors failed.

When Good Men Do Nothing (25:2–28)

Like a muddied spring or a polluted well are the righteous who give way to the wicked.

(Proverbs 25:26)

The British statesman Edmund Burke was not afraid to talk tough to both royalists and democrats. He attacked one of King George III's favourites, telling him that *"There is but one law for all, namely, that law which governs all law, the law of our Creator, the law of humanity, justice and equity."*[1] He also attacked the self-serving voters who elected him as MP, telling them that *"Your representative owes you, not his industry only, but his judgment; and he betrays instead of serving you if he sacrifices it to your opinion."*[2] The servants of Hezekiah had the same courage as Edmund Burke as they drew together the proverbs which constitute chapter 25. After 200 years of wickedness and backsliding in government, they were determined to teach the future kings and courtiers of Judah that they were rulers under God.

The Hebrew word for *king* is only used twelve times in the whole of Solomon's Top 375. It is used five times in the first six verses of chapter 25 alone. Hezekiah's servants had seen enough of Israel's history to assemble a chapter of Solomon's proverbs which warned kings not to forget that they were merely

[1] Burke said this during the impeachment trial of Warren Hastings, the former Governor-General of India, on 28th May 1794.

[2] Burke said this in a speech to the voters in his Bristol constituency on 3rd November 1774.

viceroys who ruled for God. Solomon tells rulers in verse 2 that their dual role is to seek out what is happening in the realm and how God wants them to respond.[3] He adds in verses 4–5 that their role is also to distinguish between the righteous and the wicked, expelling the wicked from their council chamber and surrounding themselves with those who will help them to govern righteously. If you carry any role of leadership – whether in government, in business or in the Church – then these verses were written for you as a reminder that you lead as one appointed by the Lord. Solomon wants you to study Scripture, to devote yourself to prayer, and to surround yourself with godly friends who will help you prosper as a leader. He wants those you lead to be able to respond as the Queen of Sheba did to him:

> *How happy your people must be! How happy your officials, who continually stand before you and hear your wisdom! Praise be to the Lord your God, who has delighted in you and placed you on the throne of Israel. Because of the Lord's eternal love for Israel, he has made you king to maintain justice and righteousness.*[4]

Hezekiah's men now turn to proverbs which focus on the role of courtiers and subjects, because the past two centuries of disaster had not simply been the fault of Judah's kings. The Hebrew word *rīb*, which means *quarrelling* or *taking somebody to court* is used six times in the whole of Solomon's Top 375 but three times here in verses 8 and 9 alone. Solomon tells us in verses 6–10 that fighting one another to gain promotion from a ruler or compensation from a judge is not the way to serve the Lord. If we act wisely and pursue righteousness, the Lord will promote us without our having to flatter and fight our way to

[3] Although God is glorified by knowing secrets which people strive in vain to understand, he also glorifies himself by revealing those things to anyone who cries out to him for knowledge (Jeremiah 33:3; John 16:14).

[4] 1 Kings 10:8–9. In his early days, Solomon embodied the message he preaches in Proverbs.

power.[5] God isn't looking to lobby his way into government. He is simply looking for humble servants he can use.

Solomon therefore tells us to submit in humility to those God has placed in authority over us. He doesn't want us to be like hairdressers and taxi drivers the world over who talk as if they know all the answers to the problems facing governments and football teams. It is far easier to comment on the decisions of others than to be decision makers ourselves. *"The hearts of kings are unsearchable"* to those who haven't walked in their shoes, Solomon warns in verse 3, so let's not fall for the fine-sounding wisdom of the critic, which is usually the voice of naïvety and folly. Edmund Burke warned that *"It is a general popular error to suppose the loudest complainers for the public to be the most anxious for its welfare."*[6] Solomon echoes the words of his friends in 24:21–22 by telling us to be friends to rulers rather than their critics.

As friends, he encourages us to influence their rule. Hezekiah's servants did this themselves and they marshal Solomon's proverbs to teach us that we can do the same. In verse 5 we read that even a bad king will make righteous decisions if he has enough godly advisers, and in verse 15 Solomon encourages us that *"Through patience a ruler can be persuaded, and a gentle tongue can break a bone."* The heart of a king may be deep in verse 3, but we already know from 20:5 that all it takes are the right questions to draw out his deepest thoughts. We also know from 21:1 that the Lord controls the heart of kings in the same way that a drainpipe controls the flow of water, and that he can influence them through us.[7] If

[5] Proverbs 4:8. Verses 6–7 may have been part of the inspiration for Jesus' parable in Luke 14:7–11. He promises that *"All those who exalt themselves will be humbled, and those who humble themselves will be exalted."*

[6] Burke wrote this in his *Observations on a Late Publication on the Present State of the Nation* (1769).

[7] If *"the Lord moved the heart of Cyrus king of Persia"* in 2 Chronicles 36:22, he is able to move the heart of even the most powerful leader through people like you and me.

we speak words of wisdom in our workplace, our town council, our city and in our nation, God will use our words to save our nation. All it takes is the faith to persevere.

Edmund Burke tried to live out the teaching of Proverbs 25 when he told the conservatives to let the American rebels have their independence and when he told the radicals not to support the French Revolution prematurely. He summed up his politics by writing that *"When bad men combine, the good must associate; else they will fall, one by one, an unpitied sacrifice in a contemptible struggle."*[8] Hezekiah's servants had something similar in mind when they assembled this chapter of Solomon's proverbs for us. They bring the chapter to its crescendo in verse 26, where Solomon warns that *"Like a muddied spring or a polluted well are the righteous who give way to the wicked."*[9] Hezekiah's servants wanted to save Judah from the same fate which had just befallen the northern kingdom of Israel. They wanted to create an alliance of the godly to influence their nation for good.

That last quotation from Edmund Burke has often been misquoted as *"All that is necessary for the triumph of evil is that good men do nothing."* Whether it is misquoted or not, it is a fair summary of what we must do with the message of Proverbs 25. Whether you are a business leader, a politician, a church leader, or simply someone who can influence a leader for good, Solomon tells you not to keep your wisdom private as a personal plaything. Bring your wisdom into the public sphere. All that is necessary for the triumph of evil is that we do nothing.

---

[8] Burke wrote this in his *Thoughts on the Cause of the Present Discontents* (1770).

[9] This verse links back to 4:23. If we muddy ourselves in compromise, we will pollute the wellspring of our nation's public debate.

The Royal Mail (25:13–14)

Like a snow-cooled drink at harvest time is a trustworthy messenger to the one who sends him; he refreshes the spirit of his master.

(Proverbs 25:13)

The paperboy who delivers newspapers to my home has been fired. When I discovered what he had been doing, it wasn't hard to see why. He was paid to deliver freebie newspapers to every home in my street but after doing so for several months he decided on an easier way to make his money. He continued to pick up his few hundred newspapers every Friday from the depot, but he threw them in the river, went home to watch TV, then went back to the depot with his empty bags to collect his money. He assumed that nobody in my road would care enough about a freebie newspaper to phone the depot, but one of my neighbours did and his suspicious manager followed him down to the river. To use Solomon's language, my paperboy was a sluggard and a fool who disregarded the message his manager paid him to deliver. Now he isn't only a sluggard and a fool. He is also unemployed.

Chapter 25 tells us that God does not give us the Spirit of Wisdom so that we can enjoy him behind closed doors. The Holy Spirit gives us *"the mind of Christ"* for a reason, and that reason is so that we can act as God's paperboys to go and make him known.[1] That's why, sandwiched between these verses about rulers and subjects needing to speak up for wisdom, we find several verses which equip us to be God's messengers.

[1] 1 Corinthians 2:16; Acts 1:8; 5:32.

Hezekiah's wise men want to teach us how to share God's wisdom with others through some simple proverbs which they found in Solomon's back collection.

Before we look at those verses, just note the difference between this extra compilation and Solomon's original Top 375. Many readers complain that Proverbs 10:1–22:16 appears unsorted and disorderly, but they can make no such complaint here. Whereas the Top 375 contains no more than half a dozen comparative parallelisms which read *"Like X is Y"*, the Top 125 compiled by Hezekiah's men contains more than that number on every page. In this chapter alone there are twelve proverbs which read *"Like X is Y"* or *"As X is Y"*, and this remains a feature of the whole of chapters 25–29.[2] On top of this, since we are talking about kings and government, Hezekiah's wise men have selected proverbs which talk about royal treasures such as smelted silver in verse 4, gold and silver in verse 11, and golden earrings in verse 12. It's as if they want to remind us that we are delivering something far more precious than a freebie newspaper. We are delivering the royal mail. We are messengers for the King.

My old paperboy reminds me of Solomon's description of a foolish messenger in 10:26. He told us that *"As vinegar to the teeth and smoke to the eyes, so are sluggards to those who send them."* Solomon recalls that proverb again here when he tells us in 25:19 that relying on an unfaithful messenger is like chewing on a broken tooth or leaning on a lame foot. He will take this one step further in 26:6 by telling us that *"sending a message by the hands of a fool is like cutting off one's feet or drinking poison"*. The implication is that we mustn't be such lousy messengers for Wisdom. Instead we must be like the trustworthy envoy Solomon described in 13:17: *"A wicked messenger falls into trouble, but a trustworthy envoy brings healing."*[3]

---

2 There are about 20 more of them in chapters 26–28.

3 Since these verses teach us to be Gospel messengers, some readers link this reference to *healing* with Paul's statement in Romans 15:18–19 that we

Hezekiah's men, therefore, gather proverbs in this chapter which teach us how to be wise messengers for the Lord. Solomon uses the word *adōnai* in verse 13 so that it is deliberately ambiguous whether the messenger has been sent by several *lords* or by *the Lord*.[4] He tells us that if we speak up for wisdom as God intends, he will find our obedience as refreshing as a harvester finds an ice-cold drink under the scorching sun. Solomon gives us several pieces of instruction in this chapter which will help us to refresh the Lord by speaking up for him wisely every day.

Solomon tells us to be *honest and frank* with people as we share God's wisdom. If we are crafty in verses 9–10 and 23, we will provoke a horrified look, both from God and from the people with whom we share. Solomon compares in verse 14 those who doctor their message and promise things God hasn't promised to *"clouds and winds without rain"* – they raise the farmer's hopes only to dash them, unlike the faithful messenger in verse 25 who refreshes them *"like cold water to a weary soul"*. The New Testament picks up on this and tells us that false teachers *"are clouds without rain… for whom blackest darkness has been reserved forever"*.[5]

Solomon tells us that we need to be *courageous* with people. He tells us in verse 12 that a rebuke in the ear is as beautiful as a golden earring, and we need to remember this when God's message isn't easy to deliver. If people persecute us for sharing it, Solomon explains in verses 21–22 how we can respond so graciously that we finally win them over.[6]

---

should demonstrate what we preach by praying for the sick.

[4] The word translated *spirit* is *nephesh*, which strictly means *soul*, so it is not a reference to the Holy Spirit. However, Leviticus 26:11 makes it clear that the Lord has a *nephesh*, so some level of ambiguity remains.

[5] Jude 12–13.

[6] Linked together with Psalm 140:10, these verses suggest that our best revenge on people is to save them! A great example of this can be found in 2 Kings 6:21–23, and Paul quotes this proverb in Romans 12:20 to teach Christians to do the same thing when they are persecuted.

Solomon tells us that we need to watch our *timing* with people. He warns us in verses 16–17 not to share for too long at any one time, since even the sweetest Gospel message can make people sick of listening if we talk too long. He warns us in verse 20 that we need to tailor our message to the circumstances of our listener. Sharing an upbeat message with someone who is grieving is like stealing a person's cloak or pouring vinegar on an open wound.[7] Just before his quotation from this chapter in Romans 12, Paul tells us to *"rejoice with those who rejoice; mourn with those who mourn"*. As messengers of God's wisdom, we need to use God's wisdom in the way in which we share.

But above all, Solomon tells us to expect our sharing to be *successful*. Although our message about God's wisdom may not seem very powerful, verse 15 tells us that a gentle tongue will break through bone if we simply persevere. Let's not get so frustrated that our tongues stop being gentle or fall silent, because Solomon promises in verse 11 that *"a word skilfully spoken"* is more beautiful than gold and silver.[8] The Holy Spirit will enable us to speak words of wisdom with divine power to change lives.[9]

So let's not be lazy, foolish messengers like my unemployed ex-paperboy. Let's be the kind of messengers who refresh the Lord like an ice-cold drink as he sends us into the harvest fields of the world. He wants to make us wise so that we can preach his wisdom to every nation. He wants to make us messengers of the King, delivering his royal mail.

---

[7] Solomon says that it is literally like pouring vinegar on *soda*. If you get a vigorous reaction when you share your faith with others, it may not be the message but the manner in which you share it. See also 27:14.

[8] This proverb echoes the one in 15:23, but Hezekiah's men include it because they know that God's messengers need fresh encouragement to persevere.

[9] Paul promises in 1 Corinthians 12:8 that the Holy Spirit will give us these *words of wisdom*.

Tomato Doesn't Go in a Fruit Salad (26:1–16)

Do not answer a fool according to his folly... Answer a fool according to his folly.

(Proverbs 26:4–5)

The Irish rugby captain Brian O'Driscoll famously told reporters that *"Knowledge is knowing that a tomato is a fruit; wisdom is knowing not to put it in a fruit salad."*[1] Hezekiah's men compiled chapter 26 because they wanted to teach us the same thing about the book of Proverbs.

The truth is that any of Solomon's proverbs can be misapplied. In fact, they often are. I have heard people justify the taking of bribes based on 17:8, despite the fact that 17:23 clarifies that this is merely an observation on the type of sin the Lord will judge. I've heard someone justify separating from his wife by quoting 21:9 and 25:24. Still others take Solomon's God-inspired observations and treat them as watertight promises they were never meant to be. That's why this chapter reminds us that knowing Proverbs doesn't make us wise. We also need to know how to apply it.

To start us off on this lesson, Hezekiah's wise men play a deliberate prank on us. They tell us in 26:4 *"Do not answer a fool according to his folly"* and then tell us at the same time in 26:5 to *"Answer a fool according to his folly"*! Which one of the two proverbs is right? Well, they both are! They have been

[1] He was quoting from the author Miles Kington at a press conference on 28th February 2009.

placed together in order to emphasize that we need some help in applying Solomon's proverbs correctly. Knowing that a tomato is a fruit is knowledge. Knowing not to put it in a fruit salad is wisdom.

This then leads into 26:7–12, which warns that being wise means far more than having the ability to reel off Solomon's proverbs. The sixteenth-century English playwright Henry Porter created a character in one of his plays named Nicholas Proverbs, who speaks nothing but proverbs yet remains an utter fool. He is the object of ridicule as people complain that *"This formal fool, your man, speaks naught but proverbs... On my life, he was never begot without the consent of some great proverb-monger."*[2] That's the kind of person that Hezekiah's men have in mind when they warn us that a proverb in a fool's mouth can no more help him than a lame man's legs, and that his proverbs are more likely to harm him than to help him, like a thorn-bush in the hand of a drunkard.

If you read these verses carefully, you will spot an underlying theme which is really rather clever. Solomon learned some of his wisdom from observing nature (1 Kings 4:33), and these sixteen verses are full of illustrations from his study of the world.[3] There is *snow* and *rain* in verse 1, a *fluttering sparrow* and *darting swallow* in verse 2, a *horse* and *donkey* in verse 3, a *thorn-bush* in verse 9, a *dog* in verse 11 and a *lion* in verse 13. They link back to Solomon's command that the sluggard should *"Go to the ant"* for his teacher in 6:6, and they remind us that all of these proverbs need to be mixed with common sense and a fear of our Creator if we are to be truly wise.

With this in mind, we can see in 26:1 why we mustn't answer back to a fool. He is likely to mistake our attention for a mark of honour, as if his foolish prating is worthy of our considered attention. Honouring a fool's chatter is as inappropriate as snow

[2] Nicholas Proverbs appears in Porter's play *The Two Angry Women of Abington* (1599).

[3] Solomon's student Agur evidently did so too in 30:24–31.

in summer or rain at harvest time,[4] which is why Jesus refused to answer the Pharisees on their own terms in Matthew 21:23–27. When they questioned his authority, he refused to grant them even the authority to ask to him questions until they had first answered a question of his own about why they had ignored John the Baptist's anointed preaching. They were forced to confess their own folly, saying *"We don't know"*, to which Jesus responded *"Neither will I tell you by what authority I am doing these things."* Studying Proverbs will help us to learn words of wisdom, but we also need to be filled with the Holy Spirit to know how to apply them well.

Proverbs 26:2 adds that a second danger in answering back to a fool is that our response will make him think that what he says really matters. David had been right in 2 Samuel 16 to ignore Shimei when he cursed him on his flight from Absalom, because a fool's chatter is worth nothing. Jesus did the same when his enemies attacked him at his trial, and his simple trust in God amazed Pilate so much that he started to wonder if this might truly be Israel's Messiah.[5] Jesus told us that silence is often the best response to folly, warning us in Matthew 7:6, *"Do not give dogs what is sacred; do not throw your pearls to pigs. If you do, they may trample them under their feet, and turn and tear you to pieces."*

Proverbs 26:3 therefore tells us that the only reason why we should answer back to a fool is so that we can show him what a fool he really is. The only thing worse than a fool in 26:12 is a person who thinks he isn't one,[6] so Solomon repeats his teaching back in 19:25 and 21:11 that such a person must have their folly beaten out of them. This is what Jesus did when

---

[4] In fact, rain at harvest time was normally disastrous, as in 1 Samuel 12:17–18. Contrast what Solomon says in 28:3 with his description of the Messiah in Psalm 72:6–7.

[5] Mark 15:1–5; John 19:7–12.

[6] See also 26:16. The word *kesîl* or *fool* occurs almost 50 times in the whole of Proverbs but 11 of them are in just 12 verses here in 26:1–12.

he responded to the foolish Pharisees with a question of his own in Matthew 22:41–46. His question was such a devastating blow that *"No one could say a word in reply, and from that day on no one dared to ask him any more questions."* Sadly, they were like the stupid dog which Solomon describes in verse 11 that returns to its vomit to eat the same meal which made it ill a little earlier. 2 Peter 2:22 quotes this verse to tell us that many people in our churches are also unconverted fools, but that if we confront their folly, at least some of them will repent and receive God's wisdom which can save them.

So study Proverbs and meditate on all that Solomon has to say, but don't forget that this is only the equivalent of learning that a tomato is a fruit. Cry out to the Lord to fill you with his Holy Spirit and to give you the mind of Christ so that you can apply what you have learned correctly. Misusing proverbs or answering fools according to their folly is like putting a tomato in a fruit salad. There will be times when we need to imitate Paul and Barnabas when they shook the dust off their feet in Pisidian Antioch in obedience to Jesus' command in Matthew 10:14. Because they refused to engage with fools who opposed their teaching in Acts 13:45–52, we read that *"All who were appointed for eternal life believed. The word of the Lord spread through the whole region... and the disciples were filled with joy and with the Holy Spirit."*

Careless Talk Costs Lives (26:17–27:6)

A lying tongue hates those it hurts, and a flattering mouth works ruin.

(Proverbs 26:28)

When rioting and looting gripped the streets of London for a week in August 2011, former mayor Ken Livingstone told news reporters, *"Something's changed in the last thirty years. We've got to find out what it is and then tackle it."*[1] Hezekiah's wise men knew that something had gone terribly wrong in their own nation for over 200 years, and they chose a series of proverbs from Solomon's collection which they hoped would tackle it for good. For the rest of chapters 26–28, they tackle three key sins which they believed had poisoned their society since the time of Solomon.

The first of the three sins was the careless way in which God's People had used their lips, tongues and ears. A famous British World War Two poster warned people that *"Careless Talk Costs Lives"*, and Hezekiah's officials could see this as they looked back on two centuries of Israel's drift away from God. Isaiah had been forced to prophesy against them for forgetting that the tongue is the strongest muscle. He confronted their sinful conversation when he warned them, *"Woe to those who call evil good and good evil, who put darkness for light and light for darkness, who put bitter for sweet and sweet for bitter. Woe to those who are wise in their own eyes and clever in their own*

---

[1] Speaking on a Sky News live broadcast on 9th August 2011.

sight."[2] Hezekiah's wise men wanted to emphasize to the people of Judah that careless talk costs lives.

In 26:17–19, Solomon tackles the ease with which we use our tongues. We need to think twice before speaking, since wading into another person's quarrel is as foolish as putting our face between the ears of a hungry street dog. We need to think twice before being sarcastic or playing tricks on one another, because words cause hurt which cannot be smoothed over simply by telling people afterwards that *"I was only joking!"* God hates mouthy talkers who fool themselves that what they say doesn't really matter, and he tells them they are like madmen who think nothing of shooting flaming arrows at their nation.[3] We must remember the immense spiritual power of our words. Solomon told us in 12:18 and 18:21 that *"The tongue has the power of life and death... Reckless words pierce like a sword, but the tongue of the wise brings healing."*

In 26:20–22, Solomon tackles the sin of gossip. We all know how easy it is for us to be blinded to the sin of talking about people behind their backs or sharing secret information *"just for prayer"*.[4] Like the people of Judah, we can forget that Solomon listed gossip alongside murder in 6:16–19. Assassinating somebody's character may not carry the same penalty as murder in our human courts, but in God's eyes it is part of the same sin.[5] In 26:22, Hezekiah's men deliberately repeat a proverb from 18:8 in order to emphasize that even listening to gossip is a sin. Because words are so powerful, gossip is like a choice morsel which goes down literally into

---

[2] Isaiah 5:20–21, prophesied in about 740 BC.

[3] Solomon warned us similarly in 16:27 that the words of the wicked are *"like a scorching fire"*.

[4] One definition of gossip from 17:9 is simply "repeating something about someone else which should have been left to be forgotten". The antithetic parallelism in 17:9 treats gossip as the opposite of love.

[5] Jesus says that hatred is akin to murder in Matthew 5:21–22. Saying things behind people's backs which we would not say to their faces is simply a cowardly form of hatred.

the *bedrooms of the belly*. Whether we like it or not, we start viewing people differently as a result of what we hear – which means that gossips are accessories to murder.[6] Eve's sin began by listening to words to which she should not have listened. So did Israel and Judah's, and so does ours.

In 26:23–28, Solomon tackles the sin of lying. When Isaiah confronted the people of Judah over their sinful conversation, he specifically accused them of promoting sin using *"cords of deceit"*. Solomon tells us that clay cups coated with a thin veneer of silver may trick fools in the marketplace, but that wicked hearts coated with lies of respectability will never fool the Lord. Lying and flattering tongues pretend to care, but Solomon tells us plainly in 26:28 that they are full of hatred. They conceal the seven abominations which Solomon listed in 6:16–19, but the Lord promises to expose their deceit and make them fall into the traps their lies have laid.[7]

In 27:1–2, Solomon tackles the sin of boasting. Although the Hebrew of 25:27 is ambiguous, it is probably a warning that nobody likes a bragger. Isaiah had addressed this as a serious issue too, telling God's People that it was evil for them to boast that *"Tomorrow will be like today, or even far better."* Boasting is in fact idolatry because it is stems from the view that we are little gods and can chart our futures without the Lord. That's why Jesus called the rich man who boasted about tomorrow a *fool* in Luke 12:19–20, and it's why James warned his Christian readers to repent of such self-worship. *"You boast and brag. All such boasting is evil,"* he writes in James 4:13–16. *"You do not even know what will happen tomorrow. What is your life? You are a mist that appears for a little while and then vanishes.*

---

[6] Proverbs 20:19 tells us that we shouldn't even associate with gossips. 20:27 and 20:30 use this same phrase *"bedrooms of the belly"* to warn us that the effect of gossip is so powerful that it can only be cleansed by the Holy Spirit or by our receiving a beating.

[7] This reference is meant to take us back to Solomon's teaching in lesson one by reminding us of 1:17–18.

Instead, you ought to say, 'If it is the Lord's will, we will live and do this or that.'"[8]

In 27:3–4, Solomon tackles the sin of speaking reckless words. The fool thinks nothing of the effect which his words will have on others, little realizing that they are harder to bear than a load of stone or sand, and that they will surely provoke the reaction he deserves. *"Anger is cruel and fury overwhelming,"* Solomon warns us, reminding us to take note of what he said in 17:27–28: *"The one who has knowledge uses words with restraint"* because *"even fools are thought wise if they keep silent, and discerning if they hold their tongues."*

In 27:5–6, Solomon ends this series of proverbs about speaking and listening with two more positive proverbs about what we should say instead. He tells us that silence is better than foolish chatter, but that loving words are even better still. Instead of flattering with kisses like an enemy, we need to speak the truth in love to one another, even if it hurts, so that we can walk the path of wisdom together.[9]

Nine months after the rioting in London, Ken Livingstone ran as an election candidate to return as the city's mayor. What was remarkable was how little he or any of the other candidates spoke about the "something" which had changed and which he had resolved only months earlier to identify and tackle. Hezekiah's wise men don't want us to be as forgetful as the candidates for London's mayor. They have identified one of the three things which destroyed their nation and which can destroy us too. Let's therefore use our lips and tongues and ears in a manner which glorifies the Lord. Let's not forget that careless talk costs lives.

---

[8] Note the way that Paul applies these words as he makes future plans in Acts 18:21 and 1 Corinthians 4:19 and 16:5–7.

[9] See Ephesians 4:15. The flatterer cares only for the short-term affection of a person, not for that person's long-term good. That's why 28:23 tells us that rebuking people will make us more true friends than flattery.

Enough is Enough (27:7–27)

Death and Destruction are never satisfied, and neither are human eyes.

(Proverbs 27:20)

It isn't just The Rolling Stones who can't get no satisfaction. Solomon tells us that this is the problem of people the whole world over. Hezekiah's men identified greed and perpetual discontentment as the second great sin which had caused their nation's drift away from God. Most of chapter 27 is a collection of Solomon's proverbs which help us to recognize when enough is enough.

Micah had prophesied against Israel and Judah in the years leading up to the start of Hezekiah's reign. *"They covet fields and seize them, and houses, and take them. They defraud people of their homes, they rob them of their inheritance. Therefore, the Lord says: 'I am planning disaster against this people,'"* he had warned them.[1] Unless we learn to be content with what we have, we will never be wise. We will be fools who leave ourselves wide open to the danger of falling *"into temptation and a trap and into many foolish and harmful desires that plunge people into ruin and destruction"*.[2]

Solomon wants to shock us with his statement that coveting and greed can never be satisfied. He compares them in 27:20 to *she'ōl* and *abaddōn*, the two main Hebrew words

---

[1] Micah 2:2–3, prophesied in about 735 BC.

[2] Paul says this as part of his teaching on godly contentment in 1 Timothy 6:6–10.

for *hell*, and tells us that greed will only be satisfied when hell no longer cries out for fresh souls. The word *she'ōl* can mean literally *demanding* and the word *abaddōn* can mean literally *consuming*, so hell is insatiable.[3] *"The unfaithful are trapped by evil desires... The greedy bring ruin to their households... A heart at peace gives life to the body, but envy rots the bones,"* we read in 11:6, 14:30 and 15:27. Our only hope, therefore, is to ask God to free us from the stranglehold of endless greed so that we can find godly contentment in the things which he has given us.

Verse 7 tells us that we need to be content with our *possessions*. We shouldn't need Joni Mitchell's song to point out to us that *"you don't know what you've got till it's gone"*. Solomon observes that what one person complains about another person dreams about, because contentment is a state of mind rather than a state of money. Solomon's earlier proverbs taught us to value relaxation, health, safety, good character, a loving home and our walk with God far more highly than mere possessions.[4] We should therefore not be hoodwinked by what Jesus calls *"the deceitfulness of wealth"* in Matthew 13:22. Only if we kill our greed instead of feeding it can we know the true joy which comes from God.

Verse 8 tells us that we need to be content with our *home situation*. Solomon tells us that a person who looks outside the home for satisfaction is like a foolish bird which builds a nest and then abandons it to another. We ought to remember the lesson of 11:22 and not let our eyes stray to the fleeting beauty of another person's partner. Nor should we foolishly light the fire of unquenchable jealousy which adultery inflames.[5]

---

3 Solomon's student Agur tells us something similar in 30:14–16. See also Habakkuk 2:5 and Ecclesiastes 5:10.

4 Proverbs 13:8; 15:16, 17; 16:8; 17:1; 19:22; 23:4. James 3:14–15 tells us that covetousness and greed are emotions which come from the Devil.

5 Since verse 12 is a verbatim repetition of 22:3, it appears to have been included here to remind us not to ignore what will happen to us if we make a husband jealous in verse 4. See also Song of Songs 8:6–7.

Jeremiah 5:8 laughs at the foolish men of Judah, where Person A lusts after Person B's wife, who lusts after Person C's wife, who lusts after Person A's wife! Instead, we should tend our marriages and make them all that they can be, since Solomon tells us literally in 27:19 that *"As water reflects the face, so others reflect your heart back to you."*[6] If you are single, Solomon has not ignored you, placing a reminder in 27:15–16 that there are far worse things than being unmarried.[7] Whatever your present home situation, Solomon tells you be content. Until the Lord unfolds his future plan, there simply isn't a better one for you out there.

Verses 9–10 tell us that we need to be content with our *friends*. Perfume isn't valuable for what it looks like but for the glorious scent which it provides, so even if your circle of friends isn't quite what you expected you should still enjoy the sweetness it provides. Verse 10 assures us that true friends can be more precious than family if we invest the time to make those friendships grow. Verse 17 adds that friendship is one of God's greatest gifts to us: *"As iron sharpens iron, so one person sharpens another."*

Verse 18 tells us that we need to be content with our *workplace*. That's important because recent surveys reveal that only 45 per cent of us are. For younger workers, those same surveys show that a mere 36 per cent of under-twenty-fives are happy with their job.[8] Solomon tells us to enjoy the job which God has given us because if we guard our bosses' interests as the owner of a fig tree guards its fruit, we will reap a certain harvest in our workplace over time.

[6] You have God on your side in this. He created marriage as a picture of Jesus' devotion to the Church and he inspired 5:18–19 because he wants to answer that prayer for you.

[7] God may well provide a partner for you (18:22; 19:14), but he warns in 12:4 that marrying badly will rot the strength out of your life as much as a refusal to be content with being single in 14:30.

[8] This data comes from a US survey by the Conference Board research group in January 2010.

Verse 21 tells us that we need to be content with our *success*. Being praised and honoured is actually far more dangerous than being ignored, since the main danger of success lies precisely in the fact that it doesn't feel much like a trial. On the contrary, Solomon tells us that it reveals the dross in our character as clearly as melting silver or gold in the fire. Be grateful that the Lord hasn't given you any more success yet than he has. He has given you as much success as your present character permits and any more success would have actually led to failure.

Therefore this chapter ends with the longest of Solomon's proverbs, a colossal ten-liner in verses 23–29. Ingrid Bergman observed that *"Success is getting what you want; happiness is wanting what you get,"* and Solomon encourages us to heed her words by making the most of what we have. He tells us to fix our eyes on our possessions in verse 23, to remember that they will not last forever in verse 24, and to enjoy the blessings which they provide in verses 26–27.[9]

Paul fleshes out Solomon's teaching in this chapter when he tells us to rejoice that everything we need is not found in flocks but in the Lamb of God. He tells us in 1 Corinthians 3:18–23 that everything is ours in Christ, and in Philippians 4:11–12 that knowing this has taught him the mystery of complete contentment. *"I have learned to be content whatever the circumstances,"* he says as a poor, single, childless prisoner. *"I know what it is to be in need, and I know what it is to have plenty. I have learned the secret of being content in any and every situation, whether well fed or hungry, whether living in plenty or in want."*

Let's not fall for the sin which destroyed coveting, grasping Israel in the centuries between Solomon and Hezekiah. Let's not be like the world which can't get no satisfaction. Let's learn from Solomon and Paul to be content with what we have, for the glory of Jesus Christ, our all in all.

---

9 Since church leaders are shepherds of the Church, it is interesting that *not loving money* is the only qualification for eldership which is mentioned in all three of 1 Timothy 3:1–7, Titus 1:6–9 and 1 Peter 5:1–4.

What God Hates About Sundays (28:9)

If anyone turns a deaf ear to my instruction, even their prayers are detestable.

(Proverbs 28:9)

Teodorín Obiang was very popular in his native Equatorial Guinea. The son of the president, he won over the nation with his speeches about how much he loved his country. He took a meagre civil servant's salary to become Minister of Agriculture, declaring that he had a vision to help even the poorest farmers to yield harvests from the African soil. He would use the revenue from the nation's oil fields to help them, making Equatorial Guinea an oasis of prosperity in a continent of corruption.

Then came the revelation from a German company in 2011 that Teodorín Obiang had just placed an order with them to build a luxury super yacht costing $380 million. Further investigations discovered that he already owned multimillion dollar mansions in America and France, a $33-million private jet and a fleet of luxury cars. Popularity turned to scandal when it became obvious that the nation's oil money had not been channelled towards helping poor farmers at all. The price tag of the yacht alone was three times the national budget for healthcare and education combined.[1]

If you find that account of Teodorín Obiang's corruption and hypocrisy sickening, you will understand the third key sin which Hezekiah's men identified behind their nation's drift

---

[1] This was reported in newspapers around the world on 28th February 2011.

away from God. The Lord hates it when people sing him worship songs like true believers then spend the rest of the week in the corrupt practices of the world. He prophesied through Isaiah that *"I cannot bear your worthless assemblies. Your New Moon feasts and your appointed festivals I hate with all my being. They have become a burden to me; I am weary of bearing them. When you spread out your hands in prayer, I hide my eyes from you; even when you offer many prayers, I am not listening."* Despite revival under Hezekiah, the Lord still warned that *"these people come near to me with their mouth and honour me with their lips, but their hearts are far from me".*[2] Hezekiah's wise men compiled a collection of Solomon's proverbs in chapter 28 which would correct this hypocrisy and corruption.

The key proverb here is in verse 9, where Solomon says that *"If anyone turns a deaf ear to my instruction, even their prayers are detestable." Tō'ēbah,* meaning *an abomination* or *a disgusting thing,* is an extremely strong Hebrew word. Solomon uses it elsewhere to describe how the Lord feels towards murder, lying, gossip, theft, crooked judges and evil in general.[3] He is therefore telling us that hypocritical prayers are among the vilest sins to God. In case we don't believe him, Jesus repeats it himself in Revelation 3:16, telling people who pretend to be on fire for God that their lukewarm disobedience makes him want to vomit.[4]

Hezekiah's men have not simply found one of Solomon's particularly fiery sayings. This message pervades the whole of Solomon's original Top 375. He told us in 15:8 and 21:27 that *"the Lord detests the sacrifice of the wicked"* and that *"the*

[2] Isaiah 1:13–15 was prophesied in about 740 BC. Isaiah 29:13 was prophesied in about 705 BC, 10 years into Hezekiah's revival. See also Proverbs 21:3.

[3] Proverbs 6:16–19; 11:1; 15:9; 17:15. The same word is used to describe how God views homosexual sex in Leviticus 18:22 and 20:13, idolatry in Deuteronomy 7:25 and infant sacrifice in Jeremiah 32:35.

[4] The New Testament repeats in 1 Timothy 2:8, 1 Peter 3:7 and James 3:9–10 and 5:16 that our obedience affects the acceptability of our prayers.

sacrifice of the wicked is detestable". He told us in 15:29 and 21:13 that *"the Lord is far from the wicked"* because *"whoever shuts their ears to the cry of the poor will also cry out and not be answered"*. Singing Christian songs on Sunday doesn't offset the sins we commit from Monday to Saturday. In fact, it can make us even guiltier. That's what God hates most about Sundays.[5]

If we read the rest of chapter 28, it becomes obvious that Hezekiah's men knew their nation's sin had been specific rather than just wickedness in general. The Lord had confronted them in Isaiah 58 by calling them to be worshippers who *"loose the chains of injustice and untie the cords of the yoke"* and who *"do away with the yoke of oppression"*. He had urged them *"to share your food with the hungry and to provide the poor wanderer with shelter – when you see the naked, to clothe them"*. That's why Hezekiah's men list a long series of proverbs that tell us specifically that our Sunday worship must be matched by the way we treat the poor and needy all week long.

We read in verse 3 that rulers who exploit their subjects like Teodorín Obiang are fools and lead their nation into economic suicide. We read in verse 5 that true believers catch God's heart for justice, and in verse 8 that those who fail to catch it will not live to enjoy the fruit of their wicked grasping. We read in verses 18–19 that those who trample over others in pursuit of get-rich-quick schemes will fall under God's judgment, because God sees their greedy coveting in verses 22 and 25.[6] We read in verse 27 that *"Those who give to the poor will lack nothing, but those who close their eyes to them receive many curses."* Let's not imagine that loud worship can ever drown out a lack of concern for the poor.

If you know that God is speaking to you, go to verse 13

---

[5] Proverbs 28:5 is directed at those who think that praying and going to church earns them brownie points with God. God tells us it doesn't in Isaiah 66:2–4; Jeremiah 6:20 and 7:21–23; Amos 5:21–22 and John 4:24.

[6] Proverbs 28:19 is largely a repeat of 12:11 because Hezekiah's men want us to grasp this very well.

where Solomon promises that if we confess our sin in this area, then God will forgive us and start delighting in our prayers.[7] Next, read the Lord's promise in Isaiah 58 that if we repent and start helping those in need, *"then your light will break forth like the dawn, and your healing will quickly appear... Then you will call, and the Lord will answer; you will cry for help, and he will say: Here am I."*

Ever since the wise men of Hezekiah compiled this chapter of Solomon's proverbs, it has brought revival to any group of believers who repent of reducing worship to the singing of choruses and who start worshipping throughout the week through their compassion towards the poor. Jerusalem after Pentecost, the first-century Roman world, the monastic movement, the Reformation, the Salvation Army: the same is true in any age.

It's so powerful that even Roy Hattersley, the former deputy leader of the British Labour Party and a self-confessed atheist, was forced to concede that it made him stop and think about the Gospel. After witnessing the work of the Salvation Army in London in 2005, he wrote that

> *Civilised people do not believe that drug addiction and male prostitution offend against divine ordinance. But those who do are the men and women most willing to change the fetid bandages, replace the sodden sleeping bags and – probably most difficult of all – argue, without a trace of impatience, that the time has come for some serious medical treatment... It ought to be possible to live a Christian life without being a Christian or, better still, to take Christianity à la carte... Yet men and women who,*

[7] Having told us literally in 28:9 that the prayers of wicked are a *disgusting thing* to him, the Lord tells us literally in 15:8 that the prayers of the upright are *a delight* to him. The difference is enormous.

like me, cannot accept the mysteries and the miracles do not go out with the Salvation Army at night.[8]

Let's rid our lives of the hypocrisy which God hates every Sunday. Let's pour out our lives to help the poor and disadvantaged the whole week long.

---

[8] Roy Hattersley wrote this in an article in the British newspaper *The Guardian* on 12th September 2005. Used with permission.

A Straight Ruler (28:1–29:27)

If a king judges the poor with fairness, his throne will be established forever.

(Proverbs 29:14)

Solomon knew that he was the son of God. Not just a son of God in general but *the* son of God in particular. Before he had even been conceived, the Lord had made a covenant with his father David, promising that *"I will raise up your seed to succeed you, your own flesh and blood, and I will establish his kingdom… I will establish the throne of his kingdom forever. I will be his father, and he will be my son."*[1] When David chose Solomon as his successor and told him he was a precursor to the Messiah, it must have felt like a heavy burden.[2]

So Solomon studied the prophecies which his father had written in his psalms, wanting to find out all he could about the true Son of God to whom he pointed. We have seen throughout Proverbs that the Lord answered his prayers, because he points to the coming Messiah again and again in the three books which he wrote of the Bible. As he tells us that we need to embrace the wisdom of God, he drops clues that one is coming who will be the true Wisdom of God. As he talks about the wise and the righteous, he hints that the true Wise and Righteous One is coming to succeed where we have failed. Hezekiah's men therefore found it easy to take

---

[1] 2 Samuel 7:12–14.

[2] We can tell this from the subject matter of the only two psalms which were written by Solomon. Psalm 72 is all about the Messiah's reign and Psalm 127 is about his hope both in the Lord and in his children.

some of Solomon's proverbs about how to be a godly king and to compile them in chapters 28–29 as a promise about the coming of the true and perfect King.

It was even more obvious to Hezekiah's men that Israel needed a Messiah than it was to Solomon when he wrote these proverbs. Solomon had not persevered in righteousness and had backslidden spiritually in his later years (we will look later at what he learned through this in the book of Ecclesiastes). The kings who followed him were even worse than Solomon on a bad day. Hezekiah was the best king for 200 years, but even he had some serious flaws which made his servants long for the Messiah who was to come. He had a disastrous episode of pride and showed a shocking disregard for what would happen to his nation under the kings who would succeed him. As for his son and heir Manasseh, there were already concerning signs that he would ignore Solomon's 500 proverbs and drag Judah back into the same spiritual wasteland as before.[3] The recurring theme in these last two chapters of Solomon's proverbs is therefore the character of godly kings and of the godly King whose reign was yet to come.

Many of these proverbs stress that kings must be righteous. The words *righteous* and *wicked* are used eighteen times in these two chapters. Many of these proverbs also stress that kings must love to help the needy. The words *justice* and *rich* and *poor* are used seventeen times.[4] Hezekiah's men are looking back to tell Jerusalem's rulers to be like David, who *"reigned over all Israel, doing what was just and right for all his people"*.[5] They are also looking forward to the future to stir up hope that a

---

[3] 2 Kings 20:12–19; Isaiah 39:1–8. Although he promised in Isaiah 38:19–20 to train up his sons, this attitude of *"peace and security in my lifetime"* made him neglect Manasseh, who became one of Judah's worst kings.

[4] In fact, 28:6 is a repeat of 19:1 except that this time the word *fool* is changed to read *rich person* instead. Note the way in which 28:11 deliberately equates *rich* with *fool*, and *poor* with *wise*.

[5] 2 Samuel 8:15. If you are unsure how much Hezekiah's servants understood about the coming Messiah, then read Isaiah 9:6–7, which was prophesied over 15 years before Hezekiah became king.

King is coming who will completely embody this description of the perfect ruler. The Messiah would completely fulfil these two chapters of proverbs and the prophecy in Psalm 45:6–7: *"Your throne, O God, will last forever and ever; a sceptre of justice will be the sceptre of your kingdom. You love righteousness and hate wickedness; therefore God, your God, has set you above your companions."*[6]

Many of these proverbs also stress that the hope of a nation is in its king.[7] More than the rest of the book, chapters 28 and 29 tell us to put our faith for deliverance in the king. Solomon tells us at least ten times that a ruler's character will bring joy or misery to the subjects of his kingdom,[8] because Hezekiah's men wanted each new king of Judah to be aware that they were sons of God and heirs of David and members of the Messiah's family tree. Paul may have been thinking about Solomon's prophecy in 29:14 when he described the righteous rule of the Messiah as *"the hope of Israel"*.[9]

The proverbs of Solomon end with three verses which call us to respond to this promise. Since the Messiah is coming, Solomon tells his readers in 29:25 *to believe*. Don't be put off by those who laugh at the Gospel, since 28:5 tells us that the wicked simply cannot understand it. Don't be put off by the cost of believing, since 28:6 tells us that poverty with godliness is worth far more than riches with rebellion. Don't be put off by the pain of confessing your sin, since Solomon promises in 28:13 that *"Whoever conceals their sins does not prosper, but the*

---

6 Note the way in which the psalmists address this future King both as God and as a ruler under God. Hebrews 1:8–9 tells us that this was a description of Jesus.

7 This was obvious to his original readers. To grasp how different Solomon's culture was from ours, note that he sees it as a good thing to promise us literally in 28:25 that *"those who trust in the Lord will get fat"*!

8 Proverbs 28:2, 3, 12, 15, 16, 28; 29:2, 4, 12, 14, 16.

9 Acts 28:20 and 23 make it clear that *"the hope of Israel"* is the Kingdom of Christ as prophesied in the Old Testament. Acts 24:14–15 and 26:6–8 add that this Kingdom was inaugurated through his resurrection.

one who confesses and renounces them finds mercy."[10] We who live after the coming of the Messiah should respond to these words with even greater urgency than the men of Hezekiah.

Since the Messiah is coming, Solomon tells his readers in 29:26 *to pray*. The people of Judah struggled as much to get access to their kings and rulers as you or I, and only a tiny percentage would ever make it past the royal gatehouse. But Solomon encourages us that we can enter the Lord's presence right now in prayer. This would be a vital promise for God's People as they suffered under wicked kings and waited for the coming of their Messiah. It is still a vital promise for us as we serve the risen King Jesus and await his return in glory.

Since the Messiah is coming, Solomon tells his readers in 29:27 *to persevere*. He repeats what he told us in 29:10, that the wicked detest the upright and will do all they can to persecute us. We need to learn to fear the Lord more than people in 28:14, and set our faces to resist the onslaught of the wicked in 28:4. If we do so, Solomon promises us in 28:1 that *"The wicked flee though no one pursues, but the righteous are as bold as a lion."*[11]

We have reached the end of Solomon's 500 proverbs, but let's not move on until we have grasped this picture of the Messiah. Solomon ends his proverbs by telling us that we must fix our eyes on him if we are to live as wise sons and daughters of God, and as servants of the King. He tells us in 29:18 that this is the vision which will keep us walking on the path of wisdom.[12]

---

[10] Proverbs 28:17 and 29:1 warn us that if we refuse to confess our sins, we will carry them with us to hell.

[11] Solomon may have been thinking back to Leviticus 26:17 and 36, as demonstrated in 2 Kings 7:5–7.

[12] Although many people quote 29:18 to assert that churches and organizations need a vision statement, note that the Hebrew word *hāzōn* does not mean human *goal-setting* but rather *revelation* of God's plan.

Solomon's Students (30:1–33)

The sayings of Agur son of Jakeh – an inspired utterance.

(Proverbs 30:1)

Forget Niagara Falls. Forget the Grand Canyon. Forget Disneyland. Jerusalem was the number one tourist destination in the world during the reign of Solomon. 1 Kings 10:24 tells us that *"The whole world sought audience with Solomon to hear the wisdom God had put into his heart,"* and the rest of the chapter suggests that many of the tourists who came to Jerusalem were converted. When Hezekiah's men added their Top 125 to Solomon's own Top 375 to complete Proverbs, it therefore appears that they also included two chapters written by two foreign authors who had been converted through visiting Solomon.[1]

We know very little about Agur son of Jakeh, the writer of chapter 30. His name means *Gathered* and his father's name means *Obedient*, but beyond that all we know is that he was not a native Israelite, since he writes in Hebrew but uses the Aramaic word *Elōah* for God instead of the Hebrew word *Elōhīm* in verse 5.[2] Verse 1 tells us that this chapter is a *massa'*, which means an *oracle* or *inspired utterance* and which is the normal

---

[1] Agur and Lemuel both call God by his covenant name *Yahweh*, but they use Aramaic words as they write in Hebrew which betray that neither of them was an ethnic Israelite.

[2] Although Hebrew writers do occasionally use this Aramaic word for God in the Old Testament, it is mainly used by the non-Hebrew Job (41 times) and by Daniel and Ezra in Babylon and Persia (95 times).

Hebrew word used to describe the words of the Old Testament prophets.[3] Hezekiah's men were issuing a very important warning. God's People do not have a monopoly on wisdom and the Hebrews needed to be humble enough to learn from the words of converted outsiders. John Calvin warned the early Protestants in a similar fashion not to be so proud of their right doctrine that they missed the wisdom of non-Christian writers in their zeal for purity:

> *In reading profane authors, the admirable light of truth displayed in them should remind us, that the human mind, however much fallen and perverted from its original integrity, is still adorned and invested with admirable gifts from its Creator. If we reflect that the Spirit of God is the only fountain of truth, we will be careful, as we would avoid offering insult to him, not to reject or condemn truth wherever it appears. In despising the gifts, we insult the Giver... Shall we deem anything to be noble and praiseworthy, without tracing it to the hand of God?... If the Lord has been pleased to assist us by the work and ministry of the ungodly in physics, dialectics, mathematics, and other similar sciences, let us avail ourselves of it.*[4]

In verses 2–4, Agur confesses that he isn't in Solomon's league when it comes to speaking words of wisdom. He will talk about the wisdom of various animals in verses 24–31, so he tells us that he is only as wise as one of those brute beasts compared to his one-time teacher Solomon. All he has going for him is the fact that at least he admits he is tired of pretending to understand.[5]

---

[3] Since there was actually a place called *Massa* in Arabia, a few translators contend that this is actually the name of his homeland.

[4] John Calvin wrote this in about 1536 in his *Institutes of the Christian Religion* (2.2.15–16).

[5] Proverbs 30:1b is best translated *"I am weary, God, but I can prevail,"* although the Masoretic Hebrew text divides those same Hebrew letters

Solomon promised us in 26:12 that this is a big step towards acquiring wisdom and, sure enough, Agur appears to grasp a whole lot more than he gives himself credit for. He understands that the Lord is the Holy One[6] and that the right response to Solomon's proverbs is for us to go looking for God's Son.[7]

In verses 5–6, Agur tells us that the only wise thing for us to do with our lack of knowledge is to believe God's Word. This may be why Hezekiah's men chose to include his writings rather than those of another visitor to Jerusalem, because they serve as an exhortation for us to pay attention to Solomon's wisdom without adding to what he has said. The kings of Judah after Hezekiah would despise and even burn the Scriptures, but this non-Israelite tells us that wisdom is ours if we accept them as the flawless words of God.

In verses 7–20, Agur admits his weakness of character and pleads with the Lord to deliver him from temptation. He recognizes that money corrupts the poor as well as the rich in verses 7–9 and asks God to protect him from being tempted by having either too much or too little. He reiterates what Solomon taught us about covetousness and greed in verses 15–16. Linked to this, he makes reference in verse 14 to the great temptation which Solomon warned about, that of oppressing the poor and forgetting that God comes to us in disguise through them. Agur talks about rebellion against masters and parents in verses 10–14 and 17, giving us an even more graphic warning against this sin than does Solomon.[8] Finally, he talks about temptation to

differently to suggest that he is talking to unknown friends named *Ithiel and Ukal*.

[6] Just like Solomon in 9:10, Agur actually uses a plural noun which can mean that he either longs to know *the Holy One* (that is, the Lord) or else *the holy ones* (that is, the Lord's People).

[7] Don't miss the astonishing insight of 30:4. Jesus is *the one who has gone up to heaven and come down*.

[8] Sadly, these four things were to characterize Judah in the years after Hezekiah: despising their parents, fooling themselves they were pure, acting proudly, and oppressing the poor and needy.

commit adultery in verses 18–20.[9] Agur may not claim to be a wise man but he has been wise enough to listen to Solomon's repeated warnings in chapters 1–29. The implication is that so must we.

In verses 21–33, Agur offers his own conclusion to this book of wisdom. He uses the Aramaic wise man's distinctive way of counting things in verses 21, 24 and 29 – the same distinctive style which Solomon used himself in 6:16 – and he uses it to rattle off lists of wise animals which ought to shame us into being at least as wise as they are.[10] We are not brute beasts like the ones which Agur referred to in verse 2, because God has made us thinking men and women. Let's therefore think about the fact that ignoring these proverbs will cause us trouble and pain as surely as twisting our nose will give us a nose bleed![11]

That's why it doesn't really matter who Agur was. He is simply one of the many visitors who had a chance to respond to Solomon's wisdom. He was not an Israelite by birth but he repented and became part of God's People. He was not intelligent by nature but he humbled himself and submitted to God's Word. He was not immune to temptation but he cried out to the Lord and received strength from the Holy Spirit to keep walking along the path of God's wisdom.

Agur was a star student in God's flight school and now he cheers us on to be the same. Let's learn from a foreigner who visited Jerusalem not to neglect the words of Proverbs. Let's apply them as fellow foreigners who have been admitted into God's heavenly Kingdom.

---

[9] Agur warns us how deceptive the sin of adultery can be. The adulteress fools herself that having a quick bath after sex has purified her. Adulterers always have their own warped rationale to justify their sin.

[10] Israel's history so far wasn't promising. Abraham had let a maidservant displace her mistress, and Jacob had despised instead of loving his wife Leah. Compare 30:23 with Genesis 16:1–6 and 29:30–35.

[11] Agur uses exactly the same word in Hebrew to describe *churning* milk, *turning* noses and *stirring up* anger. Proverbs 30:33 is an Old Testament precursor to Galatians 6:7.

Choose Your Co-Pilot (31:1–31)

A wife of noble character who can find? She is worth far more than rubies.

(Proverbs 31:10)

We have finally reached the end of Proverbs. We are about to complete lesson two in God's flight school of wisdom. As every fan of the movie *Top Gun* knows, that's the moment when we have to choose a co-pilot to fly with.

Solomon had chosen his co-pilot very badly. He was so eager to forge an alliance with Egypt that he chose Pharaoh's daughter and married outside the People of God. The marriage was a disaster. 2 Chronicles 8:11 hints that Solomon knew that he should never have married her, but he let her and his other foreign wives lead him astray into idolatry.[1]

The godliest king of Judah between Solomon and Hezekiah was Jehoshaphat, but even he had chosen his son's co-pilot badly. His passion for unity among God's People made him over-tolerant towards the northern kingdom of Israel, and he chose the daughter of the wicked King Ahab and Queen Jezebel as a co-pilot for his son.[2] Athaliah almost destroyed the royal dynasty of Judah by killing every royal prince but one so that she could steal their throne.[3] In view of this background, it really isn't

---

[1] 1 Kings 3:1–3; 11:1–13.

[2] Church unity is not a virtue if it is achieved through disobedience to God. Jehoshaphat brought trouble on Judah by allying repeatedly with Israel in its trading expeditions and in its foolish battles.

[3] 2 Kings 8:16–18; 11:1–3.

very surprising that the last chapter of Proverbs tells us how to choose our co-pilot better than Solomon and Jehoshaphat.

We know as little about King Lemuel, the writer of chapter 31, as we do about Agur who wrote the chapter before. His use of Aramaic words betrays that he is a non-Israelite, as does the fact that no king by his name ever ruled in Israel or Judah.[4] Lemuel tells us that this chapter is a record of the words which were spoken to him by his mother,[5] presumably one of the many visitors to Solomon's Jerusalem, but he adds in verse 1 that her words were also an *oracle* or *inspired utterance* which was given to her by the Lord.[6] It is fitting that this chapter of teaching on how to choose the right co-pilot should have been spoken by a woman who had herself served as co-pilot to a king.

In verses 2–9, Lemuel tells us that a good marriage starts not with the person we choose but with the person that we *are*. A marriage is only as healthy as the two people in it, so a husband needs to watch out for some particularly male sins if he wants a happy home. Lemuel's mother tells him in verses 2–3 not to look at other women, because people who do so are as foolish as sailors who torpedo their own ship before leaving harbour. The British novelist Martin Amis observed that *"If you want to know the real meaning of pornography, it is the utter dissociation of love and sex, the banishment of love from the sexual arena… They get it in high definition on the internet, and no one has any idea what the human consequences of that will be."*[7] Lemuel's mother tells him to keep his eyes on his chosen co-pilot if he wants to fly straight,

---

[4] For example, Lemuel uses the Aramaic word *bar* for *son* in verse 2 instead of the Hebrew word *bēn*.

[5] If Lemuel wrote verse 1 rather than Hezekiah's men, he truly believed Solomon's words in 17:6 that parents are the pride of their children. He was not embarrassed to admit he got his wisdom from his mother.

[6] As we noted in the previous chapter, there was a place called *Massa* in Arabia, so it is technically possible that this verse in Hebrew should read that Lemuel was the king of Massa.

[7] Martin Amis said this in an interview with *The Daily Telegraph* on 14th October 2011.

and she says the same to us. She also warns him in verses 4–7 not to drink too much wine or beer, linking drunkenness to bullying and oppression. She follows this up by reminding him in verses 8–9 that a wife will love a husband who is generous and kind.

She continues in verses 10–31 with what must surely be one of the most beautiful poems ever written.[8] It appears that she wrote it to inspire Lemuel to choose his co-pilot well, and she was a poetess of considerable skill. Ancient Hebrew poetry does not rhyme but finds its beauty in its symmetry and clever wordplay. These twenty-two verses form an acrostic poem by starting with each successive letter of the alphabet – all twenty-two Hebrew letters from Aleph to Taw. Hezekiah's men turn her poem into a final bookend to Proverbs so that it starts with Lady Wisdom calling and ends with our female co-pilot helping us to fly.[9] If you are a woman and have had to endure the very male-focused language of Proverbs, this poem should encourage you that Solomon's teaching looks just as good in female clothes.[10]

The wife in the poem has responded to lesson one of God's flight school by learning to cherish God's way. In verses 10–12, she has developed the noble character which chapters 1–9 told us was worth far more than gold and precious jewels.

She has also responded to lesson two of God's flight school by living out the detail of God's way as it is described in chapters 10–29. She is the opposite of a sluggard in verses 13–19, rising early and staying up late to tend to the needs of her growing home, and not despising manual labour such as spinning, sewing

---

8 Some commentators assume that this poem is distinct from the words of Lemuel's mother, but Hezekiah's men give us no indication whatsoever in the text that it is not still her who is speaking.

9 Note the parallel in verse 30 between 1:7 and the godly co-pilot who fears the Lord, and in verse 10 between 3:15 and 8:11 and the godly co-pilot who is worth more than rubies.

10 Chapter 31 is not meant to discourage female readers by comparing them to this ideal wife. The teaching of Proverbs is all about *sons* and *husbands* and *kings*, so it should encourage you that the two bookends of Proverbs both present its teaching as being most resplendent in a woman.

and planting.[11] She cares for the poor and needy while stewarding what money she has left very well in verses 20–22. She supports her husband in his career in verse 23, and is a working mother herself in verses 24–31.[12] She embodies what Solomon told us in 12:4 and 14:1, when he warned that *"a disgraceful wife is like decay"* which rots away a husband's strength on the inside and that *"a wife of noble character is her husband's crown"*.

Don't miss the fact that the wife's physical beauty is only mentioned in verse 30 at the very end of the poem, or that even then it is only mentioned to warn us that *"Charm is deceptive, and beauty is fleeting."* Han Solo didn't choose Chewbacca as his co-pilot in *Star Wars* because he was good-looking but because he knew how to fly the Millennium Falcon. Lemuel's mother warns us not to choose our co-pilot based on prettiness either.[13] The flight of life is too long and too risky for us to choose our co-pilot based on fleeting looks alone.

If you are married, this chapter is a description of the spouse that wisdom will teach you to be. If you are single, this chapter will help you to choose the right co-pilot. If you know that you are to remain single like Jesus or Paul, this chapter tells you what kind of Christian God calls you to be as you play your part in the Church, the Bride of Christ, and devote yourself to serving your great Bridegroom.

Lesson two in God's flight school is over. We have seen how to live God's way. It's time for us to fly with our co-pilots into lesson three and to discover more about how we can love God's way.

---

[11] Having been warned repeatedly in Proverbs against being sluggards, we are warned in verse 27 in conclusion that we should not marry a woman who *eats the bread of sluggishness* either.

[12] The Hebrew word which is used in verse 26 for the *instruction* which she gives to her children is *tōrāh*, the word which normally refers to the Pentateuch or to the Old Testament as a whole. She doesn't simply give them good instruction; she gives them God's instruction.

[13] The husband in verse 29 sees his wife as the most wonderful wife of them all. All the wives in the world cannot objectively be more beautiful than one another, but they can all be so in the eyes of their husbands.

Lesson Three:

Love God's Way

(Song of Songs)

Love Song (1:1)

Solomon's Song of Songs.

(Song of Songs 1:1)

"I have always considered marriage as the most interesting event of one's life, the foundation of happiness or misery," wrote the future American president George Washington.[1] If he was right, it shouldn't surprise us that the Bible gives us eight chapters of Solomon's wisdom on how to love God's way. I say it shouldn't surprise us, because Song of Songs is probably the most shocking and debated and least understood book in the entire Bible. It's like a prize-winning Russian novel: we know it's a work of genius but that doesn't stop it from being very hard to understand in places.

Some readers actually question whether Solomon even wrote it. They point out that the first verse of the book looks like it was added to the text later,[2] and they argue that even if it wasn't, *"Solomon's Song of Songs"* could mean a song which was written *for* him rather than *by* him. They challenge whether Solomon can truly be the shepherd of 1:7 or whether he can have written so powerfully in 8:5–7 about the exclusiveness of marriage while taking for himself so many wives.[3] We will find

---

[1] George Washington wrote this in a letter to his brother-in-law Burwell Bassett on 23rd May 1785.

[2] Song of Songs 1:1 uses a different word for *"which"* from the one which is used throughout the rest of Song of Songs. However, Solomon uses both of the two words interchangeably throughout Ecclesiastes.

[3] They also point out that the poem contains several Aramaic and Persian words, forgetting that Solomon's palace was full of foreign wives and foreign visitors.

answers to those questions in the chapters which follow, but we will not find anything which forces us to ignore the plainest reading of the Song's opening verse. *Solomon's Song of Songs* was simply the normal Hebrew way of saying *Solomon's Best Song* – like calling part of the Tabernacle the *Holy of Holies* to mark it as the *Most Holy Place*, or like calling Jesus *King of kings and Lord of lords* to worship him as the *Greatest King and Lord*.[4] 1 Kings 4:32 tells us that Solomon wrote 1,005 songs, so it appears that God inspired somebody (possibly even Hezekiah's men) to choose this as the best one. He wants to use it as lesson three in his flight school.

Other readers wonder what Song of Songs is doing in the Bible at all. It doesn't mention God by name, nor is it ever quoted in the New Testament.[5] It is shockingly frank in places about lovers consummating their love. To explain this, the Jewish rabbis taught that it was an allegorical picture of God the Husband romancing Israel his Bride. Many Christian readers follow suit and view it as an allegory of Jesus the Bridegroom and the Church his Bride.[6]

Now while it is true that the relationship between the two lovers in the Song can shed some light on our walk with Jesus, let me just call a time-out right here. Are we honestly to believe that when Solomon wrote this poem he was thinking primarily about God's love for Israel and not about sex?! Are we to believe

---

[4] Failing to understand this feature of Hebrew grammar, a few commentators have argued that these eight chapters are in fact an amalgamation of several songs – literally a song of songs! They argue this because they struggle to trace a clear plot in the Song. There is one, as I shall explain in these chapters.

[5] The only other book in the Bible which doesn't mention God by name is Esther, but at least that book is clearly about the Lord saving the Jewish nation from genocide. Perhaps as a result, some older English translations find a reference to the Lord in 8:6, although most modern ones do not.

[6] The Lord uses the same Hebrew word *dōd* to describe his relationship with Israel in Isaiah 5:1 as is used to describe the *Lover* in Song of Songs, and this also links with verses such as Hosea 2:14, 19, Isaiah 62:4, Ezekiel 16:8 and Jeremiah 31:32. Similar New Testament verses about Jesus and the Church can be found in Ephesians 5:22–23 and Revelation 19:7–9.

this despite the fact that the New Testament never quotes the Song that way? Are we to believe it despite the fact that our relationship with God is described elsewhere in intimate terms but *never* in an overtly sexual way? If we really think that, we need the wisdom which is offered by the Song even more than we realize! I have actually read commentaries which argue that *"Let him kiss me"* (1:2) is all about worship and that *"My beloved is to me a sachet of myrrh resting between my breasts"* (1:13) is all about Jesus appearing between the writing of the Old and New Testaments.[7] I didn't know whether to laugh or cry.

No. Solomon's Song of Songs has been preserved in the Bible because love and marriage and sex are as important as George Washington observed. God doesn't want believers to get their teaching on sex from movies or from rap lyrics or from awkward conversations with their friends. He has given us this book as lesson three in his flight school because it is one thing to find a co-pilot and quite another thing to learn to fly together. The idea that some parts of life do not matter to God is the very folly which the book of Proverbs sought to expose. When theologians and preachers feel uncomfortable and run to the safe ground of allegory, they simply prove how much we desperately need to be shaped by what Solomon's best song has to say. We don't have to drink out of the dirty ditch of a culture which is obsessed with sex but has lost sight of how it fits with love and marriage. Solomon has given us this divinely inspired teaching on how we are to love and make love God's way.

In 1:2–2:7, we will read about two lovers longing from a distance as they romance each other before their wedding day. In 2:8–3:5, we will read about their excitement and expectation as their wedding day approaches, before 3:6–5:1 describes what happens on their wedding day and wedding night. In 5:2–6:3, we will discover the highs and lows of love and sex within

---

[7] I am honestly not joking. They also argue that the cooing of doves in 2:12 refers to the preaching of the apostles and that *"the mountain of myrrh"* in 4:6 refers to Calvary!

marriage, before a promise in 6:4–8:4 that they should get better and better with the passing of time. This builds towards 8:5–14 and the conclusion to the Song, which tells us how to love God's way and how to enjoy his gift of sex to the full.

Queen Victoria is famous for her black clothes and her dour statement that *"We are not amused."* Along with the rest of Victorian Britain, she tends to be treated as the perfect picture of a pent-up prude when it comes to sexual love. However, even she wrote in her diary after her wedding night that

> *I **never, never** spent such an evening!! My **dearest dearest dear** Albert sat on a footstool by my side, and his excessive love and affection gave me feelings of heavenly love and happiness, I never could have **hoped** to have felt before! He clasped me in his arms, and we kissed each other again and again... To lie by his side, and in his arms, and on his dear bosom, and be called by names of tenderness, I have never yet heard used to me before – was bliss beyond belief! Oh! this was the happiest day of my life!*[8]

So if even Queen Victoria was not as scared of God's gift of sex as many church leaders and theologians, it is time for us to read and re-read Solomon's best love song. It's time for us to rediscover how God created love and sex as pure gifts to be enjoyed with the right person in the right context in the right way and for the rest of our lives.[9] It's time for us to read Solomon's Song of Songs. It's time for us to learn to love God's way.

---

[8] Queen Victoria wrote this in her journal on her wedding night, Monday 10th February 1840. Her journal can still be viewed at Windsor Castle.

[9] Hebrews 13:4 tells us that the marriage bed needs merely to be *kept* pure, not made pure.

From a Distance (1:2–2:7)

Daughters of Jerusalem, I charge you by the gazelles and by the does of the field: Do not arouse or awaken love until it so desires.

(Song of Songs 2:7)

Have you ever been to watch an enjoyable movie but found it hard to keep up with the plot? Reading Song of Songs can feel a bit like that at times. That's why it pays to know a little Hebrew. Unlike English, many Hebrew adjectives and verbs have special endings which serve as signposts as to whether the subject is masculine or feminine, singular or plural. When English translations divide the text into *his* lines, *her* lines and *their* lines, they do so based on these word endings alone. Those little details in Hebrew help us grasp that this love song is a duet between a boy and a girl, with their excited friends interjecting their own encouragements based on what the two lovers say.

The girl speaks first in 1:2–4. Unlike the book of Proverbs, which was male-focused and addressed fathers and sons and husbands and kings, we find that Song of Songs is much more even and that the girl actually sings more lines than the boy. She refers to her friends as *'alāmōth* or *virgins*, but she does not hide her longing to surrender her virginity to this boy. She uses a word to describe his love being better than wine that is more accurately translated that his *love-making* is better than wine.[1] Although the message in many churches seems to be

---

[1] *Dōdīm* is the same word which the adulteress used for love-making in Proverbs 7:18 and which the Lord uses to refer to love-making in Ezekiel 16:8 and 23:17.

that sex is a dirty and disgusting thing which we should save for the person that we marry, the girl in the Song hasn't fallen for that wrong view of sex at all! She is still a virgin like her friends but she longs to kiss the boy in verse 2, and for him to offer her a royal wedding and his royal bedchamber as quickly as possible in verse 4.

The girl's friends respond in the second half of 1:4, and they are not at all shocked by her frank declaration of her love. They use the same word for love-making to tell the girl that they delight in her (feminine), that they agree his love-making must be wonderful (masculine), and that she is quite right to adore him (masculine). They agree with what she said in verse 3 about the boy being the pin-up of all the teenage girls in Israel. They encourage her to view love and sex and marriage as a great gift, and they rejoice that she doesn't shy away from expressing her feelings.

The girl speaks again in 1:5–7, and she reveals a major problem. For all her words, she has done no more than admire the boy from afar. She isn't even sure if he will find her attractive because she has been forced to work in the family vineyard and doesn't have the fair skin which the noblewomen of Israel flaunted as a badge of honour.[2] She asks the boy to set a time for them to meet properly so that she can find out without having to act like one of the prostitutes who used to seduce shepherds away from their friends.[3]

The girl's friends – she just described them as the

---

[2] *Kedar* refers to nomadic Arabs. Since Solomon's love-making was likened to *wine* in verse 2, it is fitting that she describes her body as a *vineyard* where he can enjoy his wine.

[3] Genesis 38:13–15. Some readers are surprised to find Solomon out with the flocks here, despite the fact that his father was originally a shepherd. One of the strangest theories some of them propose is that the Song describes a love triangle between a shepherdess, a shepherd-boy and the wicked King Solomon who tries to seduce her away. Quite apart from the fact that Solomon would not cast himself in the role of villain, the concept of a love triangle is an anachronism. It only appears as a relatively modern theme in literature.

"daughters of Jerusalem" – interject again in 1:8. They show us how we should also encourage one another. They tell the girl to believe she is very beautiful and to stop waiting for the boy to make the first move. If she loves him, she needs to find him and tell him so.

The boy sings his first lines in 1:9–11, as he tells the girl that he has been longing from a distance too. Even though his ancient compliments sound strange to our Western ears, we can still grasp what he is saying. He is saying that her body looks as toned as Pharaoh's finest female horse and that, however great she looks in her earrings and necklace, she will look even better when he gives her presents from his royal treasury.

This leads into a quick-fire conversation between the boy and girl. She uses evocative language to tell him in 1:12–14 that she is overwhelmed by the smell of both of their perfumes. She longs for him to rest himself on her breasts all night long,[4] and when he compliments her in 1:15 she promises that their bed together would be lush and fruitful. There are no verbs in the Hebrew text of 1:16–17, so we should understand their talk about a lush and evergreen house to be them starting to dream about their wedding day together. Their nervous conversation is looking very promising indeed until the girl presents a problem.

She is aware that Solomon is the king and can have his pick of 10,000 beautiful women. She feels like a common flower from the plain of Sharon or from the valleys in 2:1 – one of many million virgins who might catch his eye.[5] When he tells her in 2:2 that, to him, she is like a lily and every other girl an ugly thorn, she can hardly contain her joy. She tells him in 2:3–7 that if she is a lily among thorns then, to her, he is the best tree in

---

[4] She is not promising him sex before marriage. Psalm 45:8 tells us that *myrrh* was the expensive perfume used for a royal bridegroom on his wedding day.

[5] The flower we call the Rose of Sharon is very beautiful, so many readers assume that she is paying herself a compliment. However, the Hebrew word she uses probably means a common *crocus*.

the forest. She longs for him to invite her into his banqueting hall[6] so that they can have a public date together, and she longs for the day when she can lie down in his embrace. She almost faints with anticipation in 2:5, so she finally checks herself in 2:7. She tells her friends not to let her *"arouse or awaken love until it so desires"*. True love waits for love-making in its proper place and time. Until then, they will continue their longing from a distance.

Hopefully the love lessons in this first section are quite clear. Romantic desire is good and we should not let etiquette, fear or insecurity prevent us from expressing our feelings to one another. Marriage is also good, the exciting consummation of true love, so we must not let our commitment-shy culture bully us into thinking otherwise.

This should be spiritual lesson enough, but if you are desperate to find a parallel in the passage to stir your worship for Jesus, you won't be disappointed. The perfume which the girl describes spreading its fragrance around the king at his table in 1:12 is specifically *nard* in Hebrew. This passage may well have been Mary of Bethany's inspiration when she anointed Jesus with nard as he sat at table in Mark 14:3 and John 12:2–3. If so, we would not be stretching the passage too far to believe that Jesus accepts us in spite of our sin in 1:5 and sees us as beautiful new creations in 2:2. We should worship him with the same abandon as Mary of Bethany.

What a love song. What a lover. And the great news is that this romance has only just begun.

---

[6] The Hebrew for *banqueting hall* is literally *house of wine*. This is another reference to her longing for the love-making she described back in 1:2.

Waiting for the Day (2:8–3:5)

The fig tree forms its early fruit; the blossoming vines spread their fragrance. Arise, come, my darling; my beautiful one, come with me.

(Song of Songs 2:13)

Solomon didn't divide his Song into chapters and verses. Those divisions were not added to the text of the Bible until the Middle Ages, as a study aid for much more recent readers.[1] Instead, Solomon signifies breaks in the story through repeating a chorus which calls us not to awaken love until it so desires. It signified the end of the first dialogue in 2:7, it signifies the end of this second dialogue in 3:5, and it will signify the end of the fifth dialogue in 8:4.[2] Solomon therefore marks off these verses as the second section of his Song. They describe the two lovers as they wait for their wedding day to finally come.

At only fifteen verses long, the second dialogue is in fact the shortest of the five, but it feels like the longest section of the Song to the girl as she waits for summer to come so that she and Solomon can enjoy their royal wedding.[3] She speaks thirteen of the fifteen verses, and this section focuses much more on her

---

1 An Englishman divided the Bible into chapters in 1227. A Jewish rabbi divided the Old Testament further into verses in 1448, and a Frenchman did the same to the New Testament in 1551.

2 The third and fourth dialogues take place after the lovers' wedding day, so they end not with a call to wait for the consummation of their love, but with them actually enjoying doing so.

3 Solomon doesn't name himself on purpose in this section because he wants to make it easy for us to see ourselves in the characters in the Song. He is referred to by name elsewhere in 1:5; 3:7, 9, 11 and 8:11–12, and he is referred to simply as *the king* in 1:4, 12 and 7:5.

feelings during the waiting period than it does on his. Perhaps that's because most girls tend to start thinking about their wedding day much earlier on in a relationship than most boys. The novelist Jane Austen observes that *"A lady's imagination is very rapid, it jumps from admiration to love, from love to matrimony, in a moment."*[4] Our culture may despise this, but Solomon wants us to grasp that it is actually very godly. God gave us the pull of romance and the push of desire in order to lead us by both hands towards the blessing of a happy marriage.

Even a powerful king like Solomon could not speed up the passing of time. The girl begins the second section of the Song in 2:8–13 by rejoicing that winter has given way to spring and so their wedding date is near. These verses are the Old Testament equivalent of Romeo and Juliet's famous balcony scene. The girl is cooped up in her father's house (the word used for *virgin* in 1:3 means literally *hidden one*, and she has already told us in 1:7 that in her culture an unmarried girl out on her own without an escort would be mistaken for a prostitute) so she can only look out through the lattice of her window to see if Solomon is gazing up at her window as impatiently as she is looking down. When he arrives, she compares him to a fit gazelle or stag leaping over the mountains. She tells us she can hear his voice encouraging her that winter is over and that the flowers, birdsongs and fruit trees all proclaim that their wedding day is near.[5] He isn't put off by the fact she is so eager. In fact, he encourages her.

Nevertheless, an air of caution is introduced into the Song by all this talk of love having different *seasons*. Anyone who has cultivated a vine or an apple tree will tell you that cold winters are essential if the tree is to yield a bumper crop in summer. In the same way, love's season of waiting is a time which determines how enjoyable the early days of marriage are going to be.

[4] Jane Austen in her great romantic novel *Pride and Prejudice* (1813).

[5] The mention of *vines* and *vineyards* in 2:13 and 15 refers back to the comparison between *wine* and *love-making* in 1:2. Solomon tells the girl that the vines are blossoming in anticipation of their soon drinking their wine.

Besotted though they are with one another, these two lovers never say "We're engaged now, so why wait for marriage?"[6] They remind us through the refrain of 2:7 and 3:5 that dating and engagement aren't just an arduous hold-up in proceedings, but important seasons in themselves. This is the period when a couple learn to communicate, to miss each other, to make room for each other, and to make sacrifices for each other. How we act in this period can determine whether marriage and sex will feel like heaven or hell in our early married years. God didn't tell us to save sex for marriage because he wants to frustrate us. He did so because the season of waiting is what helps a couple to build a strong relationship together before they make love.

The boy calls up to the girl's balcony in 2:14–15, telling her that he can barely wait for their wedding day either. He longs to gaze at her and to listen to the sound of her voice, and the word he uses to describe her appearance refers not just to her face but to the rest of her body too.[7] Provided that we wait until we marry before we begin to explore it, there is nothing wrong with being captivated by the sight of our loved one's body![8] The girl compared love-making to wine in 1:2 and her body to a vineyard in 1:6, so he tells her to get her vineyard ready because springtime has come and her body is in bloom. She needs to get it ready for harvest time, when he is finally allowed to enjoy its fruit.

The girl shouts back down to him in 2:16–17 that she is completely his, even as he is completely hers.[9] She tells him

[6] Even when she has an erotic dream in 3:1–4, the girl imagines herself taking Solomon back to her mother's house and bedroom – something which an Israelite bride did on her wedding day.

[7] The normal Hebrew word for *face* is *pānīm*, but instead he refers twice to her *mar'eh* in 2:14. The word means *appearance* and is the same word which the girl uses for the whole of Solomon's body in 5:15.

[8] Christian purity is about containing our desires, not about denying those which are God-given desires.

[9] Her reference to him *browsing among the lilies* should be read as a Hebrew future tense. It points back to the fact that he chose her in 2:1–2 and that he will

to go on his way now that she has seen him and to act like the fit gazelle and stag she compared him to in 2:9. She goes back inside her bedroom and goes to sleep in 3:1–4, only to dream about the future when they can finally spend the night together. She doesn't need to be explicit that this is a dream because no unmarried woman in her culture could ever actually go out in the streets of Jerusalem alone at night. The speed of the action and the similarity of these verses to the dream sequence of 5:2–8 also confirm this.[10] She wakes up so aroused that she cries out to her friends the same refrain again in 3:5 – probably as much for her own benefit as theirs – *"Do not arouse or awaken love until it so desires."* The girl aches with desire for her fiancé. Winter has passed and spring is here, but she can't wait for it to be their summer.

Solomon is talking about love and sex and marriage, not about our trying to see Jesus through the lattice-work during our devotional times with God! However, we are part of the Bride of Christ and we should feel this same sense of aching for the return of our Bridegroom and for the consummation of the age. Let's not be outdone by the girl's longing for her bridegroom king while she waits for the day when her dreams will come true.[11] We have an even better Bridegroom and we are waiting for an even better Day.

get to enjoy the most intimate parts of her body in 6:2–3 and 7:2.

[10] So does the fact she wants to make love to him in her mother's house in 3:4. Sex before marriage was punishable by death (Deuteronomy 22:13–24) so this was the last place she would bring him before their wedding day.

[11] For example, we should also deal with areas of sin (2:15), sing words which express our exclusive love for Jesus (2:16), and ignore what any critics who witness our intense devotion may say (3:1–4).

Wedding Day and Wedding Night (3:6–5:1)

> *Look on King Solomon... on the day of his wedding, the day his heart rejoiced.*
>
> (Song of Songs 3:10)

Everybody loves a royal wedding. It's estimated that over a billion people around the world tuned in on 29th April 2011 to watch at least part of the royal wedding between Prince William and Kate Middleton. Almost 3 million Facebook status updates talked about them, as did over 10 million tweets on Twitter. We all love a royal wedding, and we are about to get one in the third section of Song of Songs.

The girl describes with excitement how it feels to watch Solomon arriving for the ceremony in his wedding carriage. Prince William arrived at Westminster Abbey in a specially designed twenty-foot-long Bentley, but this could not compare with the spectacle which she describes in 3:6–10. The carriage is made of cedar wood and gold and silver, upholstered with fine purple cloth, but the best thing about it is not its decoration but *"its interior inlaid with love"*. As the smoke of the billowing dust and burning incense begins to clear,[1] she gets excited that he is so happy to be marrying her. She calls her friends to come out and look, not at the carriage or the sixty guards who flank it, but

---

[1] There is nothing effeminate about Solomon using perfume. It was the equivalent of deodorant for a rich nobleman in the hot Middle East. It also pointed to Matthew 2:11 and the greater Messiah who was to come.

at the way that King Solomon is dressed for the happiest day of his life – for *"the day of his wedding, the day his heart rejoiced"*.[2]

Solomon replies as he gets down from his carriage in 4:1–15. From now on it is mainly he who does the talking in this third section, reassuring her that she is every bit as beautiful as he promised her in 2:2 and 2:14. As guys, we need to learn from the way that he uses skilful words to melt and captivate his bride's heart. When Kate reached the altar at Westminster Abbey, Prince William could be seen to mouth to her *"You look beautiful!"*, but Solomon goes one better. He doesn't merely tell his bride that she looks beautiful in general, but lists specific observations which reveal that he has spent the days waiting for their wedding day looking at her body and feeding the desire that God has placed for her inside his soul.

Solomon's poetry seems quite strange to our twenty-first-century ears, even laughable in places, but something similar can be found in many other surviving love poems of the period. He compliments her bright eyes behind her wedding veil,[3] her long black hair,[4] her perfect white teeth,[5] her lips and mouth, her cheekbones,[6] her neck and her breasts. Since he started with the top of her head and moved downwards to her breasts, we ought to understand his reference to *lilies*, to *the mountain of myrrh* and to *the hill of incense* to mean somewhere even lower

---

[2] Some readers try to argue that the Song is not about Solomon and his bride, but about everyman and everywoman. Verses such as 3:10 show us that this view doesn't fit with the words of the Song.

[3] This compliment is actually a repeat of what he said in 1:15. We do not need to be original every time we praise our partner's looks, just sincere and genuine in what we say.

[4] It is like a flock of black goats going down from a high mountain together.

[5] Some brides did not have all their teeth in the days before toothpaste and modern dentistry. For all of them to still be as white as newly shorn sheep was even more exceptional.

[6] 1 Peter 3:1–6 warns women not to neglect the cultivation of inner beauty, but it doesn't tell them not to attend to their outer beauty at all. The bride appears to be using red lipstick and red blusher in 4:3, even as she also wears earrings and a necklace in 1:10.

down that he will discover later on that evening. The girl was worried in 1:5 and 2:1 that she might not be beautiful enough to be his royal bride, but he reassures her with carefully chosen words as soon as he sees her.[7]

Having promised to make love to her all night long in 4:6, he now talks to her about their wedding night in 4:8–15.[8] He repeats the Song's recurring theme by telling her that making love to her will be sweeter than wine, but then he amplifies the theme by telling her that it will also be sweeter than fine perfume and spices, milk and honey, fresh fruit and fresh water. He asks her to come close and tells her literally in 4:13 that she is his own private *paradise*.[9] When he rejoices that she is a virgin – a *locked up garden* – and that they have waited for their wedding night to make love for the first time, she can't contain her gratitude either.[10] Their wedding day is over and their wedding night has begun by the time she tells him in 4:16 to *"come into his garden and enjoy its choice fruits"*.[11] This third section ends in the first half of 5:1 with Solomon's excitement that they have just made love and that he has finally enjoyed

[7] Solomon calls her flawless in 4:7, even though 1:5 told us that her culture's view of beauty said her body was flawed. He is telling her that, in his eyes at least, she simply couldn't look better. He doesn't treat her mean to keep her keen, but tells her in 4:9 that one glance is all it takes for her to steal his heart.

[8] We find it strange that Solomon calls his new bride his *sister*, but this was not uncommon in Middle Eastern love poetry. The Song may be reminding us that the best lovers are first and foremost best friends.

[9] The reference to Lebanon and its high mountains in 4:8 need not mean that the girl was Lebanese. Solomon may simply be saying that she has seemed so far away until today that now he wants her very close.

[10] Our culture despises virginity – think of the movie *The 40-Year-Old Virgin* – but the Song tells us that virginity is a very sacred thing. There is nothing better than to save it for your wedding night.

[11] Note that 4:16–5:1 agrees with 1 Corinthians 7:3–5 that a wife's body belongs to her husband and that a husband's body belongs to his wife. Deliberately to withhold sex from one another is a form of theft.

her garden with its myrrh, spices, milk and wine.[12] In the second half of 5:1, the girl's friends have the last word as they celebrate sex in its proper context.[13] They encourage the newlyweds literally to *get drunk* on their love-making together. Their time of waiting is over. Harvest time has now begun.

One of my friends had a disappointing experience on his wedding night. He arrived at the hotel and discovered that he and his new bride had been given a twin room with narrow beds and dirty sheets. He naturally complained, but Solomon wants to challenge us whether we are putting up with a shabby marriage bed ourselves.

He doesn't want us to spoil our future wedding night by experimenting with sex beforehand. If we are married, he doesn't want us to accept the view among some Christians that sex is dirty and should not be celebrated with the happy laughter of 5:1. He doesn't want us to settle for second-rate marriages because we fail to stoke the flames of our romance by speaking specific words of encouragement like the ones he models for us in 4:1–7. He doesn't want us to forget that sex within marriage is a treasure worth far more than all the jewels possessed by the British royal family.

If you have already polluted your wedding bed, Solomon wants want you to read these words in faith that it can yet be cleansed through faith in the blood which was shed by the true and better Bridegroom. Kate Middleton was born a commoner but her Sarah Burton wedding dress transformed her into a princess. Do you honestly think that a pricey dress from a London fashion house might be better at covering a bride's blemishes than the priceless blood of Jesus is able to cover

---

[12] Solomon teaches husbands not to charm their wives into sex and then simply roll over and start snoring afterwards. He is just as charming after making love in 5:1 because he genuinely loves his bride.

[13] Hebrew poetry expressed its beauty through symmetry. Note therefore that the lovers consummate their marriage 111 lines into the Song and 111 lines away from the end.

yours? No. Whoever you are and whatever you have done, Jesus will forgive you, cleanse you and restore you to the picture of sexual purity which Solomon sings about in this Song: *"You are altogether beautiful, my darling; there is no flaw in you."*[14]

[14] 1 John 1:8–9 tells us that Jesus doesn't merely forgive us for our sin. He also cleanses its filth away too.

The Wake-Up Call (5:2–6:3)

I have taken off my robe – must I put it on again? I have washed my feet – must I soil them again?

(Song of Songs 5:3)

Lady Hillingham wrote in her diary in 1912: *"I am happy now that Charles calls on my bedchamber less frequently than of old. As it is, I now endure but two calls a week and when I hear his steps outside my door I lie down on my bed, close my eyes, open my legs and think of England."*[1] Perhaps that's why the fourth section of Song of Songs is a completely female affair. Solomon plays an active role in 5:2–6:3 because both husband and wife must take responsibility for the state of their marriage, yet he doesn't speak in order to leave the focus on his bride. It appears that several months or even years have passed since the excitement of their wedding day. This section warns us that love and sex and marriage need to be protected and nourished if we are to keep enjoying them as God intends.

The fourth dialogue begins with Solomon's wife having a second dream, this time as a married woman.[2] She dreams that Solomon comes to her room in the palace complex and tries to get into her bedroom to make love to her again.[3] She is slow

---

[1] Quoted from her diary by Jonathan Gathorne-Hardy in *The Rise and Fall of the British Nanny* (1972).

[2] She tells us it was a dream in 5:2, and it would have been unthinkable for a queen to walk the streets of Jerusalem alone at night, let alone for her to be attacked by the night watchmen.

[3] This and 6:8 are the only two clues in the Song that Solomon took other wives besides the girl. She had her own room in a palace full of other wives too, but this is downplayed to help us identify with the two lovers.

to respond because the routine of life has begun to put out the fire of love which she expressed in the earlier chapters. The French writer Honoré de Balzac observed that *"Marriage must contend unceasingly with a monster which devours everything: familiarity."*[4] She illustrates what Balzac means by complaining in her dream that she is in bed and doesn't want to get dressed, and that she has had a bath and doesn't want to get dirty again.[5] By the time she remembers how magnificent their love-making can be and opens the door excitedly, her husband has gone.[6] She has missed the moment and she is so mortified that she hunts through the dark streets of Jerusalem to find him.

If you are a husband, these verses were not written to justify your complaints that your wife is not as interested in sex as you are. Sorry. The problem in this chapter is that Solomon makes a move but doesn't persevere when his wife takes longer than expected to become aroused. A wise husband understands that arousing his wife can take time in the midst of running a home, pursuing a career and looking after children. In the classic sitcom *I Love Lucy*, it is Lucille Ball and not her husband who complains that *"Ever since we said 'I do', there are so many things we don't."*[7] If your marriage has become routine and joyless and unphysical, the solution is not to complain about your wife. It is to persevere as Solomon should have in this fourth section of the Song, and it is to keep romancing your wife as Solomon does in the fifth section. Husbands with really good wives are often those who have taken personal responsibility to keep on loving God's way.

For now, however, the main focus of this fourth section

---

4 Balzac wrote this in his treatise *The Physiology of Marriage* (1829).

5 The word translated *feet* in 5:3 is a Hebrew euphemism for the woman's private parts, so she is saying that she doesn't want to make love because she doesn't want to have to take another bath.

6 The *dripping myrrh* on her fingers in 5:5 links back to her *mountain of myrrh* in 4:6. She is so excited that her body is ready for love-making by the time she opens the door.

7 *I Love Lucy*, Season 1, Episode 1 (1951).

of the Song is on the wife and how she feels long after the last piece of the wedding cake has been eaten. It tells us that wives are responsible for the health of their marriage too. She has become so entangled with the stuff of life that her husband is no longer centre-stage, but as soon as she shifts her focus away from her to-do lists and back onto him she starts to rekindle her love's flame. If you are a wife, don't make the same mistake as Solomon's bride in her dream in 5:2–8 by failing to adore the husband you have until you lose him. Make a conscious decision to focus on his best qualities, no matter how many or few they may be, and you will find that your love is rekindled, just as hers is when she follows her friends' advice in 5:9 and begins to describe what made her fall in love with him. Her words in 5:10–16 are the counterpart to his description of her in 4:1–7. She describes his face, head, hair, eyes, cheeks, lips, arms, torso, legs, stature and mouth – and then finishes by saying that despite his being so handsome, he is first and foremost her best friend. Husbands have a responsibility to keep their bodies in shape and to have the godly character which attracts a wife far more than mere externals.[8] But wives also have a responsibility to feed their eyes and their thought lives on their husbands.

The Song reminds wives what they will get to enjoy if they treat this dream as a wake-up call and persevere in loving God's way. By the time her friends offer to help her find her husband in 6:1, she has already found him. She ends this section by describing in 6:2–3 how he has returned to persist in his advances towards her and how this time she has happily agreed. Lady Hillingham's description of sex as a conjugal chore for women is a million miles away from this celebration of femininity as God intends it. The same God who created the clitoris, which has no biological use except to give a woman sexual pleasure, wants to teach you to delight in being in the bedroom with your husband. She is not

[8] Note that Solomon's descriptions of his wife in 4:1–7 and 7:1–9 focus on her tender feminine beauty, whereas her description of him focuses on his manly strength and energy.

lying back and thinking of Israel, but restating that she belongs to him and he belongs to her. She is enjoying the fact that he has gone back inside her garden and she closes the section with excitement that once again he is *browsing among her lilies.*[9]

If you are single, this passage should encourage you that the grass isn't always greener on the other side. Relationship misunderstandings and sexual frustration are often married people's issues too. If you are a husband, this passage should remind you to persevere and help your wife to move out of the shallows of mundane matrimony into the deep end of enduring and life-consuming love.

But if you are a wife, this passage is particularly for you. It should serve as a wake-up call to stop you from making the same mistakes as Solomon's wife in her dream, or the same mistake as millions of married women across the world today. The British philosopher Bertrand Russell speculated that *"the total amount of undesired sex endured by women is probably greater in marriage than in prostitution".*[10] Don't be a reluctant lover, so consumed with your jobs and household tasks that you neglect to let your husband into your garden. Set a date night. Put a lock on the door. Get a cleaner. Do whatever it takes. Let this wake-up call cause you to set your heart on discovering in a new way every day what it means to spend your entire life learning to love God's way.

[9] We saw earlier that *lilies* probably refers to the wife's private parts, so 5:13 is probably a reference to very intimate kissing. This ties in with her reference to *garden**s*** in 6:2, speaking of variety in how they make love.

[10] Bertrand Russell in *Marriage and Morals* (1929).

Vintage Love (6:4–8:4)

At our door is every delicacy, both new and old, that I have stored up for you, my beloved.

(Song of Songs 7:13)

Vintage wine sells at astronomical prices. Most wine buffs I know swear that the greatest of them all is a vintage Bordeaux from 1945 called the Château Mouton Rothschild. It's seventy years old but don't let that fool you into thinking that it has lost any of its taste with the passing of time. A twelve-bottle case of it sold at an auction in Hong Kong in 2010 for over US$200,000.

Perhaps that's why Song of Songs repeatedly compares love and sex to wine. It simply won't accept our culture's pessimistic expectation that marriage and sex will get worse as we get older. Frank Sinatra quipped that *"A man doesn't know what happiness is until he's married. By then it's too late."*[1] Mike Myers warns his best friend in the movie *"Wayne's World"* that *"Garth, marriage is punishment for shoplifting in some countries."*[2] The fifth section of the Song sets out to end such foolish pessimism in 6:4–8:4. Solomon and his wife are now many years into their marriage and they show us what vintage love can be like if we learn to love God's way.

Much has changed between Solomon describing his wife on their wedding day in 4:1–7 and his doing so again in 6:4–7:9. He confesses that he now has sixty wives and eighty concubines,[3]

---

[1] He said this in the movie *The Joker Is Wild* (Paramount, 1957).

[2] *Wayne's World* (Paramount, 1992).

[3] This dates this part of the Song to about 950 BC, probably 20 years into their marriage. In the backslidden last two decades of his reign he increased this to 700 wives and 300 concubines (1 Kings 11:3).

but despite this sin (more on that next, in Ecclesiastes) he is still as captivated by his first love as he ever was before.[4] He still compliments her eyes, her long black hair, her perfect white teeth and her cheekbones in 6:4–9, just as he did back in 4:1–7. His wife's friends interject in 6:10 and in the first half of 6:13,[5] but he returns to his description of her body in 7:1–9, only this time he starts with her feet and works upwards. He compliments her feet, her legs, her private parts, her breasts, her white neck, her eyes, her straight nose, her head and her hair. Far from finding her body less attractive with the passing of time, he tells her that, to him at least, it looks even better. She bore herself like a commoner when he first met her, but they have grown together and he tells her in 7:1 that she now moves her limbs with the bearing of a *prince's daughter*. He loves the fact that he knows her body so well, and wouldn't swap it for any of the teenage virgins of Israel whose looks are two-a-penny (6:8–9).[6]

If you are a husband, this is a lesson in how to grow old with your wife and enjoy the taste of vintage love. First, Solomon doesn't describe her body ("you are five foot six and wear a size-eight dress") so much as describe the way he *feels* about her body ("I get a bit scared because you take my breath away").[7] Bodies change but feelings needn't if we make the same covenant with our eyes as Job did in Job 31:1. If we want to

---

[4] The main reason some readers question whether Solomon truly wrote Song of Songs is that his polygamy ought to disqualify him to speak on marriage. Yet 6:8 insists that Solomon really wrote this book. His wisdom was God-given and it should sober us that he himself forgot it and became the fool of Ecclesiastes.

[5] *Shūlamīth* in 6:13 is simply the feminine form of the name Solomon. Rather than translating it *Shulammite*, we ought to see it as a pet name for Solomon's little *Solomina*.

[6] He compares her to *Tirzah*, meaning *Delightful*, the old capital city of Israel, and to *Jerusalem*, the ancient capital of Judah. Like Rome or Venice, her beauty just gets classier with the passing of the years.

[7] Solomon says this in 6:4–5. This communication of feelings rather than facts is best seen in the way he compares her jet black hair to a *royal tapestry* in 7:5.

delight in the wife of our youth as Solomon told us to in Proverbs 5:18–19, we need to keep our eyes off other girls to make our wife our shifting definition of true beauty. Second, Solomon's enjoyment of sex doesn't make him neglect the whole scope of what marriage ought to be. He makes great conversation, builds deep friendship, is very happy simply kissing,[8] and wants to explore her entire body with his very patient foreplay. They have great sex because they love each other so deeply. Don't fall for our culture's lie that it ever works the other way around.

Solomon's wife gets to speak in the second half of 7:9 and she completes the rest of this section of the Song. She eagerly consents to his kisses, tells him she is still completely his, and expresses her delight that he still wants her even after all these years. Solomon was surprised in 6:11–12 and 7:8 that examining her body reignited his desire to keep drinking from her vineyard, and we can tell that listening to his words has had the same effect on her.[9] She asks him to take her away from the busyness of the palace to explore the wine of their love-making undisturbed.[10] Perhaps the key verse in this fifth section of the Song is her promise of vintage love in 7:13.[11] She tells him that their years of love-making have taught her exactly what he likes, so she can guarantee him *"every delicacy, both new and old, that I have stored up for you, my beloved"*.[12]

The two lovers escape to their private getaway and

---

[8] The word for mouth in 7:9 is *hēk*, which means literally the roof of her mouth. See also 4:11.

[9] This is important. If we wait until we are "in the mood" before making love, it might not happen. If we set time aside to make it happen, speaking loving words to one another can always get us in the mood.

[10] This isn't being pushy. Solomon tells wives that if they want their husband to do something, they should go ahead and ask him!

[11] When she talks about the blossoming vines in her vineyard in 7:12, she uses the same word *dōđım* to promise that their *love-making* will be better than the wine which she compared it to in 1:2.

[12] *Mandrakes* were a plant associated with fertility (Genesis 30:14–17) and the Hebrew word for them is *dūdāʾım*, which sounds very similar to *dōđım* or *love-making*.

discover that their love-making is all they hoped that it would be. It makes Solomon's wife wish in 8:1–2 that she could have him all to herself a lot more often, far away from the prying eyes of the courtiers in the palace and the busyness of Jerusalem.[13] Vintage wine isn't simply wine that is old, it is wine which has been lovingly preserved. We should learn from these verses to schedule date nights, unhurried hours alone, and weekends away without the children. This fifth section ends with Solomon's wife repeating the refrain that we must not awaken love until it so desires. Since love and sex can be this good after years of marriage, we must save sex for marriage, make time for sex in marriage, and guard sex like a fine wine which gets better and better with each passing year.

If we do this, we will defy the marriage cynics, like Frank Sinatra and Mike Myers. We will find that marriage isn't a disappointing main course after a delicious hors d'oeuvre, but rather the kind of dessert which keeps us wanting to come back for more and more. This of course makes sense, since Ephesians 5 says that our marriages are a picture of Jesus' union with the Church for evermore. Jesus opened his ministry with a wine-based miracle which provoked onlookers to comment that *you have saved the best till last.*[14] We will find this to be true in our marriages as well as when we reign alongside Jesus the royal Bridegroom as his eternally loved Bride.

So enjoy the way that your marriage improves with each year and becomes like a vintage wine. As you do so, you proclaim to the world that Jesus isn't tired of his Church and that he still promises his People that the best is yet to come.

---

[13] It seems very strange to us that she wishes Solomon were her brother, but she is simply saying that she wishes they could kiss and show their affection in public, something married couples couldn't do.

[14] John 2:1–11.

Love's Conclusion (8:5–14)

Many waters cannot quench love; rivers cannot sweep it away. If one were to give all the wealth of one's house for love, it would be utterly scorned.

(Song of Songs 8:7)

I have a board game which I play with my children in which you have to guess objects from ridiculously close-up photos. You can only see a very small part of the object and it is normally magnified many, many times. The objects are fiendishly difficult to guess until you flip over the card and see the object through a normal lens. That's what Solomon tries to do in the conclusion to his Song in 8:5–14. He soars away from the detail to give us an overview of what he has taught us about how to love God's way.

Song of Songs 8:5 reminds us that we have learned that *love is immensely significant*. The woman's friends sing the first half of the verse and what they describe is a very commonplace sight: a boy and a girl walking along with their arms around one another. The woman picks up the song in the second half of the verse and reminds us that this commonplace sight is in fact extremely holy. She talks about Solomon's mother conceiving him – a thought which is likely to dampen his mood for romance rather than kindle it! – but she mentions his mother for a reason. She points out that the previous generation saw people fall in love, get married, make love and have children; they are now repeating what their parents did, and they will conceive children of their own to repeat the cycle. Let's not allow our highly individualistic culture to blind us to the obvious point that Solomon's wife is making: the choices we make about love and marriage and sex are some of the most destiny-laden choices we will make in our entire lives. When we talk of love, we are talking about shaping human history.

That's why it shouldn't surprise us that a book of the Bible is devoted to teaching us how to love God's way. It doesn't matter that the book does not refer to God by name; his handiwork as love's Creator shines through on every page.[1] If Agur admitted that he couldn't understand love in Proverbs 30:18–19, and if even the great detective Sherlock Holmes confessed that *"Woman's heart and mind are insoluble puzzles to the male,"*[2] it should excite us that God has invited us to travel on a journey of discovery with his Holy Spirit and Song of Songs as our guide. The fact that Solomon wrote the book and yet mismanaged his own journey is a sobering reminder that love deserves our passionate attention.

Song of Songs 8:6 reminds us that we have learned that *love is immensely powerful.* It can make a king pine for a glimpse of a commoner on her balcony and it can catapult a peasant girl from the fields to the palace. Solomon's wife knows this from personal experience and she reminds us that *"Love is as strong as death, its jealousy unyielding as the grave."*[3] It is as powerful as a blazing fire and able to resist a mighty torrent.[4] Lovers would rather die than relinquish it, and jealous husbands and wives would rather kill than forgive those who intrude on it. God has given it to us in order to point to Jesus' love for his

[1] Some older English translations find a reference to the Lord in 8:6. I am not convinced but it would be nice to believe them, because if God ignited the flame of love, it means we can trust him to help keep it alive.

[2] Sherlock Holmes says this to Dr. Watson in Sir Arthur Conan Doyle's "The Adventure of the Illustrious Client" (1925).

[3] Her desire to become a *seal* on Solomon's heart in 8:6 means that she wants to stamp her exclusive ownership on his affections (2:16; 6:3; 7:10). With rival queens at the palace, she wants to bar access to anybody else.

[4] We should turn the first half of 8:7 into a prayer because God is able to protect our marriages from the raging power of neglect, adultery and divorce.

Church, so it shouldn't surprise us that it carries awesome power. Human love is second only to the divine love of Jesus himself, which proved even stronger than death and even more unyielding than the grave.

Song of Songs 8:7 reminds us that we have learned that *love is immensely valuable.* Solomon's Song has rescued sex and marriage from their detractors, presenting both as beautiful God-given delights which are more precious than all of Solomon's royal treasures. True love can't be bought from an unmarried man or woman, and nor can it be compensated for if it is stolen from a married one through an act of adultery. The thing which symbolizes Jesus' relationship with his Church is the most expensive commodity on the planet. No wonder, when it points to the thing which cost the priceless blood of God's own Son.

In view of this, the girl's friends respond by telling us in 8:8–9 that *sex must be saved for marriage.* They can see why God tells us to treat it as his wedding present and why sexual sin cannot produce the exquisite love and love-making enjoyed by the ageing lovers in the fifth section of the Song. They tell us literally that they will *besiege* their little sister to stop her from being a fool and giving up her virginity before her wedding day.

Solomon's wife picks up the song again and responds to this conclusion by telling us in 8:10–12 that *sex must be nourished within marriage.*[5] The author Jonathan Swift commented that *"The reason why so few marriages are happy is because young ladies spend their time in making nets, not in making cages."*[6] Solomon's wife, at least, isn't satisfied that she has got her ring on Solomon's finger. She took the initiative to start the Song and she will take the initiative to end it too. She took the initiative to look for her husband in 5:8 and she took the initiative to suggest

---

[5] In 8:10 she picks up on her friends' reference to *walls* and *towers*, telling them that she is an example of what their little sister can expect if she guards her virginity in order to love God's way.

[6] Jonathan Swift wrote this in his *Thoughts on Various Subjects* (1706).

that they go away together for a holiday in 7:11. In these closing verses she takes the initiative to look after the vineyard of her body so that Solomon can continue to enjoy its fruit.[7] If love and sex and marriage are as important as this Song suggests, we cannot afford to take any less initiative ourselves.[8]

The two lovers therefore end the Song with a reminder in 8:13–14 that *sex must be enjoyed for the glory of God.* He calls to her in 8:13 and tells her that he loves the sound of her voice and the parts of her body which they both called her *secret garden* in 4:12–16. She ends the Song by calling back to him in 8:14 and telling him that she loves his agile body as much now as she did before their wedding day in 2:8, and that she wants him to whisk her away to enjoy what he referred to in 4:6 as her *mountain of myrrh.*

So there we have it: how to love God's way. Remember how significant, powerful and valuable it is. Save it for marriage, nourish it within marriage and enjoy it throughout marriage. That's lesson three in God's flight school of wisdom. It's how you and your chosen co-pilot can enjoy the best of life's journey together.

---

[7] The reference to fruit farmers in 8:12 is slightly confusing, but she appears to be telling Solomon that he and his tenants can keep their money, as it is nowhere near as valuable as the love she gives him for free.

[8] *Baal Hamon* was a place in the winegrowing hill country of Ephraim but, since it meant *Husband of a Multitude*, it is probably also a hint that her vineyard is more precious to Solomon than his many other wives.

Lesson Four:

Keep to God's Way

(Ecclesiastes)

Flight 007 (1:1)

The words of the Teacher, son of David, king in Jerusalem.

(Ecclesiastes 1:1)

Solomon wasn't merely the star student in God's flight school. By the time he wrote the book of Ecclesiastes towards the end of his life, he was also one of its greatest disappointments. The man who had received at the Tabernacle such unsurpassed wisdom from the Lord that he wrote and compiled Proverbs and Song of Songs to help us *learn God's way, live God's way* and *love God's way* failed to take his own advice and started acting like a fool. Shortly after the Queen of Sheba took her caravan of camels back down south, the ace pilot Solomon became just like the pilot of Korean Airlines Flight 007.

The pilot didn't notice any problems on 31st August 1983 when his Boeing 747 took off from Anchorage, Alaska, en route for Seoul, South Korea. He didn't spot that there was a problem with his plane's navigation system. The error was so small that after half an hour his plane was only six miles farther north than it should have been, but small errors can cause terrible diversions over time. After two hours, those six miles had become 100 miles; after three hours, they had become 180 miles; and after five and half hours, they had become 390 miles. By that time – while the pilot was still entirely unaware of his navigation error – the plane was so far north that it had entered Soviet airspace on a day when the Russians were testing a secret new missile below. Tiny navigational errors across the course of a five-and-a-half-hour flight had led the Boeing 747 into a place of severe danger. The Soviets concluded that the object on their radar must be a US spy plane, so they scrambled one of their Su-15s and shot the Boeing down, killing the pilot and all of his 268 passengers.

Like the pilot of Flight 007, Solomon hadn't noticed his navigation errors. We saw some of them at the end of Proverbs and in Song of Songs. His sobering example made Hezekiah's wise men finish Proverbs by pointing us to a better Teacher, and he himself confessed in Song of Songs 6:8 that he had taken sixty wives and eighty concubines. We discover in 1 Kings 11 that these early errors spelt disaster in the last two decades of his life:

> *King Solomon... loved many foreign women besides Pharaoh's daughter – Moabites, Ammonites, Edomites, Sidonians and Hittites. They were from nations about which the Lord had told the Israelites, "You must not intermarry with them, because they will surely turn your hearts after their gods." Nevertheless, Solomon held fast to them in love. He had seven hundred wives of royal birth and three hundred concubines, and his wives led him astray. As Solomon grew old, his wives turned his heart after other gods, and his heart was not fully devoted to the Lord his God, as the heart of David his father had been. He followed Ashtoreth the goddess of the Sidonians, and Molek the detestable god of the Ammonites. So Solomon did evil in the eyes of the Lord.*

We can tell from chapter 12 that Solomon was an old man by the time he wrote Ecclesiastes. By that time he had drifted so far from wisdom's flight path that some readers even question whether this can truly be the same man who authored Proverbs.[1] They point out that the author refers to himself as

[1] Although Solomon's folly is shocking, Ecclesiastes refuses to let us doubt his authorship. Chapter 1:16 links back to 1 Kings 3:12 and 4:30, and 2:7–9 links back to 1 Kings 10:23–29.

Israel's *qōheleth*, or *Teacher*, and that he criticizes the way the king oppresses Israel.[2] They are in danger of missing the tragic lesson of Ecclesiastes, which is that even the wisest man in the Old Testament acted like the pilot of Flight 007. If even Solomon failed to persevere on the path of wisdom, we are even greater fools if we ignore the danger. He wants us to read and learn from his mistakes, treating them as the fourth and final lesson in God's flight school. He wrote Ecclesiastes to teach us to *keep to God's way*.

The author of Ecclesiastes tells us straightforwardly in 1:1 that he was indeed the *"son of David, king in Jerusalem"*. Since subsequent kings of Judah might have used that same title, he clarifies further in 1:12 that he was *"king over Israel in Jerusalem"*. The ten northern tribes of Israel broke away from Judah at the end of Solomon's reign,[3] so only David and Solomon could ever say that they ruled over ***Israel*** from Jerusalem. To clarify still further, he tells us in 12:9 that he was the compiler of many proverbs.[4]

The Hebrew word *qōheleth*, which in Greek is *ekklēsiastēs*, is so much at the heart of the book's message that the translators of the Septuagint made it the book's title. The word means *Teacher*, or more literally *one who addresses the assembly of Israel*.[5] Solomon therefore wrote this book as instruction for God's People, and as the fourth and final lesson in God's flight

2 For example, in 4:1–2, 5:8–9, 8:2–4 and 10:20. Yet 1 Kings 4:7–19, 5:12–16 and 12:1–4 tell us that Solomon *did* foolishly oppress the ten northern tribes by overtaxing them and press-ganging them into his slave army.

3 1 Kings 10:9–13 and 12:1–4 tells us this was not just Rehoboam's fault, but also God's judgment upon Solomon. He confesses his own injustice towards the ten northern tribes and towards others in Ecclesiastes.

4 Solomon could refer to rulers of Jerusalem before him (1:16 and 2:7–9) because Jerusalem had been ruled by the Jebusites for centuries and because he and David saw themselves as successors to Melchizedek and his ancient dynasty (Genesis 14:18–20; Psalm 110:4).

5 It comes from the word *qāhāl*, which is the normal word for the *assembly* of Israel in the Old Testament. The Greek equivalent is *ekklēsia* – the word Jesus chose as the name for his *Church*.

school. He describes the utter meaninglessness of life without God in 1:2–11 and the futility of running after pagan idols in 1:12–2:26. He contrasts this with the hope of the Gospel in 3:1–15, before flitting between gloomy unbelief and happy faith throughout 3:16–6:12. He gives us fifteen wise observations on life as an old man in 7:1–8:8, then fifteen more in 8:9–11:6, but even as he does so he continues to lurch between faith and unbelief, between hope and despair. One of my close friends was converted through reading Ecclesiastes and being helped to see the pointlessness of living without God, but Solomon wrote it primarily to instruct believers to keep to God's way.

That's why we still desperately need the message of Ecclesiastes today. The American writer Eugene Peterson observes that

> *It is useful to listen to people who come into our culture from other cultures, to pay attention to what they hear and what they see. In my experience, they... see a Christian community that has almost none of the virtues of the biblical Christian community, which have to do with a sacrificial life and conspicuous love. Rather, they see indulgence in feelings and emotions, and an avaricious quest for gratification.*[6]

We need to read how Solomon felt after reaching the heights of fame and fortune and science and success – all that people strive for in our culture – and how he regretted being ensnared by their empty allure. We need to read these regrets and reflections from the aged Solomon and to be inspired by them to keep to God's way.

As we read them, we will discover that by God's grace Solomon's life was not shot down like Flight 007. We discover in the book's finale in 11:7–12:14 that Solomon spotted the

[6] Eugene Peterson in *The Contemplative Pastor* (1989).

error in his flight path just in time, that he returned to the Lord, repented of his sin and rejoined the path of wisdom just in time for touchdown. He turned his years of folly into lesson four in God's flight school of wisdom. He wrote down his spiritual testimony in the book which we call Ecclesiastes.

Life Minus God (1:2–11)

"Meaningless! Meaningless!" says the Teacher.
"Utterly meaningless! Everything is meaningless."
(Ecclesiastes 1:2)

If you have ever used a spreadsheet on your computer, you know how easy it is to make an error in one of the formulas. All it takes is a plus or minus sign in the wrong place and you get an error message which tells you that you need to go back and double-check your formula. Solomon uses the language of spreadsheets to describe Ecclesiastes in 7:27, and we find error messages popping up on every page. Solomon had mistakenly put in four foolish plus signs and one very foolish minus sign.

The first set of error messages should be obvious to any reader. The Hebrew word *hebel*, which means *meaninglessness* or *emptiness* or *vanity*, occurs thirty-eight times throughout the book – more times than the rest of the Bible put together. This is intensified to *hebel hebālīm* in 1:2, meaning *vanity of vanities* or *the emptiest thing of them all*.[1] Whenever you come across the word *meaningless* or *vanity* in Ecclesiastes, therefore, you should understand it as a sort of error message which warns you that the sums of life don't add up without God.[2]

The second set of error messages should also be obvious, but experience shows that it isn't. Ecclesiastes makes lots of bizarre statements which don't look as if they ought to be in the

---

[1] Ecclesiastes 1:2 serves as a summary verse for the whole of Ecclesiastes, just as 1:7 did for Proverbs.

[2] *Hebel* is the Hebrew word for *Abel*, who was born shortly after the Fall. Paul uses the same Greek word which translates *hebel* in the Septuagint in order to describe the fallen world as *futile* in Romans 8:20.

Bible and superficial readers often latch onto them to justify their folly. The greedy person latches onto 10:19 and argues that the Bible says *"money is the answer for everything"*. The misogynist takes 7:28 as his proof text that Scripture states that women are inferior to men. The humanist takes 3:19 as confirmation that that *"Surely the fate of human beings is like that of the animals; the same fate awaits them both."* What all of them fail to grasp is that these are error messages which show that Solomon has got his formulas wrong. They are not statements of what God says is true, but an expression of how foolish it is to take God out of the equation.

The third set of error messages should also be obvious, but some people use them as an excuse to ignore the message of Ecclesiastes altogether. If you read Solomon's words carefully, you will see that he contradicts himself several times. He tells us that wisdom can't beat death in 2:16, then promises that wisdom can save us from death 7:12! He tells us it is better to die than live in 4:2, but then argues that living is better than dying in 9:4! Confused yet? You are meant to be, because Solomon is himself confused. These are error messages because he is trying to add up life's sums without God.

They show us that life *plus foolish friends* doesn't work. Very few of Solomon's 700 wives and 300 concubines were godly co-pilots like his bride in Song of Songs. Most of them were foreign idolaters who led him so far away from his earlier devotion to the Lord that he even turned the Mount of Olives into a centre for idolatry. 1 Kings 11:7–8 and 2 Kings 23:13 tell us that on the very hill where his great descendant Jesus would later pray to the Father *"not my will, but yours be done"*, Solomon built shrines to the detestable false gods Chemosh and Molek.[3] If you find the book of Ecclesiastes confusing, you may understand it

[3] Luke 22:42. Jesus also ascended to heaven from the Mount of Olives in Acts 1:9–12.

better than you think. It seeks to demonstrate that the sums of life don't add up with foolish friends.

These error messages also show that life *plus a pagan worldview* doesn't work. Ecclesiastes is quite similar to a piece of Mesopotamian wisdom literature known as the *Dialogue of Pessimism*, which was written at about the same time as Solomon came to the throne in 970 BC. 1 Kings 4:30 and 10:24 suggest that this similarity may be down to Solomon's study of Eastern and Egyptian philosophy, and due to his constant stream of visitors from all over the world. Solomon influenced many of his visitors but, sadly, they influenced him too. The Hebrew text of Ecclesiastes contains several clues that its author has been studying works in Aramaic, collating books of pagan wisdom to go alongside his proverbs.[4] Studying pagan works can be helpful, but imbibing them is not. The sums of life do not add up with a pagan worldview.

These error messages also show that life *plus human reason* doesn't work. Solomon refers to things *"under the sun"* over thirty times in twelve chapters, even though this phrase does not appear anywhere else in the Bible.[5] As he does so, he betrays his failure to think in terms of heaven and of God. He is much more like Peter in Matthew 16:23, when Jesus had to rebuke him because *"You do not have in mind the things of God, but the things of men."* Perhaps his study of botany and zoology in 1 Kings 4:33 had made him start to view the world through the narrow lens of science alone. However it started, the end result was that the sums of life didn't add up with human reason.

The error messages also show that life *plus trust in money* doesn't work. Money itself isn't sinful – the Lord had promised

---

[4] The *Dialogue of Pessimism* is a conversation between a Mesopotamian master and his slave which also emphasizes the entire futility of human existence. Similar Aramaic influence can be seen in Song of Songs, probably due to the amount of time which Solomon spent with his foreign wives and foreign visitors.

[5] He says *"under the sun"* 29 times and *"under heaven"* 3 times.

to make Solomon rich in 1 Kings 3:13 – but relying on money is idolatry. That's why the Law of Moses forbade kings from accumulating horses to stop them relying on human strength instead of on the Lord.[6] Solomon flouted this in 1 Kings 4:26 and Ecclesiastes reveals the price which he paid. He discovered that the sums of life don't add up with trust in money.

But most of all, these error messages show us that life doesn't work minus God. Solomon constantly repeats the phrase *"I saw"*, but never once does he remind us about what *"the Lord said"*. In fact, he doesn't even call God *"the Lord"* in Ecclesiastes at all. He appears less influenced by the Law of Moses than he is by the logic of Mesopotamia, and less in tune with the Exodus generation than with the Egyptian slave-masters they left behind. As Solomon laments the pointlessness of life here in these first eleven verses, he reminds us that the sums of life can never add up without God.

So don't be surprised that Ecclesiastes is strewn with confusing statements and error messages for the reader. They are reminders that Solomon wrote for us to learn from his folly, not for us to copy it. Ecclesiastes teaches us that life plus foolish friends, plus a pagan worldview, plus human reason or plus trust in money does not add up. It teaches us that no one can explain the world through any formula minus God.

[6] Deuteronomy 17:16 and Psalm 20:7. 1 Kings 10:23 may also be hinting at this when it tells us that Solomon was great in *riches and wisdom* rather than in *wisdom and riches*. He began to have more money than sense.

Well-Fed Fools (1:12–2:26)

I became greater by far than anyone in Jerusalem before me… Everything was meaningless, a chasing after the wind.

(Ecclesiastes 2:9–11)

If you ever thought consumerism was a modern-day phenomenon, Ecclesiastes warns you to think again. Solomon and his contemporaries were voracious consumers. The problem was that no matter how much they consumed, they still felt empty.

In 1:12–18, Solomon tells us that he consumed wisdom literature. He devoured the works of the best pagan philosophers from around the world, convinced that wisdom was the only thing worth consuming.[1] He thought he was doing what he told us to do in Proverbs, but he wasn't; he was merely becoming a well-fed fool. He forgot that he told us in Proverbs 1:7 that all true wisdom starts with fearing the Lord, and as a result his studies merely made him blame the Lord for human suffering in 1:13. He treated wisdom as a commodity which he could acquire through extensive study and forgot that he had told us that true wisdom only comes through being guided by God's Spirit. He found that the wisdom literature which he devoured in the last two decades of his life was *"meaningless, a chasing after the wind"* – a Hebrew phrase which means literally *"a feeding on the wind"*. When Solomon found that the pagan wise men were more miserable than their students, he grew disillusioned. The

---

[1] Solomon told us this in Proverbs 4:7, 16:16 and 18:15. However, studying pagan philosophy had actually turned his wisdom into folly.

wisest man in the Old Testament concluded that his studies had merely made him a well-fed fool.

In 2:1–11, Solomon tells us that he consumed pleasure instead. He envied the fools around him who lived for the moment and decided that he would deny himself nothing.[2] He filled his life with wine and building projects and creating royal gardens, but he found that when the momentary euphoria passed it left him feeling just as empty as before. Even the glorious Temple he had built for the Lord on Mount Moriah and the magnificent palace he had built for himself on Mount Zion couldn't satisfy him. He acquired an army of slaves, vast flocks and herds, lavish treasures, the best court musicians and a massive harem of women, but he still felt empty. *"What does pleasure accomplish?"* he moans, as he tells us that this too was *"meaningless, a chasing after the wind"*.

In 2:12–16, Solomon concludes that wisdom is better than folly,[3] but that neither is enough to give life meaning. Death remains the greatest enemy of humankind, laughing at all our pleasures and accomplishments, and stripping our short lives of any purpose. The wise are as foolish as fools, he concludes, because *"Like the fool, the wise too must die!"*

In 2:17–23, Solomon tells us that he consumed ambition. He worked hard and was successful, but success still left him feeling empty because he knew there is no such thing as a successful corpse. He looked at his son Rehoboam and despaired that his hard work would undoubtedly be squandered by his errant son.[4] Solomon limits his gaze in these two chapters to what he can see *"under the sun"*, so he is in fact quite right to dismiss worldly ambition and success as largely pointless. Since

2 Solomon should have known better than this, since he himself taught us in Proverbs 27:20 that greed and lust can never be satisfied. He had spent so much time with foreign kings that he forgot his own wise words.

3 The Hebrew word which Solomon uses for a *fool* in 2:14–16 is *kesîl*. It is the normal word for *fool* in Ecclesiastes, occurring almost 20 times.

4 Rehoboam was born in 971 BC (1 Kings 14:21) and Solomon compiled Proverbs in about 950 BC. He could therefore probably tell by the time he wrote Ecclesiastes in about 931 BC that his son hadn't listened.

he ignores God's judgment and his promise of life beyond the grave, he concludes that earthbound hopes and dreams are also *"meaningless, a chasing after the wind"*.

C. S. Lewis famously observed that

> *Creatures are not born with desires unless satisfaction for those desires exists. A baby feels hunger: well, there is such a thing as food. A duckling wants to swim: well, there is such a thing as water. Men feel sexual desire: well, there is such a thing as sex. If I find in myself a desire which no experience in this world can satisfy, the most probable explanation is that I was made for another world. If none of my earthly pleasures satisfy it… probably earthly pleasures were never meant to satisfy it, but only to arouse it, to suggest the real thing.*[5]

We need to understand that even Solomon's depressed observations in these two chapters were inspired by God to make us reach out for the only thing which can truly satisfy. In case we doubt this, God sprinkles these verses with a series of clues for anyone who will listen.

The constant refrain in these verses is that consuming what this world has to offer is like *"chasing after the wind"*. The Hebrew word which Solomon uses for the *wind* is *rūach*, the normal Old Testament word for God's Holy *Spirit*. It's as if the Lord is winking at us over Solomon's shoulder as he writes Ecclesiastes, telling us that the answer to Solomon's blinkered frustration is for us to stop chasing the *wind* and to chase God's *Spirit* instead. It is to grasp that Solomon felt empty because he was eating from the Tree of the Knowledge of Good and Evil, and that we can be filled and satisfied by eating from the Tree of Life and drinking from the River of Life instead.[6]

---

[5] *Mere Christianity* by C. S. Lewis. Copyright © C.S. Lewis Pte. Ltd. 1942, 1943, 1944, 1952. Extract reprinted by permission.

[6] Genesis 2:9; 3:22; Proverbs 3:18; 11:30; Revelation 2:7; 21:6; 22:1–2, 14, 17, 19.

Another clue is in 2:5, where Solomon despairs that building *pleasure parks* did not satisfy him. He uses the Aramaic word *pardēs,* which means *paradise* and which is probably the same word which Jesus used to tell the thief on the cross in Aramaic that *"Today you will be with me in Paradise."*[7] Even as Solomon despairs that no earthly garden can ever satisfy, the Lord points us to the Garden in the age to come which will satisfy forever.

Still another clue is in 2:8, where Solomon despairs that his *private treasure collection* cannot satisfy him. He uses the Hebrew word *segūllāh,* which is the same word which the Lord used in Exodus 19:5 and in Deuteronomy 7:6, 14:2 and 26:18 to tell his People that they were his *treasured possession.* Solomon therefore does more than simply expose the folly of consumerism in these two chapters. He also shows us a better way. He tells us that consuming the things of this world will leave us feeling empty, but that being consumed by God and his eternal plan is more than enough to satisfy anyone.

Solomon may tell us pessimistically in 2:17 that he hates life and its conveyor belt of sorrow and frustration, but he also unwittingly gives us the answer to his searching. Life minus God *is* meaningless and death *is* the great enemy of mankind, but the Gospel is the answer to both problems. The Lord has recorded Solomon's miserable search for meaning in order to point us upwards to his Spirit, to Paradise and to his plan to make us his treasured possession. He calls us to repent of our empty consumerism and to be consumed by his eternally satisfying plan.[8]

---

[7] Luke 23:43. It is also the Aramaic word which Solomon used in Song of Songs 4:13.

[8] This explains Solomon's sudden burst of optimism in 2:24–26. With God back in the equation, Solomon returns to his teaching in Proverbs 13:22 and 28:8 that the wicked store up wealth in order to hand it over to the godly.

The Return of Mr Incredible (3:1–15)

I know that everything God does will endure forever; nothing can be added to it and nothing taken from it. God does it so that people will fear him.

(Ecclesiastes 3:14)

"No matter how many times you save the world, it always manages to get back in jeopardy again," complains Mr Incredible in the Disney movie.[1] *"Sometimes I just want it to stay saved, you know?! I feel like the maid: 'I just cleaned up this mess! Can we keep it clean for ten minutes? Please?'"*

Solomon had been Israel's Mr Incredible. The first half of his reign had been a golden age in which God's People finally enjoyed the full extent of the land which the Lord had promised them through Moses. He ruled with breathtaking wisdom, composed worship psalms and love songs, and made more scientific discoveries than all the previous rulers of Israel put together. He built the Temple and turned it into a worship centre which blessed Israel and made Israel a blessing to the nations. He hoped that the successes and progress of his early years had irreversibly changed Israel for good.

Sadly, he discovered that they hadn't. He had watched the greatness of his kingdom implode in the latter years of his reign. The reason he complains in 1:3–11 that the sun which rises also goes down and that the rain which falls also evaporates is that his own star had fallen and his own spirituality had run dry. Like

---

[1] *The Incredibles* (Walt Disney Pictures, 2004).

Mr Incredible, Solomon felt like the maid and grew disillusioned by the meaningless life cycles of a world minus God. But now, as we start chapter 3, we find that a glimmer of hope returns.

Maybe Solomon had spotted some of the clues which God inspired him to include in the text of 1:12–2:26. We can't know for sure, but we can see a sudden change of tone in 2:24–26. He mentions God for only the second time in the book so far, and for the first time in a positive way. He begins to explain that, although life minus God is meaningless, life plus God is entirely different. This launches him into the most famous section of Ecclesiastes. For a brief moment, Solomon returns to his earlier fear of the Lord and it results in the wisdom of 3:1–15.

Without God, Solomon echoed the two-dimensional wisdom of the pagan philosophers, dividing the world into *positives* (living, planting, building, laughing, dancing, gathering, loving and peacemaking) and *negatives* (dying, uprooting, demolishing, weeping, mourning, scattering, hating and fighting). With God back in the equation, Solomon suddenly rediscovers the three-dimensional wisdom which he taught us years earlier in Proverbs.[2] What we are witnessing as we read these verses is Solomon's slow return to the Lord. The old and cynical king is turning back into Israel's Mr Incredible.

Solomon remembers *that God has a plan*. He tells us in 3:14 that *"Everything God does will endure forever; nothing can be added to it and nothing taken from it. God does it so that people will fear him."* Yes, life consists of endless cycles of repeated activity, but that isn't to say that life's repetitions serve no purpose. The question most people ask in their forties and fifties is "Is there more to life than this?", and the question most people ask in their sixties is "Was it worth it?" Solomon answers both of those questions by reminding us that God fulfils his purposes through the seemingly pointless ebb and flow of people's lives.

[2] In God's three-dimensional wisdom, timing is crucial. That's why wisdom is not gained simply by learning to recite proverbs, but by gaining the same *hearing heart* as Solomon describes in 1 Kings 3:9.

Solomon remembers that *God has a strategy*. He tells us in 3:11 that God *"has made everything beautiful in its time"*, because his three-dimensional strategy can use everything for good. That's why these verses are often read at funerals to encourage mourners that God is in control, or at weddings to prepare the happy couple to trust God during life's rollercoaster ride. When Abraham, Isaac and Jacob died still trusting God, their deaths were not tragedies but a beautiful part of God's strategy for the world.[3] When Israel was uprooted from the Promised Land because of sin, it was a day of hope because it meant that the Lord was felling deadwood in order to make room for fresh shoots of life to grow.[4] Solomon married many times amid great celebrations, but he reflects that love and marriage are only beautiful if they are part of God's plan. There is *"a time to embrace and a time to refrain from embracing"*.[5] When Solomon embraced a godless, two-dimensional view of good and bad, he grew depressed. But with God back in the equation, he rejoices in both good and bad as part of God's overarching plan.

Solomon remembers that *God grants eternal life*. He told us several times in chapter 2 that the greatest enemy of humankind is death and he says very little about the promise of life beyond the grave. Now he suddenly remembers that *"God will call the past to account"* on judgment day and that *"everything God does will endure forever"*. By implication, he reminds us that all he taught us about heaven and hell in Proverbs is completely true. There is a reason why these verses are quoted more than any other part of Ecclesiastes. They record Solomon's rediscovery of the truth he expressed in Proverbs 14:32: *"When calamity*

[3] Hebrews 11:13.

[4] Deuteronomy 29:28; 1 Kings 14:15; Luke 13:6–9. It is not always a bad thing for a church or Christian organization to close down. Revelation 2:5 tells us that it is Jesus, not the Devil, who does the closing.

[5] This also explains why it was right for Jesus to hate wickedness in Psalm 45:7 and Hebrews 1:9, and wrong for Saul to spare Agag's life in 1 Samuel 15:9–33. Similarly, a just war may be better than an unjust peace.

comes, the wicked are brought down, but even in death the righteous have a refuge."

Finally, Solomon remembers that *God wants to save us and to give our lives meaning*. He reflects on the empty speculations of the pagan philosophers and concludes that God has placed a hunger for himself in the hearts of people all around the world. He tells us in 3:11 and 14 that God has *"set eternity in the human heart... God does it so that people will fear him."* Fish don't notice they are wet because they were born to swim in water, but we do sense this world's emptiness because we were born for another world. We weep at funerals because we know it isn't enough to console ourselves that "they had a good innings". We know deep down that they were created for eternity and we rage against death as the great imposter. Some individuals may feel this less than others, but they are simply like colour-blind people in an art gallery or tone-deaf people in an opera hall. Their failure to sense this primal instinct doesn't alter what God has made plain, deep down, to everyone. God is eternal and he has created us to be with him for eternity.

Solomon therefore returns to the things he rubbished in chapters 1–2 and tells us that with God in the equation we *can* in fact enjoy them. We can be satisfied with eating and drinking if we thank God for the fruits of our labour (2:24). We can be satisfied with wisdom and knowledge if we receive them as a gift from the Lord (2:26). We can enjoy hard work and success if we embrace them as gifts from God (3:13).[6] Our lives are brief and repetitious, but God infuses them with great meaning.

---

[6] Although human sinfulness has transformed *work* into hard *toil* and *labour* (Genesis 3:17–19), God created work as a good thing and wants to help us to enjoy it (Genesis 2:5).

Darkness and Light (3:16–6:12)

I said to myself... I also said to myself...

(Ecclesiastes 3:17–18)

Solomon flickers so quickly between darkness and light in 3:16–6:12 that these verses ought to come with a warning about the use of strobe lighting. Solomon's mind is a battlefield on which the cynicism of his old age fights against the resurgent faith of his younger years.[1] One moment Solomon has put God back in the equation and he speaks words of hope and wisdom. The next moment, he is back to life minus God and lurches into pessimism and deep despair. These chapters contain as much darkness as they do light. We are witnessing the fight for Solomon's soul in the final years before he died.

Solomon's thoughts were pretty dark in 1:12–2:23. We found death lurking behind every corner as Solomon lamented that life has no meaning. Light broke into the darkness in 2:24–3:15, as Solomon reconnected with the faith of his younger years. He told us that God is far greater than death, that there is life beyond the grave and that our actions matter in this life because they determine what will happen to us throughout eternity. For a moment it looked as if Solomon had repented of his backsliding and returned wholeheartedly to the Lord, but repentance and surrender usually involve a battle. The fight for Solomon's soul rages on for the whole of these three chapters.

---

[1] The Lord promised Solomon in 1 Kings 3:14 that he would live to a ripe old age if he followed him wholeheartedly. Tragically, because of his backsliding, Solomon's "old age" was in his fifties. He died in 930 BC, aged only about 58.

Darkness descends again in 3:16–4:12, as Solomon doubts his own conclusions and returns to the emptiness of living without God. Like many people today, his faith is suffocated by the sight of so much suffering in the world. Is God strong enough to stop it but too uncaring to do so, or is he caring enough to stop it but too weak to do so? Either way, it's heads-I-win-and-tails-you-lose for God. Solomon starts debating with himself in 3:17 and 3:18, telling us that *"I said to myself"* one thing but *"I also said to myself"* another. He concludes that there can be no final judgment and that human beings are nothing more than two-legged animals.[2] *"As one dies, so does the other... Everything is meaningless... Who knows if the human spirit rises upward and if the spirit of the animal goes down into the earth?"*[3] He therefore concludes in 4:1–3 that the dead are luckier than the living, and that those who were never born are even luckier still. Solomon's words are not without wisdom – life truly has no meaning in the absence of God, and life truly is pointless without an afterlife – but his main point is utterly flawed. He says this because he doubts that God is a Comforter to the weak, but Scripture tells us repeatedly that this is exactly what he is.[4]

Suddenly there is a flash of light in 4:12. When Solomon concludes that worldly success is pointless,[5] he turns to human relationships in his search for life's meaning. He remembers the days before he took 700 wives and 300 concubines, and tells us that in this pointless life *"Two are better than one... If two lie down together, they will keep warm... Though one may be*

---

[2] This is a terrible reminder that we must guard our hearts from lies (Proverbs 4:23). Solomon talked clearly about heaven and hell in Proverbs, yet his pagan friends managed to make him doubt it was true. See also 6:6 and 9:1–3.

[3] Solomon is right to say that both animals and humans have a *rūach* or *spirit*, since we are also told this in Genesis 7:15 and 22. However, he forgets that Genesis 1:26–27 also says that human spirits reflect God's image.

[4] See Psalm 34:18; 147:3; Isaiah 61:1–3; Jeremiah 8:18; John 14:16; Romans 8:35–39.

[5] Even as he speaks folly, Solomon echoes some of the genuine wisdom he spoke in Proverbs 6:6–11 and 15:16.

overpowered, two can defend themselves." Solomon's nostalgia suddenly reminds him of the faith he had when he wrote Song of Songs in his younger days as a faithful follower of God. *"A cord of* ***three*** *strands is not quickly broken,"* he continues as he remembers walking with his bride before the Lord. The light of truth bursts into the darkness of his depression.[6]

The battle for Solomon's soul isn't over, however. He nosedives back into cynicism in 4:13–16. Is he thinking about himself when he laments in 4:13, *"Better a poor but wise youth than an old but foolish king who no longer knows how to heed a warning"*? Although he generalizes in 4:14–16, he sounds very much like an old king who knows he has become unteachable. He seems to fear that for all Rehoboam's popularity as crown prince, a great disaster will befall his kingdom under his son.

Humbled by this thought, a fresh burst of light fills his mind in 5:1–7. As the former builder of God's Temple, Solomon warns us not to *"offer the sacrifice of fools, who do not know that they do wrong"*. He seems to be convicted that every sacrifice he has offered, every rash prayer he has prayed and every empty chorus he has sung in the past two decades of backsliding have been meaningless too. *"It is better not to make a vow than to make one and not fulfil it,"* he warns us. *"Therefore fear God."*[7] He warns us in 5:6 that God's judgment is real, as his faith in the Gospel refuses to die.[8]

Darkness falls again in 5:8–6:12. Solomon is convicted in 5:8–9 that one of his gravest sins has been to oppress the poor in the ten northern tribes of Israel, coveting their money despite all of his own warnings in Proverbs. He repeats those warnings

---

[6] We misquote 4:9–12 if we use it to celebrate friendship or marriage without God in the equation. Solomon warned us in Proverbs 18:24, 19:4 and 19:7 that godless relationships will also disappoint us.

[7] A tragic example of this is 2 Chronicles 34:31–32 and Jeremiah 3:10–11. Another is Nehemiah 10:29–39 and 13:1–31.

[8] The word *mal'āk* could mean *[temple] messenger* but its normal meaning is *angel*. Solomon is not merely talking about the earthly repercussions of sin, but about eternal ones.

here, telling us that no amount of riches can ever satisfy – in fact they cause problems which poor people never know.[9] He comes close to repenting of his greed but fails to go far enough, telling us instead in 5:19–20 that all he now wants is enough money to keep his mind off life's big issues.[10] He still refers to life in 6:12 as *"the few and meaningless days they pass through like a shadow"*, and he still argues in 6:3 that a stillborn child is better off than anyone who has a chance to live.[11] He isn't simply telling us that we cannot take riches with us to heaven when we die, but doubting in 6:6 if there is even a heaven at all. Evening falls on the battlefield of Solomon's soul as these verses end in darkness.

If you have read this far into Solomon's writings but have not yet surrendered your life to Jesus, I want to congratulate you on persevering in your reading. But I also want to warn you not to become like Solomon yourself. This same battle is presently raging for your own soul and the Devil will play dirty to keep you blinded by the darkness. Solomon's words are full of half-truths and fleeting insights which get throttled by the weight of cynicism and habitual unbelief. God has included these verses in the Bible to warn you that Christian conversion is never easy. He calls you to embrace each ray of truth which he shines into your mind and to reject the dark thoughts which try to choke them. As we will see in a few chapters' time, Solomon responded to the Gospel and returned to God. Don't waste the opportunities you have to do the same today.

---

9 Ecclesiastes 5:11 may refer to 1 Kings 4:22–23 and to the vast entourage of servants and courtiers which Solomon had to feed every day. 5:10 and 6:9 recall the proverbs we examined in the chapter "Enough Is Enough".

10 Since Solomon refers to *God* four times in 5:18–20, these verses are more positive than most of this section, but they simply don't go far enough.

11 Job 3:16 says something similar.

Fifteen (7:1–8:8)

All this I tested by wisdom and I said, "I am determined to be wise" – but this was beyond me.

(Ecclesiastes 7:23)

As the battle rages for his soul, Solomon decides to make a run for safe ground. He wrote 3,000 proverbs in his younger days, so he hopes to make a breakthrough in the battle if he writes some more. *"I am determined to be wise,"* he confides in us in 7:23 during an interlude which explains this collection of fifteen new proverbs. He has been so influenced by foreign writers that only a few of them are two-liners like his Top 500 in Proverbs; they are far more like the writings of the non-Hebrew Agur in Proverbs 30. But as Solomon begins to write them he finds the breakthrough he is looking for.

The first proverb in 7:1–6 is much more positive than chapter 6. Although he still thinks that death is the greatest enemy of humankind, he tells us that this makes funerals better than birthday parties.[1] We are all going to die but we tend to fool ourselves we won't, so it is good for us to experience suffering and mourning. Earlier this week, I went to visit a friend on his death bed and prayed with him as he sank into unconsciousness and died. I am still in awe of what I witnessed as my friend passed from this world to the next, and that's what Solomon has in mind here. Fools are happy to be entertained to death instead of staring death in the face and being spurred on

---

[1] There is a play on words here in Hebrew since a *good name* is *tōb shēm* and *fine perfume* is *tōb shemen*. An obituary smells better than a birth announcement.

to lay hold of life. Solomon's point is that no one is complacent about the meaning of life next to a coffin.[2]

The next three proverbs in 7:7, 7:8–9 and 7:10 are Solomon's reflections on how he has made a mess of his life. His second proverb attributes it to his listening to rich pagan visitors who brought him gifts, since 1 Kings 10:25 tells us that each one *"brought a gift – articles of silver and gold, robes, weapons and spices, and horses and mules"*. These foreign visitors came to catch some of Solomon's wisdom but their presents infected him with their folly.[3] His third proverb reminds us that how a matter ends is more important than how it begins – whether an angry remark or a proud decision to follow the way of the world rather than the way of the Lord. His fourth proverb tackles some of the nostalgia that he feels for the years when he walked with God: *"Do not say, 'Why were the old days better than these?' For it is not wise to ask such questions."*[4]

Solomon's strategy is working. His return to writing proverbs is helping him to rediscover the path of wisdom. His fifth and sixth proverbs in 7:11–12 and 7:13–14 are both expressions of the Gospel. The fifth one retracts his statement in 2:16 that wisdom cannot save a soul from death. Instead, he argues that wisdom is better than money because *"wisdom preserves the life of its possessor"*. The sixth proverb points out that God is sovereign over the bad times as well as the good times and that we need to trust him with our future. Solomon is beginning to sound much more like the young king who wrote the book of Proverbs. However, get ready for

---

[2] David and Moses also teach that wisdom comes from looking death in the face in Psalms 39:4–5 and 90:12.

[3] The early Christians refused to take money and allowed their possessions to be confiscated rather than stray from the path of wisdom (Acts 8:20; Hebrews 10:34).

[4] Nostalgia almost always requires a selective memory. For example, in Numbers 11:4–6 the Israelites remembered the fish and vegetables of Egypt but forgot that they were slaves there!

strobe lighting again, because Solomon lurches back into the darkness of his depression.

The seventh proverb in 7:15–18 is the only one of the fifteen in which he sounds more like the sceptic of chapter 6 than the believer of Proverbs. Contrasting good times and bad times makes him repeat his angry displeasure towards God for not putting an end to all the suffering in the world. He despairs of *"this meaningless life of mine"* in which bad things happen to good people and good things happen to bad people, and his solution echoes the folly which he spouted in chapters 1–2. He counsels us to be neither "over-wicked" nor "over-righteous" – to be as wary of too much religion as we are of too little religion.[5] Even in the safe ground of writing proverbs, Solomon finds the battle for his soul rages on.

Light bursts back in for the next three proverbs in 7:19, 7:20 and 7:21–22. The eighth one praises wisdom above physical strength.[6] The ninth one confesses that *"there is no one on earth who is righteous, no one who does what is right and never sins"*.[7] The tenth one argues that, in view of this, we should turn a blind eye and a deaf ear to other people's sins towards us and forgive them, since we have committed those exact same sins ourselves.

This leads into an interlude in 7:23–25 during which Solomon admits that he has tried to become wise but has failed. No longer wise in his own eyes, he confesses that *"this was beyond me"*, and this humble confession edges him closer

---

[5] This is a great example of why we need to be careful how we quote from Ecclesiastes, just as we do the speeches of Job's friends. How is it possible for us to be literally *"excessively righteous"*?! The point of this verse is to expose Solomon's folly, not to teach us to embrace it.

[6] Paul may have 7:19 in mind when he tells us in 2 Corinthians 10:3–5 that we can use God's wisdom to tear down whatever strongholds of wrong thinking oppose the Gospel.

[7] Although it appears that Ecclesiastes is never explicitly quoted in the New Testament, this is such a clear Gospel verse that Paul may be quoting from here instead of from Psalm 14:1 in Romans 3:10.

to repentance. As a result, his eleventh and twelfth proverbs in 7:26 and 7:27–29 are a frank confession of his sin.[8] He admits that he has been ensnared by his many wives and by his foolish choice of pagan wise men as his friends. Only one in a thousand of his companions has been a good influence on him, and not even one of his many foreign wives.[9]

Therefore the last three proverbs in 8:1, 8:2–6 and 8:7–8 are all expressions of the Gospel. The thirteenth one reminds him to smile instead of grieving that the Lord has disciplined him. The fourteenth one reminds him that subjects obey kings as part of their oath towards God, and that kings therefore ought to obey the Lord.[10] The fifteenth proverb tells us that no one has power to decide the day of their death or to hold onto their own spirit.[11] We will all die precisely when God determines it is time for him to judge us. Although he accused God of not judging the wicked only a few verses ago, he changes his mind and admits that God is as unlikely to release the wicked from hell as a general is to demobilize his army on the eve of battle.

Fifteen proverbs. Fourteen steps forward and only one step back. Solomon comes very close to repentance and to renewing his backslidden faith in Yahweh. Now, just as it feels as though the battle is over, darkness makes one final, last-ditch attempt to destroy Solomon's soul...

---

[8] He calls himself the *Teacher* (Hebrew *qōhelet* and Greek *ekklēsiastēs*) in 7:27 for only the fourth time after 1:1, 1:2 and 1:12. He confesses that he tried to become wise through deductive reasoning rather than by continuing to rely on the Holy Spirit, which is one of the reasons why he failed.

[9] We noted in Song of Songs 4:8 that the girl in the Song was not necessarily a foreigner. She was probably an Israelite – perhaps the only godly wife among them all.

[10] Ecclesiastes 8:3 links back to Proverbs 29:26 to remind us that God is the true King and that we are fools if we rush through our prayer times with him. See also Luke 10:41–42.

[11] Once again, the Hebrew word *rūach* can refer here either to grasping the *wind* or holding onto our own *spirit*.

Fifteen More (8:9–11:6)

The quiet words of the wise are more to be heeded than the shouts of a ruler of fools.

(Ecclesiastes 9:17)

Movie villains don't die easily. Nor does the villain Folly in Ecclesiastes. As Solomon starts to see the light, Folly quickly fights back and makes a last-ditch attempt to repulse the advance of Wisdom. The battle still rages for Solomon's soul. Darkness and depression invade his thoughts again in 8:9–9:12.

Folly spots a weakness in Solomon's defences when he promises in 8:8 that God will judge the wicked. One of his biggest problems with faith in God throughout Ecclesiastes is his frustration that God doesn't seem to judge the wicked enough! Evil people often die with honour (8:9–10) and even those who reap what they have sown are often judged far too little and far too late (8:11).[1] *"When the sentence for a crime is not quickly carried out, people's hearts are filled with schemes to do wrong,"* he complains,[2] implying that it is God's fault that injustice thrives in Israel because he has not done enough to judge it. The battle rages in Solomon's soul as he debates with

---

[1] Note Solomon's inconsistency here. He complains in 8:10 that the wicked are not punished but he also complains in 8:9 that they don't get to enjoy their ill-gotten treasures!

[2] Solomon is right about this principle. When governments fail to bring criminals to book and when church leaders fail to discipline troublemakers, sin multiplies. However, Solomon is wrong to accuse God of wrongdoing by inference. Matthew 13:24–30 and 2 Peter 3:3–9 explain that God delays patiently to save many.

himself whether God is just (8:12–13), unjust (8:14) or simply too difficult to comprehend at all (8:15–17).[3]

Folly has Wisdom on the run, but now she overstretches herself. Solomon may sound humble when he claims in 9:1–3 that no one can be sure if there truly is a heaven and a hell, but he is actually contradicting his own teaching in Proverbs. When he starts to argue in 9:4–10 that life therefore has no meaning except to enjoy food and drink and marriage and hard work, even he can tell that he is contradicting himself in 1:12–2:23.[4] His words in 9:7–9 are remarkably similar to a section of the Babylonian poem *The Epic of Gilgamesh*, but Solomon is wising up to the way that his pagan friends have misled him.[5] He exclaims in 9:11–12 that this is a dead-end conclusion which robs life of any meaning in the face of time and random chance and sudden tragedy. Folly has overplayed her hand and has driven Solomon back into the arms of Wisdom. He has come too far on his fresh journey of faith to return to his thoughts in the opening verses of Ecclesiastes. He resists the darkness by launching into fifteen more proverbs like the fifteen which went before.

The sixteenth, seventeenth and eighteenth proverbs express his resolve to fight off these renewed attacks of Folly. The sixteenth proverb in 9:13–18 repeats the same message as the eighth one in 7:19, telling us that wisdom is better than strength. Noisy doubts must not be allowed to drown out the quiet words of wisdom, because it isn't too late for Solomon

---

[3] Solomon is wrong to argue that no one can discover the meaning of life. That is only the case if we try to do so without God. In fact, God promises to reveal it to us in Proverbs 3:32, Psalm 25:14 and Jeremiah 33:3.

[4] Atheism naturally leads to moral apathy and to the cry "Eat, drink and be merry for tomorrow we die" (Isaiah 22:13; 1 Corinthians 15:32). Only belief in God can make us listen to Solomon when he says in 9:10 *"Whatever your hand finds to do, do it with all your might."* See Colossians 3:23.

[5] *The Epic of Gilgamesh* was written 750 years before Ecclesiastes in about 1700 BC, but it is such a famous work of eastern literature that Solomon must have been very familiar with it.

to lay hold of wisdom and save his backslidden nation.[6] The seventeenth proverb warns in 10:1–3 that it only takes a little folly to destroy a wise man, and that Solomon needs to be radical with every foolish argument which sticks to his tangled mind like flies landing in ointment. The eighteenth proverb reminds us in 10:4 to keep our heads in a crisis and not be panicked into foolish action. Solomon resolves to close his ears to the loud noise of Folly and to come through to the faith he almost rekindled through his previous fifteen proverbs.

The nineteenth to twenty-fourth proverbs therefore strengthen this resolve. He reminds himself in 10:5–7 that kings must be wise because the welfare of their kingdom depends on their winning the battle for their own mind.[7] He adds in 10:8–9 that if he persists in sin at this late stage, he will surely be harmed by his own folly.[8] He resolves to take time out to think in 10:10,[9] to finish thinking in 10:11, to be silent in 10:12–14a and to be humble before God in 10:14b. Solomon strengthens his determination to surrender to Wisdom and reject the voice of Folly. As a result, light shines into the darkness of his mind and he comes to the brink of repentance.

The twenty-fifth to twenty-ninth proverbs remind us of what Solomon has learned. He has learned not to get worn down

[6] We have examples in 2 Samuel 20:15–22 of a wise woman doing as Solomon says and in 2 Kings 6:14–23 of a wise man doing so. We should be encouraged that it only takes one wise person to repulse the enemy.

[7] In saying this, Solomon returns to the wisdom he expressed in Proverbs 19:10, as echoed by Agur in 30:22.

[8] We should not understand 10:8–9 as a commendation of the risk-averse excuse making which Solomon roundly condemned in Proverbs 22:13 and 26:13. After all, Solomon condemns such sin again here in his thirtieth proverb in 11:4. Rather, Solomon is repeating what he said in Proverbs 26:27 and 28:10 – that those who do evil will suffer judgment through the evil they commit.

[9] Ecclesiastes 10:10 contains a very important principle for us. Time spent in study and in listening to God is no more wasted than a woodcutter wastes time in taking a break from chopping trees to sharpen his axe. The person who prays for 55 minutes and works for 5 will achieve far more than the person who works for an hour.

by folly in 10:15, not to get distracted by pleasures in 10:16–17 and not to get defeated by laziness in 10:18. We need to learn these same lessons because Ecclesiastes is the fourth lesson in God's flight school of wisdom, and it tells us that we need to *keep to God's way*. Solomon learned not to fall for expensive pleasures in 10:19,[10] and not to speak flippantly about the true King of Israel in 10:20. If we also learn to resist the siren voice of Folly like Solomon, we will be ready to graduate in style.

The thirtieth and final proverb in 11:1–6 lifts our eyes to see that this battle between Wisdom and Folly rages in soul after soul across the world. It encourages us to keep on sowing seed and trusting God that Wisdom will finally overcome. Solomon gave us these thirty extra proverbs – the same number of proverbs as he gave us in the sayings of the wise in Proverbs 22:17–24:22 – in order to do far more than bring his total number of proverbs in Scripture up to 530. He gave us them to offer us a ringside seat on his own personal battle, and to enlist us in the air force which God is training to take his Gospel to the world. As we prepare to graduate from God's flight school of wisdom, Solomon tells us we are not pleasure pilots. We have been trained and equipped to proclaim this Gospel throughout the embattled world.

[10] Ecclesiastes 10:19 confuses many readers because Solomon seems to be advocating money as the answer to everything, even though it fails to satisfy. There is no need to be confused if we place this alongside 7:1–6. Money does bring many pleasures but we must not let pleasure distract us in our quest for wisdom.

Fighter Pilots (11:1–6)

Sow your seed in the morning, and at evening let your hands not be idle, for you do not know which will succeed, whether this or that, or whether both will do equally well.

(Ecclesiastes 11:6)

In one of the Lord of the Rings movies, the wizard Gandalf leads the outnumbered fellowship to a brilliant victory over the orcs. As he surveys the battlefield in the aftermath of victory, he declares: *"The battle for Helm's Deep is over; the battle for Middle Earth is about to begin."*[1] Solomon wants us to grasp this principle as we watch him triumph in his battle between Folly and Wisdom. He tells us that his own life is simply one battle of many. We are called to be wise pilots who play our role in God's great plan to win this same battle in the hearts of men and women in every nation of the world.

Strictly speaking, Solomon's thirtieth proverb in 11:1–6 is all about farming. He talks about *grain* and *sowing* and *planting* and *reaping,* but this is the same terminology which Jesus uses throughout the gospels to illustrate the way in which we must participate in his mission to spread the Gospel message. It doesn't detract from the usefulness of these verses to farmers when we note that they form the final proverb of these thirty for a reason. Solomon told us throughout the book of Proverbs that God turns wise people into trees of life through which he

---

[1] *The Lord of the Rings: The Two Towers* (New Line Cinema, 2002).

saves the souls of many.[2] Now, as he wins his own internal battle and draws the fourth lesson of God's flight school to a close, he trains us to be fighter pilots armed with wisdom who know how to use it to defeat folly.

In 11:1, Solomon tells us that we need to speak truth *expectantly*. Every farmer knows that sowing seed requires faith, since it is easier to eat seed today than to scatter it in hope of reaping more seed tomorrow. Every businessman knows that shipping grain requires faith too, since it is safer to eat the grain than load it into trading vessels bound for rich markets overseas. The book of Ecclesiastes was written almost 3,000 years ago but it is full of reasons why we should expect the Gospel to be successful in our culture. Our pleasure-seeking but dissatisfied age is desperate to discover life's true meaning. Since we know that the gods of our culture cannot satisfy, we must share the Gospel expectantly so that the Lord can surprise us with a generous return.

In 11:2a, Solomon tells us that we need to speak truth *lavishly*. He points out that every farmer who sows seed knows two things: that not every seed sown will bear fruit and that those seeds which do bear fruit will yield as much as 100 times what was sown. He therefore encourages us not to be measured in communicating *"Christ the power of God and the wisdom of God,"*[3] as if evangelism somehow fails unless it yields an instant harvest. He warns us that we normally need to *"invest in seven ventures, yes, in eight"* in order to see a single person saved from Folly.

In 11:2b, Solomon tells us that we need to speak truth *urgently*. We simply do not know how long people have to listen to the voice of Wisdom calling them before God's

---

[2] He says this in Proverbs 11:30, but he also urges the wise to warn the foolish throughout Proverbs.

[3] 1 Corinthians 1:24. Paul continues by stating that, in the Gospel, *"the foolishness of God is wiser than human wisdom, and the weakness of God is stronger than human strength."*

judgment puts an end to their lives of folly. In January 2009, Chesley Sullenberger became an international hero when US Airways Flight 1549 hit a flock of birds and lost both engines. He was piloting the plane and instantly grasped the urgency of the situation, managing to save all 155 passengers and crew by gliding to a perfect landing on the Hudson River. He told reporters afterwards that *"I've been making small, regular deposits in this bank of experience: education and training. And on January 15 the balance was sufficient so that I could make a very large withdrawal."*[4] Solomon tells us that God wants to make us wise so that we can make urgent withdrawals of our own to save the lives of those he has placed into our care.

In 11:3, Solomon tells us that we need to speak truth *realistically*. Rain falls where clouds are heaviest, and trees lie where the wind blew them over. In the same way, if 2.7 billion individuals have no indigenous church which can tell them the Gospel, then some of us are going to have to move home in order to reach them. If 340 million individuals do not have the Bible in their language, some of us are going to have to go and live among them and start translating or they will die without ever hearing God's words of wisdom.[5]

In 11:4, Solomon tells us to *take risks* to share the truth. A farmer who waits for the perfect wind will never plant, and a farmer who fears the onset of rain will never harvest. Don't exaggerate the risks of sharing your faith like the sluggard in Proverbs,[6] and don't wait for the perfect opportunity to share. Paul tells us in 2 Corinthians 6:2 that *"now is the time of God's favour, now is the day of salvation"*. Let's take risks to reach new individuals and new people groups, convinced that this is true.

---

[4] He said this in an interview with the CBS programme *60 Minutes* on 8th February 2009.

[5] This is 2011 data from the websites of the Joshua Project and Wycliffe Bible Translators. Proverbs 20:4 tells us that only a sluggard would ignore such facts yet still expect a Gospel harvest around the world.

[6] Proverbs 15:19; 22:13; 26:13.

In 11:5, Solomon encourages us to share truth *full of faith in God*. No farmer understands the path of the wind or what makes his seed grow, just as no parent understands how a baby's body is knitted together in its mother's womb. In the same way, we do not understand how God turns wicked fools into forgiven wise men and women through the power of his Spirit. We simply need to share the Gospel in faith that God uses it to change the world one life at a time.[7]

In 11:6, Solomon challenges us to share truth *consistently and tirelessly*. If God can even win back a stubborn backslider like him, we must share both day and night, not knowing which conversation will yield a harvest. We are not to be part-time pilots, who fly the occasional sortie but spend most of their time boasting about it at the bar. We are to be pilots who give nothing less than total dedication to our role in God's great battle against Satan's folly. We are to be those about whom the Lord will be able to say when he returns to sound an end to this great Battle of Wisdom:

> *Undaunted by odds, unwearied in their constant challenge and mortal danger... Never in the field of human conflict was so much owed by so many to so few.*[8]

---

[7] Solomon is probably making a deliberate play on words in 11:5, since the Hebrew word *rūach* means either *wind* or *spirit*. Jesus may have been thinking of this passage in Luke 8:11.

[8] Winston Churchill said this of British pilots during the Battle of Britain on 20th August 1940.

The Return of the King (11:7–12:14)

Now all has been heard; here is the conclusion of the matter: Fear God and keep his commandments, for this is the duty of all mankind.

(Ecclesiastes 12:13)

Everybody loves a happy ending, so it's great to discover that Ecclesiastes has one. Much of the book so far has felt more like a tragedy than a story with a happy ending. The star student in God's flight school of wisdom looked poised to be its greatest failure, so we are meant to be excited to get this news in the final verses before our own graduation day. Solomon returned to faith in the Lord before he died, and he retook his place as one of Wisdom's greatest teachers.

Light has been battling with darkness throughout Ecclesiastes, and light finally triumphs in Solomon's life in 11:7–10. We have been using the two words to contrast wisdom and folly, but Solomon uses *light* and *darkness* in 11:7 to contrast life with death, the great enemy which has dominated the book so far. It was old age and the thought of death which sent Solomon into a spiral of depression in the early chapters of Ecclesiastes. Now he insists that *"youth and vigour are meaningless"* too, but he does so with a sense of hope which was missing when he wrote his darkest chapters. Gone are his complaints that death is the end, that God doesn't judge sin, and that consequently stillborn babies are far luckier than the living. Instead, he says this to encourage young people to forget the petty cares of youth in the knowledge that their precious lives have massive meaning. He urges young readers in 11:9 to remember that God will judge them for what they do with their short lives on the way to eternity.[1] Solomon at last sounds like the same man who wrote in Proverbs 12:28 that *"In the way of righteousness there is life; along that path is immortality."*

Having talked about judgment and eternal darkness, Solomon now addresses young people forcefully in 12:1–7. His renewed faith in the Lord makes him want to warn the next generation of Israelites not to waste as many years in folly as he did. He warns that days are coming when their lives will not be as pleasurable as they are now. Life's charms will fade (12:2a), pain will be a constant companion (12:2b), muscles will wither (12:3a), teeth will fall out (12:3b) and eyes will fail (12:3c). Ears will grow deaf (12:4a), sleep will be broken (12:4b), hearts will fear (12:5a), hair will go white (12:5b), energy will fail (12:5c) and sex drive will disappear altogether (12:5d). They mustn't let their youth delude them that they have long before they *"go to their eternal home"* (12:5e), and to stress this he reels off a series of vivid metaphors in 12:6–7. The silver cord on which their life hangs will be severed. The golden bowl from which they drink the water of life will be broken. Their jug will be shattered so that they can gather no more life from this world's springs, and the wheel which drops the bucket down into the well of life will not function for them any more. The God who made their bodies from dust will return them to the dust,[2] and the God who sent their spirits into the world will recall them to the world beyond the grave. *"Everything is meaningless!"* he warns young men and women in 12:8, but he does so to communicate a message which is as positive as he was negative before. He wants young

---

[1] Don't misunderstand Solomon's reference to *darkness* after death. He is not saying there is no afterlife, since he says the darkness will last for *many days*. Ecclesiastes 12:5 and 14 show us he is talking about two kinds of *"eternal home"*.

[2] Solomon has already referenced Genesis 2:7 and 3:19 in Ecclesiastes 3:20–21.

people to learn the lesson of his own foolish life so that they can graduate from God's flight school and keep to God's way.

Solomon pleads in 12:1 with his readers to *"Remember your Creator"* from an early age. Gone is the folly of chapters 1–2, where he barely mentioned the Lord except to complain about him. He no longer calls life meaningless because he despises it, but because it is too precious for us to be satisfied with anything less than life eternal.[3] He tells us in 12:5 that when each person dies they *"go to their eternal home"*, and he therefore warns us in 12:6–7 to *remember God* during all the days we have left before our spirits return to God for the final judgment which he described in 11:9. God is real; God has made both heaven and hell; and life has great meaning because God will judge us for what we did or didn't do with the brief lives he gave us as a foreword to our eternity.

Like a good book or movie, the message of Ecclesiastes finally makes sense in its final seven concluding verses, in 12:8–14. Solomon summarizes the message of the book in 12:8, using the same words which he used to begin it in 1:2: Life is utterly meaningless if we try to live it without God, but *"the conclusion of the matter"* is that this simply shows us we have done our sums wrong. He tells us in 12:13–14 that God will judge every deed committed by each person – both those we think he knows about and those we think he doesn't – and so the meaning of life is to *"Fear God and keep his commandments, for this is the duty of all mankind."* He told us at the start of Proverbs that wisdom begins with fearing the Lord, and he repeats this at end of Ecclesiastes. If we obey the Lord, repent of our sins, and submit to the Gospel, our brief lives will merely be the cover page to a far greater story which will unfold for us beyond the grave.[4]

---

[3] Solomon used the phrase *"under the sun"* 30 times in Ecclesiastes when his vision was restricted to this world alone. He does not even use the phrase once in these two chapters of conclusion.

[4] 1 John 3:23 sheds light on 12:13 when it tells us that *"This is his command: to believe in the name of his Son, Jesus Christ, and to love one another as he commanded us."*

Solomon gives you three reasons in his conclusion why you need to treat this message as the call of Wisdom. First, he insists in 12:9–10 that he is the *Teacher* of God's People.[5] He compiled Proverbs and Ecclesiastes because God gifted him to impart true wisdom to the world. He claims his words are divinely inspired, saying literally that they are *pleasing [to God], a statement of what is right*, and *words of truth* for anyone who will listen.[6] Second, he tells us in 12:11 that his writings and his compilations of wise sayings are in fact words *"given by one Shepherd"* – the Lord who shepherded Israel throughout the Old Testament and who would later appear in the flesh as Jesus the Good Shepherd.[7] Third, he sees through our excuse in 12:12 that we need to study further before repenting. The seventeenth-century English writer Francis Bacon warned that *"To spend too much time in studies is sloth"*,[8] and Solomon warns us that it can often be the sluggard's way of putting off an important decision to a day which never comes. Solomon draws a line under our sums and tells us it is time for us to give the Lord our answer. Life minus God is meaningless but life plus God leads to delights which will never end.

You have enough data to finish life's sum and to pass the final test to graduate from God's flight school of wisdom. Don't put off complete surrender to the Lord as Solomon did in his wasted years. Learn from the king who returned to the God of his youth, and make the most of the time you have left between now and death and final judgment.

---

[5] The Hebrew word *qōhelet*, translated *ekklēsiastēs* in Greek and *Teacher* in English, occurs seven times in Ecclesiastes: three times in the introduction, once in the main body, and three times in this conclusion.

[6] Ecclesiastes 12:10 is therefore an Old Testament precursor to 2 Timothy 3:16–17 and 2 Peter 1:20–21.

[7] Genesis 49:24; Psalm 23:1; 80:1; Isaiah 40:11; Ezekiel 34:23; John 10:14; Hebrews 13:20; 1 Peter 5:4.

[8] Francis Bacon in his essay on studies, published as part of his *Essays* in 1625.

Conclusion: Life Works God's Way

The words of the wise are like goads, their collected sayings like firmly embedded nails – given by one Shepherd.

(Ecclesiastes 12:11)

Even if you aren't as big a fan of eighties movies as I am, you've still got to love the Tom Cruise classic *Top Gun*. The pilots at the elite training school at Air Station Miramar in California look pretty good at flying until Tom Cruise enrols and flies planes on a whole new level. About 925 years after Solomon died, a Top Gun pilot enrolled in God's flight school of wisdom and did the same. He got a perfect pass in all four of the lessons which Solomon compiled, even though the teacher who compiled them had personally failed.

The new Top Gun pilot passed lesson one perfectly by *learning God's way* as described in Proverbs 1–9. He was so eager to learn wisdom from an early age that Luke's gospel tells us *"the child grew and became strong; he was filled with wisdom, and the grace of God was on him"*. At the age of twelve, he went missing from a family trip to Jerusalem in order to take his thirst for learning further. When his parents finally found him asking questions in the Temple, he asked them incredulously, *"Didn't you know I had to be in my Father's house?"* Despite their puzzlement, he obeyed his parents as completely as Solomon commanded us to do in lesson one of God's flight school. Luke tells us that he *"grew in wisdom and stature, and in favour with God and man."*[1]

The new Top Gun pilot also passed lesson two perfectly by *living God's way* as described in Proverbs 10–31. Luke tells us that he was a better son of David than Solomon, and a far better heir to God's covenant with David in which he promised *"I will raise up your offspring to succeed you, your own flesh and blood... and I will establish the throne of his kingdom forever. I will be his father, and he will be my son."*[2] He had such an unblemished record by the age of thirty that God shouted the results of his lesson-two exams from heaven: *"You are my Son, whom I love; with you I am well pleased."*[3] By way of proof, the Top Gun pilot spent forty days and nights fasting in the desert during which he resisted the temptations which had toppled the teacher who wrote the bulk of Proverbs. Solomon was filled with wisdom from God to draft these four lessons, but he failed to practise all he preached. This new pilot – Jesus of Nazareth – was so much better than his predecessor that he told the crowds who flocked to hear his wisdom and called him Teacher that others *"came from the ends of the earth to listen to Solomon's wisdom, and now one greater than Solomon is here"*.[4]

The new Top Gun pilot also passed lesson three perfectly by *loving God's way* as described in Song of Songs. When God called him to be single while all his childhood friends married and had children, he perfectly obeyed its chorus call not to arouse or awaken love until its proper time. Instead of focusing his love and affection on a single woman, he became betrothed to God's People as a whole and did for them what Solomon

---

[1] Luke 2:40, 49, 51–52.

[2] 2 Samuel 7:12–14. Compare this with Luke 1:27, 32, 69; 2:4, 11; 3:31; 18:38–39.

[3] Luke 3:22. Interestingly, Jesus spent much of his life ministering to people in the very region which had suffered most in 1 Kings 9:10–14 from Solomon's foolish overspending on his lavish palace.

[4] Luke 11:31.

promised to do but failed to deliver. Song of Songs 8:6 says that *"love is as strong as death"*, but Jesus demonstrated what that verse means by laying down his life to save and sanctify God's People. He fulfilled the call to love God's way so completely that his followers could simply state that *"This is how we know what love is: Jesus Christ laid down his life for us."*[5]

The new Top Gun pilot also passed lesson four perfectly by *keeping to God's way* as described in Ecclesiastes. Whereas Solomon started strong but couldn't go the distance, Jesus obeyed God even when it meant betrayal, torture, crucifixion and shameful death – and as he did so he answered Solomon's cry in Ecclesiastes. The great enemy of humankind throughout the book is death and its menacing shadow lurks on every page, but Jesus' death and resurrection broke the power of death so completely that Paul celebrates: *"'Death has been swallowed up in victory.' 'Where, O death, is your victory? Where, O death, is your sting?' The sting of death is sin, and the power of sin is the law. But thanks be to God! He gives us the victory through our Lord Jesus Christ."*[6]

Even though Jesus fulfilled Proverbs, Song of Songs and Ecclesiastes almost 1,000 years after Solomon wrote them, these final verses point to his coming. The truth is that you and I are far more like Solomon than Jesus. We haven't set our hearts fully to learn God's way, live God's way, love God's way and keep to God's way. In short, we have sinned like Solomon and deserve the divine punishment which he warns about throughout the book of Proverbs and at the end of Ecclesiastes. We need more than to be told in Ecclesiastes 12:11 that *"The words of the wise are like goads, their collected sayings like firmly embedded nails – given by one Shepherd."* We need a Shepherd who was beaten

---

5 1 John 3:16.

6 1 Corinthians 15:54–57.

by the goad of judgment for our sin and who surrendered his hands and feet to the firmly embedded nails of Calvary.[7]

Jesus' victory on the cross should excite you far more than watching Tom Cruise save a ship full of sailors by shooting down several Russian MiGs at the end of *Top Gun*. It made the apostle Paul so excited that he wrote letter after letter about *"the mystery of God, namely, Christ, in whom are hidden all the treasures of wisdom and knowledge"*. Even now he tells you to believe this Gospel message that Jesus is *"the wisdom of God"*, and promises that if you do so, *"you are in Christ Jesus, who has become for us wisdom from God – that is, our righteousness, holiness and redemption"*.[8] He tells us that Jesus is the voice of Wisdom which speaks in Proverbs 1–9 and the wise man who fulfils the lifestyle of Proverbs 10–31, that he is the one who laid down his life for God's People with a greater love than that which is described in Song of Songs, and that he fills us with the Holy Spirit – the Spirit of Wisdom[9] – so that we can keep on living God's way by the power of one greater than Solomon living inside us.

So don't put down this commentary and treat these three books of the Bible as nothing more than clever maxims or a list of rules or a lofty description of unattainable ideals. God has sent the perfect Top Gun pilot to fulfil the message of these three books of the Bible. Don't put down this commentary without surrendering your life afresh to Jesus as your King and Teacher. Tell him right away that you choose Wisdom instead of Folly and that you believe with all your heart that life works God's way.

---

[7] Solomon was probably telling us that God had defined wisdom immovably in these three books in order to drive us along the path of wisdom. However, God inspired his choice of words to hint at the one who would bring us forgiveness whenever we listen to the voice of Folly and fail.

[8] Colossians 2:2–3; 1 Corinthians 1:24, 30.

[9] Deuteronomy 34:9; Isaiah 11:2; Ephesians 1:17.

TITLES IN THE **STRAIGHT TO THE HEART** SERIES:

OLD TESTAMENT

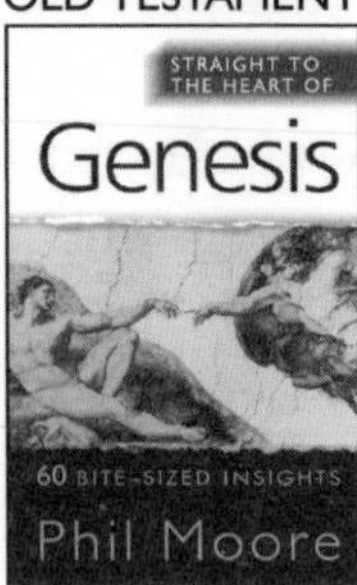

ISBN 978 0 85721 001 2

ISBN 978 0 85721 056 2

ISBN 978 0 85721 252 8

ISBN 978 0 85721 428 7

ISBN 978 0 85721 426 3

NEW TESTAMENT

ISBN 978 1 85424 988 3

ISBN 978 0 85721 253 5

ISBN 978 1 85424 989 0

ISBN 978 0 85721 057 9

ISBN 978 0 85721 002 9

ISBN 978 1 85424 990 6

For more information please go to **www.philmoorebooks.com** or **www.lionhudson.com**